A History
of
Eton Fives

The Chapel steps at Eton, site of the original fives court: from a painting by Herbert Marshall, 1896

A History of Eton Fives

of
Eton Fives

Dale Vargas and Peter Knowles

The Kinnaird Cup Final 2009: Tom and Peter Dunbar (second and third from the left) v. Howard Wiseman and James Toop

ISBN 978 1 899163 98 4
Copyright © 2012 Dale Vargas and Peter Knowles
First published 2012

Published by
JJG Publishing
Sparrow Hall
Hindringham
Norfolk NR21 0DP

Designed by Graham Hiles
Printed in China through Colorcraft Ltd., Hong Kong

Contents

Acknowledgements

The authors are most grateful to a large number of people for their help in the production of this history. The former Provost of Eton, Sir Eric Anderson, gave his blessing to the project and was generous in his encouragement, allowing us access to the College archive and the photographic archive. His successor, Lord Waldegrave of North Hill, has kindly extended this access. We are therefore particularly indebted to the College Archivist, Penny Hatfield, for sharing her profound knowledge of Etonian matters with us and for all her useful advice. For most of its history, Eton fives has been a school game and we have therefore relied heavily on school records. In caring for these records, some schools are better equipped than others: some have full time professional archivists, in others the school librarian has a dual role; many rely on alumni as part-time archivists but in others it falls to a master with a full teaching timetable. To them all we express our gratitude for their patience with our demands for information and images, and for their tolerance of our repeated pestering.

In particular we wish to thank Rosemary Baldwin, Archivist at Queen Elizabeth's Grammar School, Barnet; Molly Barton of the Old Aldenhamian Society; Sam Bellringer, Research & Database Manager, Mill Hill School; Michael Bevington, Archivist at Stowe School; Andrew Bishop, Deputy Headmaster of Summer Fields; Rita Boswell, Archivist at Westminster School and Harrow School; Peter Boughton, Bursar of Ipswich School; Richard Brett, Archivist at St Columba's College, Rathfarnham; Ellen Broughton, Archivist at Ipswich School, John M Brown, Old Olavians EFC; Nancy Crisp of St Columba's College; Leigh Cunningham, Development Officer, Framlingham College; Tom Dawson, Headmaster of Sunningdale School; Anne Drewery, Archivist at Lancing College; Marian Delfgou, Archivist at Chigwell School; Jonathan Evans, Archivist at the Royal London Hospital; Mike Fenn, Former Secretary of the Eton Fives Association; Dirk Hey of Old Zuozers Fives Club; Deborah Jennings, Archivist at Portsmouth Grammar School; Lynne Johnson, Archivist at Wolverhampton Grammar School; Stephen Jones, former Headmaster of Dover College; Tony Jones, Archivist at Emanuel School; Mervyn Joyner, Archivist at Wrekin College; Jenny Kohnhorst, Archivist at Berkhamsted School; Liz Larby, Archivist at Gresham's School, Holt; Mike Leach, Sports Master at Rydal Penrhos School; Suzanne Mann, Archivist at Cranleigh School; Patrick Mileham, Editor of *Wellington College, The First 150 Years*; Mike Morrogh, Archivist at Shrewsbury School; Richard Meunier, Deputy Archivist at the Royal London Hospital; James Newton, Archivist at Highgate School; John Ottley, Secretary of the Old Burians Association; John Puddefoot, Warden of St Thomas' College, Mount Lavinia; Chris Potter of the Old Wellingtonian Society; Anthony Reeve, Archivist at St Bees School; John Reynolds of the Old Citizens EFC; Terry Rogers, Archivist at Marlborough College; Jerry Rudman, Archivist at Uppingham School; Curt Schmitt of the Lyceum Alpinum, Zuoz; Alan Shrimpton, Archivist at Bryanston School; Catherine Smith, Archivist at Charterhouse; Elizabeth Spicer, Information Officer at Exeter College, Oxford; Paul Stevens, Archivist at Repton School; Gordon Stringer of the Old

Citizens EFC; Stuart Tate, Archivist at Aysgarth School; Pamela Taylor, Archivist at Mill Hill; Judith Thomas, Librarian at St Bartholomew's School, Newbury; Christine Vickers of the Photographic Archive at Eton College; Michael Weaver, Archivist at Woodbridge School; Jane Wells, Archivist at St Olave's Grammar School, Orpington; and Alison Wheatley, Archivist at King Edward's School, Birmingham.

We would also like to thank the following who have contributed photographs or reminiscences:

Gerald Barber, John Batting, Tony Beadles, Alison Brunner, Gareth Hoskins, Rodney Knight, Robin Moulsdale, Charles Robins, Michael Stewart, Kitty Turnbull, Derek Whitehead, Peter Worth and Mark Yates.

We have also been grateful for advice on the text or proof reading by Richard Barber, Ross Beckett, Richard Black, Michael Constantinidi, Mike Fenn, Kirsty Shanahan, Krystyna Vargas and Mark Williams.

The authors and publishers are also grateful to the following school archives for permission to print copies of photographs and other images:

Aldenham School Archive: pages 48 top, 55 lower and 104 lower;

Old Burian Association: page 38 top left;

Charterhouse Archive: pages 29, 34 lower left and right, 39 top right, and 94;

Eton College Photographic Archive: pages 13, 14, 15, 16, 17, 31, 32, 33, 34 top right, 44, 45, 54, 74, and 92.

Gresham's School Archive: pages 9 and 39 lower;

Harrow School Archive: pages 4, 28 top left, 37 lower, 38 right top left and right, 38 lower, 40, 56 left, 66, 72, and 117;

Highgate School Archive: pages 28 top right, 36 right, 39 top left, 47, 70 and 89;

King Edward's School, Birmingham, Archive: page 100;

Lancing College Archive: pages 34 right, lower right, and 85

Rugby School Archive: page 65;

Shrewsbury School Archive: pages 6, 28 lower left, 34 right lower left, 46, 69, 80 and 90;

St Columba's College, Rathfarnham, Archive: pages 23 and 24

Repton School Archive: page 28 lower right;

Uppingham School Archive: pages 25, 26, 27, 48 lower, and 86;

Westminster School Archive: pages 7 and 23

And to the following who have allowed us to reproduce images from their private collections: Gerald Barber (page 103), Alison Brunner (page 2), Gareth Hoskins (page 148 and cover picture), David Pedley (page 113), Gordon Stringer and the Old Citizens' Fives Club Archive (pages 52, 88, 91, 96, 98, 99, 104 right, 105, 109 lower left, and 145), Kitty Turnbull (page 114 top left), Derek Whitehead (page 95), Peter Worth (pages 43 and 109 all at top left) and Mark Yates (pages 30, top and bottom, 37 top, and 79)

Permission to use their work has also been given by professional photographers Allen Warren (page 110), and John Thompson (page 116) and *The Times* newspaper (page 97, upper and lower)

Photographs have also been reproduced from publications by the *Badminton Library of Sports and Games*: (pages x and 35); *The Lonsdale Library* (all on page 61); *Lionel Ford* by CA Alington, published by SPCK, 1934 (page 42); *Percy Chapman – a Biography* by David Lemmon, published by Queen Anne Press, 1985 (page 48, top left and right); *Many a Slip* by Colin Ingleby-Mackenzie, published by Oldbourne Book Co. Ltd., 1962 (page 100, lower)

Most of the other images have been taken from the Eton Fives Association Archive.

Foreword

Richard Barber OBE, President of the Eton Fives Association

Eton Fives is the best court game in the world. That is some claim to make, but I have high authority on my side for saying so. William Hazlitt, one of the greatest writers in our language, describing the game of fives as it was played in the 1820s, wrote:

It may be said that there are things of more importance than striking a ball against a wall — there are things indeed which make more noise and do as little good, such as making war and peace, making speeches, and answering them, making verses and blotting them; making money and throwing it away. But the game of fives is what no one despises who has ever played at it. It is the finest exercise for the body, and the best relaxation for the mind. ... He who takes to playing at fives is twice young. He feels neither the past nor future 'in the instant'. Debts, taxes, domestic treason, foreign levy, nothing can touch him further. He has no other wish, no other thought, from the moment the game begins, but that of striking the ball, of placing it, of making it!

In the 1870s a master at Eton made a still more extravagant claim for the game when he wrote, "the evolution of the Eton Fives court ...was the most valuable contribution ever made by the School to the well-being of mankind." In more recent times, my uncle Alan Barber, who was Chairman of the Eton Fives Association in the 1960s, played in a match to inaugurate a school's new fives court, at the end of which the school's master in charge of sport said to him that fives was all very well but it wasn't a patch on squash. Alan rounded on him. "Nothing could be further from the truth," he said, and then emphasised fives' comparative merits in detail.

- alone of all games, fives fully exercises both right and left sides of the body at the same time,
- fives' teaching of speed of foot and all-round hand and eye coordination is second to none, a peerless training for all ball-games,
- fives is a far safer game to play than squash or rackets,
- with four players on court you need to use your head at fives twice as much as at squash, with a social dimension to match,
- fives allows people of widely different ages to play together on equal terms,
- fives costs virtually nothing to take part, the only equipment required being a pair of gloves,
- fives can be played to a far greater age than squash,
- alone of all games, Fives requires no referee or arbitrator, thereby putting a high premium on learning fair play and courtesy at an early age,
- and, as a game of hazard, the unexpected is a part of every Eton fives rally, "a very mirror of Life itself".

I do not believe that any other game on earth can make such extravagant claims as that! It is therefore long overdue that such a game should have its own history.

Dale Vargas and Peter Knowles have done a huge service to the game in writing this fascinating book, taking the story from the game's emergence in "fives places" in the precincts of parish churches (to the horror of many an 18th century vicar) into a game played in the early 19th century by Eton boys against an outside corner of their College Chapel and, through a panoply of extraordinary personalities, evolving gradually into the game we know today, played by men and (increasingly) women throughout England and in a number of countries around the world.

A major theme which threads its way through the story is the role played by headmasters in the 19th and early 20th centuries, who had played the game themselves, realised its unique merits and introduced it into their schools as it spread beyond the confines of Eton College to a wider playing population. Today in the 21st century the role of headmasters in giving the game visible and energetic support at their schools remains the decisive influence, above all others, in keeping Eton fives alive and thriving. It is through their enthusiasm, allied to the support of the Eton Fives Association, that the game will continue to flourish wherever it is played, and so ensure that this story of Eton fives will be enjoyed by an ever-widening population of players far into the 21st century and beyond.

Sketch by Lucien Davis of the courts at Eton in about 1900

Chapter 1

Introduction

One wonders why it is that some games attain national and international popularity while others remain a minority interest or wither on the vine. Why did rugby football become a national and international game, but not the Eton field game or Winchester football? The same question could be asked of squash, rackets and fives, or of lawn tennis and real tennis. It might be observed that modern rugby football bears as little similarity to its original form as soccer does to the Eton field game, but the answer is not simply that these 'better' games have forced their way to wider participation. Could it just be chance?

For Eton fives the question is in three parts: why did the game break out from Eton College to be adopted by other schools? Having broken out, why did it not become a universal game? How has it managed to survive as a minority pursuit?

Many of the readers of this history will be familiar with Eton fives and will require no explanation, but for those who are not, here is a brief introduction. It should perhaps be noted that there are two other forms of handball known as 'fives' currently played in Britain: Rugby fives and Winchester fives are played in differently configured courts with different rules. Also note that, for convenience of description, the masculine form, 'he' and 'his', is used, although today an increasing number of women play Eton fives.

Eton fives is a hand-ball court game. It is played between two teams of two players. Players wear padded leather gloves since the ball, which is slightly larger but lighter than a golf ball, is made of rubber and cork and is quite hard.

The Eton fives court has three walls, the back of the court being completely open. The inside of the court is quite complicated in design, being based on a bay formed by the buttresses at the base of the Chapel steps at Eton College, where the game originated.

The court is divided into two parts by a step, which is positioned about one-third of the length of the court from the front wall. The front part of the court is variously known as the 'top step' or 'front' or 'upper court'. Because of the step, the front court is a few inches higher than the rear part, which is known as the 'back court' (or 'lower court'). The end of the back court is defined by another small step.

While there are no actual rules about where the players must stand during a game – except during the service – it is usual for two players (one from each team) to be in the front court, whilst their partners play in the back court, although a player may hit the ball in either court during the course of a game.

A bevelled ledge runs around the three walls, about four-and-a-half feet above the floor. On the front wall, the lower angle of this ledge is the 'line', on or above which the ball must be played to be 'up'. The walls in the front court have an additional flat ledge about two feet from the floor. The upper limit of the three walls is defined by the 'coping': the stonework at the top.

The most obvious feature of an Eton fives court is the large projection on the left-hand side, called the 'buttress' or, less commonly, the 'pepper pot' or 'pepper'. The shape of the buttress defies description – the name 'pepper pot' is not much help – but is derived precisely from the end of the banister at the bottom of the steps of the Eton College Chapel and is best seen in the photographs. It is located at the left-hand side of the step and extends into both the front and back courts. Where the buttress meets the step it forms a small three-sided space, originally a drain, called 'the dead-man's hole' or just 'the hole'. This is a natural place to try to send the ball when playing, as the ball is then often irretrievable but, because it is very small, it requires great accuracy to direct the ball there successfully.

The game is played by players from each side hitting the ball in turn, called a 'rally'. A rally is lost when a player fails to return the ball onto the front wall above the line before it bounces twice, or hits it 'out'. If the winning team is serving (or 'up'), then that team wins a point. If the winning team is not serving, then it in turn becomes the server.

The service and return are important parts of the game and are unusual. The server stands on the top step and throws the ball high into the angle between the front and right-hand walls so as to fall just below the step. The important condition is that he must do this to meet the requirements of his opponent, the 'cutter'. The 'cutter' stands below the step in the back court and hits the ball into the same angle so that it hits the

Schools' Championships Semi-finals 2008: Highgate 2 (TM Nicoll & AK Yanovski [in red]) v Shrewsbury (MM McKeever & RF Griffiths)

front wall above the play line (the 'cut'). If he chooses not to accept the service or fails to return the ball above the line, this does not matter and nothing happens. The server serves again. Once the cut has gone 'up', the ball is in play and, if the server or his partner can return the ball above the line, a rally begins.

Eton fives is the only remaining game where the serve (as the word originally meant) is a service to the opponent and not a weapon to win a point on its own or an advantage in the ensuing rally.

This brief description will only have given the reader a rough idea of Eton fives. It is a strange

AC Ainger, a Master at Eton from 1864-91 and a champion of fives, personified the concept of games in that era. He wrote a *Song of Fives*; it is typical of the allegorical style of school songs of the period, espousing games as lessons for life:

Smooth and square and dry the wall;
White, elastic, round, the ball;
Two on that side, two on this;
Two hands each to hit or miss –
.....Two hands each to hit or miss,
What more need we to possess,
Two good hours of happiness?
.....What more need, &c.

Send the service slow and high;
Hold your tongue and mind your eye;
Turn and twist, and duck and dance;
Volley, when you see your chance –
.....Volley, when you see your chance
Hit them hard, and hit them low;
Thus your score will upwards go!
.....Hit them hard, &c.

Aces after aces get;
Shun the unprogressive let;
Slowly, surely onward crawl;
Set the game at 'fourteen all' –
.....Set the game at 'fourteen all'!
Blackguards gain not honour, but
Honour gain by 'blackguard cut'!*
.....Blackguards gain, &c.

From the moment you begin;
Do your level best to win;
Cheer your partner; wipe your shoes;
Keep your temper, win or lose –

.....Keep your temper, win or lose.
If you miss it, don't be vexed;
Badly this time – better next!
.....If you miss it, &c.

Oft you'll think, in after lives;
What is life? – a game at Fives;
Partners to their partners true;
Courteous to their rivals, too –
.....Courteous to their rivals, too.
Here and there alike the aim
In the end to win the game!
.....Here and there, &c.

Oft in life you'll meet with knocks
'Gainst a harder pepper-box;
Fingers scraped and fingers bruised;
Ball and player roughly used –
.....Ball and player roughly used.
Till 'cut down,' or slow or fast,
Into 'dead man's hole' at last!
.....Till 'cut down,' &c.

So let Fives its lessons teach;
Hit all balls within your reach;
If you fail for want of pluck,
Don't abuse your rival's luck –
.....Don't abuse your rival's luck!
Everyone can win who tries,
For the struggle is the prize.
.....Everyone can win, &c.

---

* A 'blackguard cut' is a 'fault' because it has hit the front wall on the wrong side of the 'blackguard line'. See Laws (Appendix 6) for full explanation.

fact that complicated games have complicated rules: examples are real tennis and chess. Are they 'better' games than lawn tennis and draughts? Who can say? It is really a matter of preference. The design of the Eton fives court, with its profusion of ledges and angles, adds marvellous complexity to the game and puts a huge premium on the elusive quality of 'court craft'. Skilful players make great use of the features – especially the buttress – to confuse and deceive their opponents. Simple shots often become unpredictable ricochets. The front court is particularly difficult to play in, as the ball may easily change direction several times during its travel.

Eton fives played well is an extremely fast game, but it is also a game of great skill – players practised in its subtleties and nuances will nearly always beat those who rely mainly on brute force and speed. A pair including a left-handed player is often considered to have an advantage but, as the ball may be hit with either hand, the truly ambidextrous have the greatest advantage of all.

A further characteristic of Eton fives is worth mentioning, as it goes against all the trends in modern sport. Although players play to win, there is a strain of chivalry running through the game, that is an essential part. The server serves to the requirements of the cutter: there is no such thing as a winning serve or an ace. Second, in a crowded fives court collisions and obstructions tend to occur, and it is a well established principle that a 'let' (whereby the point is played again) should be offered to the opposition before it is requested. The game is played without a referee, the players keeping the score and resolving disagreements among themselves. Only in very rare and exceptional circumstances, such as where two pairs have an acrimonious relationship, is a referee appointed but even then his role is just that: someone to whom irresolvable disputes are referred. Third, when a team reaches one point short of game (known as 'game ball') it is required to place itself at a disadvantage by serving with one foot in the lower court until the ball

Cutting and receiving cuts are crucial features of Eton fives

is cut, and allowing the opposition to cut the ball anywhere on the front wall above the line.

To some this may seem odd, even perverse, but then Eton fives is a Victorian game with Victorian values: cheating is anathema and generosity to an opponent is a sight seen all too rarely in modern sport.

In the pages that follow, we shall be tracing the

The step and ledges of the Eton fives court add to the skills required for the game.

path of Eton fives from an informal game played by boys in tailcoats hitting a ball up against a wall of the Eton College Chapel to its adoption by other Public Schools in the second half of the nineteenth century; to its wider spread to schools of varying stripe in the early years of the 20th century; through a surge of popularity in the 1920s and 1930s when it was adopted as an adult game and exported overseas to some very unlikely places; to the organisation of the game by a proper governing body.

We shall trace its path through the cataclysmic events of the Second World War, the years of austerity and the 'fives ball crisis'; through the recovery years, the flirtation with sponsorship, the awareness of the possibilities of Eton fives as a game that can be played and enjoyed beyond the narrow stratum of society that has been its traditional home; through its acceptance as a women's game; to the formation of a charitable trust to try to achieve such a spread of interest and the construction of courts in a public sports centre. It is a strange tale that threads its way through the ups and downs of the social history of the last two centuries.

It will come as no surprise that many of the best exponents of Eton fives have also been good at other games, in particular cricket: many of the skills are similar. It will perhaps be unexpected that no fewer than six England cricket captains have been first-class Eton fives players: the Hon Ivo Bligh, the Hon FS Jackson, APF Chapman, RWV Robins, PBH May and JM Brearley. Many other familiar names will find their way into the story – but we must not jump ahead. To see how the game of Eton fives evolved, we need to go back even before the Victorian era, back nearly two hundred years.

Chapter 2

The Games of Fives

The name "Fives" has, for many years, been given to games played by hitting a ball with the hand, usually against a wall. The commonly accepted belief is that the word 'fives' came from a 'bunch of fives', being a slang term for a hand or fist, although other theories have been suggested. However, until the second half of the 18th century, the terminology was imprecise, as were the conditions of play. Hitting the ball over a net strung across the middle of the court was common practice (the forerunner of the game that was to become real tennis) and *jeu de paume* (hand-ball) was played in many forms, with the hand, a bat or a racquet. Research suggests that the bat or racquet was preceded by winding a form of string round the hand, not for protection, but to be able to hit the ball harder. This newspaper advertisement was published in 1742:

> To all Gentlemen that like the exercise of Tennis, Fives or Billiards.
>
> *There is a complete Tennis-Court, with a Tambour and everything that makes it as good a Tennis-Court as any in England at 1s. a Set single or 6d. a Set double; with Fives-playing in the Tennis-Court and Billiards at the same place. Its near the Bull and Gate Inn, Holborn... next door to Adlam's Coffee-House, opposite Little Turnstile. It's kept by Thomas Higginson, Who keeps a Fives Court at the bottom of St Martin's Street... Its for Fives-playing only either with Racquets, Boards or at Hand-Fives at 2d., 3d. or 4d. a Game.*

The term 'Fives Court' seems to have been used to describe many rectangular spaces and early prints show them being used for all sorts of activities, notably boxing, in addition to ball games. Hazlitt's famous essay tribute to Jack Cavanagh, the fives player, written in 1819, is interesting in that he *assumes* that the readers know what fives is, without either explaining the name or describing the game that he played.

Handball games have been played all over the world since time immemorial – John Lolkama lists 45 in his *Handball Games of the World* – the closest relatives to fives being the Basque games of Pelota, and Irish handball. In the west of England, judging by the number of notices prohibiting ball games in their precincts, 'fives places' seem to have been very common in the 18th century. Church walls were the most popular, but play there caused endless problems with broken windows and the like. Parish records are full of

A print of the Old School at Shrewsbury showing fives courts on the right of the picture, 1811

entries such as: "For digging up ye Fives place 3s 6d." The following is a notice from the "Vestry of the Parish of St. Peter Portesham" in 1751:

We whose names are underwritten taking into our Serious Consideration the Many Damages done to the Church as also the Invasion of Private Property, together with the Nuisance and above all the Prophanation arising from the Scandalous Practice of Playing at Vives [fives] in Church Yarde have this Day agreed to put a Stop to so Infamous a Practice in respect of That belonging to our Parish. This therefore is to give Notice That Whoever shall presume to Play Vives in this Church Yarde from the Day of the Date hereof will be prosecuted with the Utmost Rigour of the Law, as so Complicated an Insult upon God and Man calls for and demands at our Hands...

Fives was usually played against the north wall, known as the 'devil's side' as there were normally no graves there. The story is told of Paylor Matthew Proctor, vicar of Newland in Gloucestershire, who took extreme measures to stop games being played in the churchyard by directing that he should be buried at the spot where the parishioners played.

Wiltshire, Somerset and Dorset were dotted with fives walls at this time, many of which still survive. The oldest school court still standing is to be found at the former Lord Weymouth Grammar School, now Warminster School. An early brochure states that the court "was built before 1787". This court consists of a single high wall with 'wings' protruding at 135 degrees on each side.

However, it is not the purpose of this book to make a study of these various forms of fives. Rather we shall restrict ourselves to the particular game played at Eton College in England and now known as 'Eton fives' – but some background is necessary.

Like rugby football and squash, Eton fives

Little Dean's Yard at Westminster, 1843

began as a school game. Unlike the other two, it has remained largely so, only recently breaking free of the school playground. Quite why it should have been constrained within this strait-jacket is a matter for conjecture. Some have suggested that the intricacies of the court – a joy for experienced players but a deterrent to beginners – and the necessity of four players for a game have impeded its spread. Others have suggested that Eton fives has been perceived as a toffs' game – although why that should restrict its popularity is unclear: the jibe about a hooligans' game being played by gentlemen did nothing to restrain the popularity of rugby football. Whatever the reason, the close relationship between Eton fives and schools has meant that the story of Eton fives is closely entwined with the evolution of education in this country, particularly in the schools that came to be known as 'public'.

In the course of the 18th century, boys attending these schools found a set of circumstances that led them to become extremely inventive at ways of amusing themselves. First, they were away from home and, second, the hours devoted to study were quite short. Around 1770, the normal academic programme was five hours of school each day, but no lessons on Tuesdays and numerous whole holidays, allowing plenty of time for the 'extra', and for masters more profitable, activity of private tuition. The boys meanwhile were left to their own devices with masters paying little attention to what those might be.

Many of these "ways of amusing themselves" were destructive if not actually criminal, such as throwing stones at birds and windows; others were harmless. In *Nugae Etonienses*, published in 1766, the author lists over thirty games in vogue at that date. As it was not unusual for the younger boys at the time to be no older than six, many of these are what we would now consider to be childish games. There were top spinning, hoop rolling, hopscotch and banister sliding. Less familiar were 'headimy', 'peg-in-the-ring', 'trap-ball', 'chucksteal baggage' and 'puss-in-the-corner'. When Lord John Russell went to Westmin-

ster in 1803 he found "the boys play at hoops, pegtops and pea-shooters". Harrovians were inveterate stone throwers: it was said that no dog could live on Harrow Hill. 'Toozling' was the chasing and killing of young birds and Jack o'Lantern was a sort of chase whereby a boy with a lamp was hunted through the fields and woods. At Shrewsbury 'fox hunts' were popular with boys playing all parts, including the fox, and to this day the cross country club is known as the 'Royal Shrewsbury School Hunt'. 'Boar hunts' were also conducted, chasing and killing a young pig. Various forms of football also began to take shape, much of it brutal; there was a lot of fighting, and bullying was rife. The novel *Tom Brown's Schooldays* gives a flavour of the period.

The industrial revolution made the 19th century a time of social upheaval in the country generally but it was a time of fundamental change in the Public Schools. The famous Dr Thomas Arnold, credited with the civilising of Rugby School, was Head Master from 1828-42. He was no enthusiast for games himself – he preferred the chapel and the classroom – but he saw that they provided him with an opportunity to channel the energies of adolescent boys more fruitfully. Arnold's policy of encouraging the senior boys themselves to organise sporting activities proved a success and was taken up by his disciples, in particular Charles Vaughan at Harrow and George Cotton at Marlborough. In 1852 Vaughan set up the Philathletic Club to organise school games. The following year Cotton (the model for Tom Brown's 'young master' at Rugby), sent out a circular to parents setting out his vision for the place of games in education, and Edward Thring, who was to play an important role in the history of Eton fives, arrived at Uppingham. Masters were now encouraged to take part in games, which soon were to become compulsory.

The Clarendon Commission was appointed in 1863 to investigate the perceived mismanagement, out-of-date practices and financial irregularities in the public schools. One of the problems was that many were tied into ancient char-

The fives court at Gresham's Old School, Holt. In this picture they are playing with racquets, but hands would have been more normal. Eton fives courts were built at the new site but demolished in the 1960s

ters and statutes, for example restricting the teaching to Latin and Greek; many had also long departed from their founder's purpose to provide a free education for the poor of the parish. The Commissioners took as their sample the nine 'Great Public Schools': Charterhouse, Eton, Harrow, Merchant Taylors', Rugby, St Paul's, Shrewsbury, Westminster and Winchester. The Public Schools Act of 1868 freed these schools (and others) from the yoke of Crown, Church or Government and granted them independence over their administration.

The wind of change blowing through the old public schools, the growth in numbers and prosperity of the British middle class and their acquisition of wealth propelled a scramble for education in the second half of the 19th century. The appeal of the ancient foundations under these more enlightened regimes widened and new schools appeared: Cheltenham (1841), Marlborough and Rossall (1843), Radley (1847), Bradfield (1850), Wellington (1853), Clifton, Malvern and Haileybury (1862), Cranleigh (1865), and the Woodard Foundation which

gave birth to Lancing (1848), Hurstpierpoint (1849), Bloxham (1860) and Denstone (1873) among others.

The rapid growth of the industrial cities led to increased anxiety about pollution and contagious diseases, especially cholera, that threatened the middle classes as well as the poor. The growing numbers, the desire for open countryside and the space to play games provoked a number of schools to move out of the cities; for example, St John's School (to Leatherhead in 1872), Charterhouse (to Godalming in 1874), Shrewsbury (across the river to Kingsland in 1882), Emanuel (to Wandsworth in 1883) and Christ's Hospital (to Horsham in 1897). All these schools, in addition to the 'new' schools above, were equipped with fives courts of one sort or another.

The games evolving in the public schools at this time were cricket, various forms of football, rowing (if there was a river nearby), athletics, cross country running in the form of beagling or other hunting, shooting, rackets and fives. Fencing and gymnastics were to come later. Lawn tennis was considered a 'soft' game and in some schools was actually banned. Games promoted manliness and character. The team games were top of the list for character forming; they taught corporate spirit, reliance of one player on another, the merging of the individual into the team.

A related preoccupation of the Victorians was health. In one of its early reports, Clarendon commended the public schools "on their love of healthy sports and exercise". The medical profession grew enormously in the first half of the 19th century, producing more university-trained doctors in this period than in the entire preceding history of the profession. There was widespread belief that mental disorders had their origins in defects of the body and the clichéd phrase, 'Mens sana in corpore sano', became a byword for healthy living. Physical exercise was seen to be important in the practical business of turning out boys who were healthy in mind and body, and Public School masters, who hitherto had spent their time "divided between Latin verse and patriotic doggerel", embraced the athletic revolution with enthusiasm. "[Fives] gives grand exercise to all parts of the body," pronounced the

Hon EH Lyttelton, Old Etonian, Head Master of Eton and one of the great pundits of his day.

As the century wore on, there were other notable changes: players of games began to wear more suitable clothing by the standards of the day – no longer top hats, waistcoats, boots or braces on the fives court!

The rules of games were written down rather than passed by word of mouth. The laws of cricket had been first written down in 1774 when the game began to be played widely, but it was some years before rugby football followed in 1846; the first association football rules were devised in 1863. The rules of Eton fives were not written down until 1877 for the simple reason that there had been no need to; everyone who played the game had learned the rules as part of the Eton way of life.

Finally and most significantly, communications improved: the railway, the telephone, the wireless telegraph, the motor car and tarmac roads all helped schools to look beyond their boundaries, and to exchange ideas and practices. It even made travel between them possible.

Chapter 3

Shirking Walls

The Origin of Eton Fives

What idle progeny succeed
To chase the rolling circle's speed
Or urge the flying ball?

The writer of these lines was Thomas Gray, who was at Eton in 1730. The first reference is probably to hoop-rolling; the second could be any ball game, possibly fives.

The first three games listed in *Nugae Etonienses* are Cricket, Shirking Walls and Fives. Cricket is known to have been played at Eton in the early years of the 18th century. Horace Walpole who entered the College in 1726 later wrote that "cricket was a common occurrence" at this time. There were certainly matches between Eton and Westminster played at Tothill Fields in the 1790s and the 1805 Eton and Harrow match at Thomas Lord's first ground became widely known because the poet Byron was in the Harrow team and wrote about it afterwards. But 'Shirking Walls' needs some explanation.

The matter of 'bounds', that is, where boys were allowed to go, seems to have been one of constant dispute at Eton for many years. Indeed, controversy between assistant masters and sixth form praepostors on this subject seems to have been one of the main causes of a rebellion in 1768. The streets of Eton and Windsor were officially 'out of bounds' and boys found there and in the neighbouring countryside by a master were likely to be sent back to College. A 'lower boy'

Dr Edward Hawtrey, Head Master of Eton, 1834-53. It was during his headmastership that the first fives 'walls' were built

might be similarly treated by a sixth former unless he had been given permission known as 'liberties'. This led to a strange custom known as 'shirking'. Maxwell Lyte, in his *History of Eton College 1400–1910*, explained: "If a boy saw a master coming towards him in the High Street he was expected to dive into a shop to allow him to pass.... On the other hand he might safely follow a master at a respectful distance, etiquette forbidding the latter to turn round or go out of his way in search of delinquents.... The real offence was a failure to 'shirk'."

Quite how the buttresses against the wall of College Chapel came to be known as 'shirking walls' is not clear. The Provost, Joseph Goodall, writing to his former pupil CT Metcalfe in 1816, alludes to the "steps near the shirking walls" as a place where stray copies of *Horace* or of the *Poetae Graeci* might often be picked up. Presumably, College Yard was 'in bounds' thereby removing the need to shirk. On the other hand, the word later took on the more general meaning of 'to avoid' and there were no doubt many unpleasant duties such as fagging to be avoided. To 'shirk a boy' – that is to fail to answer the fag master's call – was a serious offence.

During the first half of the 19th century, the Head Master and Lower Master used to take 'Absence' once or twice a day, standing on the Chapel steps in School Yard. This was quite a lengthy procedure as the masters read out a list of the boys' names, checking who was missing: it could take up to an hour. Meanwhile, the boys, bored by waiting to have their names called out, would play with a ball in the bays between the buttresses. These handball games became known as 'shirking walls' and 'fives': 'Upper and Lower Fives' are mentioned. The game was described as "flourishing" by George Lyttelton in 1825, "the favourite time being before 11 o'clock school, when a ring of spectators would assemble to watch good players". He spoke of the skill required to return a ball from the far end of the 'off wall' (lower step) while actually jumping off the steps descending from the Chapel entrance.

Such was the popularity of the game that some replicas of the 'doubles court' were built at some of the boarding houses. William Rogers in his *Reminiscences* (1888) wrote, "During the first half of the 19th century the game gradually became popular at Eton... Certain Houses built more or less exact replicas of the Chapel court...." The remnants of one of these, known as the 'Pigsty' because of its position next to a piggery, could still be seen as late

as the 1930s. However, the Hon EH Lyttelton in *Fifty Years of Sport at Eton, Harrow & Winchester*, published in 1920, declares that the first courts were built in 1840 "on the Wick Road" claiming them to be four or six in number.

Maxwell Lyte: "Two of the paved 'courts', assuredly not made for any such purpose, could be used only by two players apiece; but at the foot of the stairs leading up to the north door of the chapel there is a larger space, partially obstructed on the left by the end of a stone balustrade, the prototype of the 'pepper box' which to this day forms an essential feature of the Eton fives court. There four boys could play together, two of them between the buttresses, and the other two behind them on a level platform, a few inches lower down. It is not improbable that the name of 'Fives' was originally limited to the game as played by two boys and that the game played by four boys on the larger 'court' corresponded to 'shirking walls', the second game on the list in the *Nugae Etonienses....*"

Shirking Walls? This space at the foot of the steps to the College Chapel became the basis for the Eton fives court

The *Eton College Magazine*: "The formal recognition already accorded to boating was in 1847 extended to the unpretending game of Fives, hitherto played exclusively in the School Yard. At the instigation of Mr EH Pickering and Mr JG Mountain, Dr Hawtrey laid the foundation stone of some new fives courts in Trotman's Garden on the Dorney Road on 4 December 1847 and declared the site 'within bounds'. As soon as the ceremony was over the Lower Master, Richard Okes, stepped forward

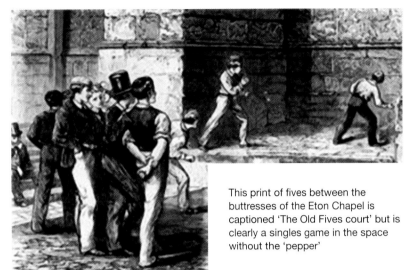

This print of fives between the buttresses of the Eton Chapel is captioned 'The Old Fives court' but is clearly a singles game in the space without the 'pepper'

and delivered a Latin oration containing many puns and good-humoured banter on the Head Master's unfamiliarity with athletic sports. Some verses and epigrams in five languages, Greek, Latin, French, German and Italian by different Assistant Masters, were printed as a memorial of the occasion." In spite of this declaration by the Head Master, it appears that some of the Assistant Masters "persisted in requiring boys to 'shirk' them on their way".

We can then reasonably deduce from these fragments that the game conceived at the foot of the Chapel staircase, spawned replicas around the Houses that grew into the Eton fives courts we know today. And it is to Dr Edward Hawtrey, Head Master 1834-53, that credit for giving Eton fives full status as a game, must go. As anyone who compares the Eton fives court with the original Chapel bay can easily detect, some important decisions were made at this time and changes were made to improve the game. The continuation of the

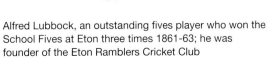

Alfred Lubbock, an outstanding fives player who won the School Fives at Eton three times 1861-63; he was founder of the Eton Ramblers Cricket Club

side walls below the step has generally been considered essential but the bevelled ledges along these side walls and the protruding pillars at the back have been more controversial. The slight slope of the floor, introduced to expedite drainage before the days of covered courts, has become a standard feature of the court. In fact it was not long before the dimensions had to be altered further. The first replica walls were built in sandstone, a material that quickly erodes, and the re-facing with plaster reduced the dimensions by two inches on each surface.

The new fives 'walls' (note the terminology – it was only much later that they came to be known as 'courts') quickly became extremely popular but four 'walls' were completely inadequate for a school of 740 pupils (811 by 1863). 'Lower boys' didn't stand a chance and even seniors resorted to such tactics as asking a master, who had a free period at the end of the morning, to play with them and thus 'bag' a court.

'Singles fives', probably a hang-over from the days of play in the 'singles bays' on the Chapel wall, survived until the late 1850s. However occupation of a court by just two boys when spaces were scarce was not tolerated. An accepted procedure was for new arrivals to announce themselves: "Four wall, holes innings, finge ball." This seemingly incomprehensible patter can be translated as, "We're making up a four, I'm serving and we'll play with your ball." No compromises there! As boys had to buy their own fives balls this last assertion was important.

Arthur Kinnaird, 'Fives Champion' at Cambridge University in 1869; Scotland football international 1873; President of the Football Association 1890-1923. In 1924 his son, Kenneth, donated the challenge cup for the Eton Fives Championships, thereby ensuring the perpetuation of the Kinnaird name in the world of Eton fives

Chapter 4

Etona et Hic Noster Ludus

The Development of Fives at Eton 1850-1900

"Of all the decades in our history," wrote GM Young in his *Victorian England: a Portrait of an Age*, "a wise man would choose the 1850s to be young in." The Great Exhibition of 1851 was a symbol of the country's progress and achievements. Britain was the centre of world manufacture, commerce and banking. It was a prosperous time for factory owners and land owners; in spite of the Crimean War (1853-56) the country was secure and confident. In the schools it was a time for expansion and building and at Eton that included fives courts. In 1863, after an appeal for contributions, the Dorney Lane courts were improved and two new ones built. Only payers of school subscriptions (including Old Etonians) were permitted to play on these courts and there was also a plea for players to "wear proper shoes". The wearing of "boots of the toughest description" was deplored: three years later it was deemed necessary to introduce a fine of one shilling for not wearing 'fives shoes'. Serious – but not as serious as using a bat or racquet: fine 2s 6d.

Enthusiasm for fives was gathering apace. The School Fives competition began in 1857 when the first winners were TE Bagge and FE Norman. It is difficult to know how good they were, but both went on to win cricket blues at Cambridge, Norman in 1858-60; Bagge in 1859-61 and captain in his last year. This was not such an achievement as it would have been a hundred years later but they were certainly good games players. The following year the winners were WM Hoare and WH Gladstone. Hoare was an unusual winner as he was a 'wet bob' and

Four Eton Masters who played influential supporting roles in the early days of fives

Rev JL Joynes, Assistant Master 1849-77, and one of the earliest supporters of fives. He donated the challenge cup for School Fives in 1865. The Lubbocks were in his House

Henry Salt, Assistant Master 1875-84; he was the son-in-law of Joynes and wrote his biography. He said that he left Eton because he could not tolerate the meat-eating habits of his colleagues. He may have been a little eccentric

GR Dupuis, Assistant Master 1858-75 and House Master, "One of the most famous amateur coaches of cricket and a keen fives player"

'Johnnie' Yonge, Assistant Master 1840-75; the 'fluke shot' was named after him

A C Ainger

A C Ainger (1841-1919) was educated at Eton where he was a 'Newcastle Select', that is winner of the most prestigious classics prize. He was a scholar at Trinity College, Cambridge, where he obtained a 'first class' in the Classical Tripos. He then returned to Eton as an Assistant Master in 1864, remaining there until his retirement in 1901. He was a prolific writer of songs and hymns for use at Eton, as well as books on the classics and the history of the College. Not many of the hymns have survived into modern hymn books but the best known are probably *God is working his purpose out* and *Let all God's people join in one*. He wrote *The Song of Fives* which is reproduced here and was the author (with HG Wintle) of the *English – Latin Verse Dictionary*. He produced *Eton in Prose and Verse* in 1915 and *Memories of Eton Sixty Years Ago* two years later.

Arthur Ainger was a champion of all things Etonian: he was largely responsible for the explosion of court building at Eton in the second half of the 19th century, persuading the College to build but also leaning on House Masters to build their own. It was he that assembled the committee to draft the first *Laws of Eton Fives* in 1877 and he contributed the chapter on Eton fives in the *Badminton Library of Sports & Pastimes*. Unsurprisingly he was a traditionalist and became involved in some tetchy correspondence in the *Eton College Chronicle* after he had retired from the College: "The ball should be bowled not thrown – overarm not underarm – at service," he wrote. "It requires practice but is the only correct way." This claim was contested the following week by a correspondent signing himself Senex, who claimed, "In my day the ball was always thrown…" And so on.

A former colleague described Ainger as "one of the most distinguished and useful of Eton masters, a man of clear head, controlling character, wide accomplishments, a fine and habile scholar of the old school, with a remarkable memory, an incisive speaker, a good critic, fertile in suggestion, complete in execution. He preserved admirable and friendly discipline by means of a dry and ready irony, which was never harsh or unamiable (sic). He set no punishments, and his justice, courtesy, and unruffled good humour won the respect and admiration of the boys."

stroked the Oxford boat between 1861 and 1863, when he was President. Gladstone, the eldest son of the future Prime Minister, played for Scotland against England in the first soccer international between the two countries.

When the Hon GC Lyttelton won with AE Pedder in 1860, he was the first of a family of exceptionally talented games players to make his mark on the fives court. His father, George, the fourth Baron Lyttelton, like many prosperous Victorians, was a prolific breeder. He sired eight sons and four daughters by his first wife, Mary, and then ran out to game (old scoring method: game at 15 points) with his second wife, Sybella. If he hadn't committed suicide by throwing himself down the stairs of his home, Hagley Hall, aged 59, there is no saying where it would have ended. All eight Lyttelton sons played county cricket, all but one (who left early) played in the Eton XI, four won blues at Cambridge and four won the School Fives. The eldest GC, later Viscount Cobham, and the youngest Alfred were

Presidents of the MCC. Edward, the seventh son, won the School Fives with his younger brother, Alfred, in 1873 and again with WF Forbes the following year. He was Head Master of Eton from 1905 to 1918.

In 1861 LW Dent and the "celebrated" Alfred Lubbock won the School Fives. Edward Lyttelton doubted "whether there had ever been a better player than Alfred Lubbock." Lubbock won the School Fives three times and in his last two years he was "so good he could have played with anyone." In 1862 he played with his brother, Edgar, who was a fifteen-year-old at the time, and in 1863 he played with Quintin Hogg "more for the fun than with any expectation of winning, as he was not a first class performer. By making him keep out of the way and taking as many shots as I could manage, we got into the final." They won the Final too against SF Freemantle and JB Walter, who were strong favourites.

It is difficult to tell how these players played their fives in the early days as this is rarely described in reports, but one can build up a broad brush picture. The greatest changes in games occur through advances in technology: the construction of the racquet has been the single factor in transforming lawn tennis. In cricket, the preparation and covering of wickets, the design of the bat and to a lesser extent the ball, have had a huge effect on the creation of a game unrecognisable to that played 150 years ago. Advances are also inspired by international competition and the urge to make money. None of these factors has occurred in Eton fives, at least up to 1960: the courts were the same, the ball was the same and any change in the design of the gloves was of no significance. In all likelihood, the game played by the Lubbocks and the Lytteltons was very similar to that played by Langton and Burrows, and the best Etonian players of the 1950s, and that is well within living memory. Their play concentrated on 'cutting' the ball into the pepper box to a length, that is to hit the nick and go dead; in the upper court, volleys were hit hard into the 'pepper' at every opportunity – but length was more impor-

tant than power. While the emphasis was on consistency and accuracy, constant use was made of variation of pace and angle.

In the 1860s and 1870s competition for 'walls' was becoming fierce: a booking system was devised "to stop unseemly rush out of Chapel to 'bag' walls", but it seemed to meet with no one's approval. In particular, there was an argument over unfair allocation of walls to Collegers and Oppidans. The informality of the organisation of games at this time is illustrated by the way in which two new walls were built in 1864: it was left to the Captain of the Oppidans to raise the necessary £300 and to commission the building. Old Etonians were banned from taking 'walls'

These four were members of the group of "clear-headed friends" who drafted the first rules of Eton fives in 1866

AC Ainger

RAH Mitchell

EC Austen Leigh

E Lubbock

The Hon Ivo Bligh

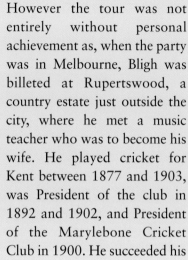

The Hon Ivo Bligh (1859-1927) was at Eton; he won the School Fives with J Lubbock in 1876, and with H Whitfield in 1877; he also won the Public Schools Rackets Championship in 1877. At Trinity College, Cambridge, he won cricket blues from 1878 to 1881, and was captain in his last year. Bligh was Amateur Rackets Champion (doubles) in 1878; (singles) in 1879 and 1880; he was also Tennis Champion (doubles) in 1878; (singles) in 1879 and 1880. Bligh is perhaps best known for captaining the English Test team that regained the Ashes in 1882-3. His Test career of four matches was hardly triumphant: he scored 62 runs at an average of 10.33. However the tour was not entirely without personal achievement as, when the party was in Melbourne, Bligh was billeted at Rupertswood, a country estate just outside the city, where he met a music teacher who was to become his wife. He played cricket for Kent between 1877 and 1903, was President of the club in 1892 and 1902, and President of the Marylebone Cricket Club in 1900. He succeeded his elder brother as Earl of Darnley in 1900 and became an Irish representative peer in 1905.

during term time. An entrance fee for the School Fives of three shillings per pair was introduced in 1863 and thirty-five pairs entered for the challenge cup donated by the Rev JL Joynes in 1865. Joynes had been Alfred Lubbock's tutor described by him as "not only a splendid player but a very enthusiastic devotee of the game." Junior cups were donated by the Marquis of Lorne and Quintin Hogg. A year later a House Cup was proposed: a letter in the *Chronicle* called for 'Cocks of College' – "as Harrow, Rugby, Marlborough and indeed all Public Schools play for Cock House at Rackets & Fives".

The first rackets court at Eton was built in South Meadows Lane in 1866. In many schools, notably Harrow, the popularity and success of rackets, being a court game appealing to players with the same sort of talents, has had a detrimental effect on fives. This was not so at Eton. A letter to the *Chronicle* in 1882 complains about the "small list of subscribers at the rackets courts. Unless this game is supported as warmly as any other it will eventually go to the wall." (Presum-

ably the pun was unintended!) The magazine reported the following year that the "popularity of rackets was declining".

Edgar Lubbock won the Schools Fives for the third time in 1866 with CR Alexander, and Alexander won the next year with CI Thornton. Thornton won with CJ Ottaway in 1868 and Ottaway won again in 1869 with J Maude. These two, Thornton and Ottaway, were formidable sportsmen: Thornton was a huge hitter of a cricket ball, reputedly having recorded a hit of over 160 yards at Hove in 1876; Ottaway was regarded by his contemporaries as perhaps the most versatile sportsman of his generation.

A further indication of the growth of status of fives was the setting up of an order of 'choices'. 'Choices' at Eton are recognition of the best players; in other schools they have more usually been called 'colours'. In 1871 a master, AC Ainger, himself an Old Etonian, persuaded Old Etonians to subscribe sufficient money to build twelve new courts and then "saddled each House with the task of building a court for itself." The new courts were built at the side of The Field, also known as Sixpenny, which has been the site of the fives courts ever since. In 1875 there were 45 pairs entered for the School Fives, won by J Wakefield and J Oswald – "strong evidence of the increasing popularity of the game". The Hon Ivo Bligh won in the next two years, with J Lubbock in 1876 and H Whitfield in 1877. Bligh is best known as the captain of England's cricket team in Australia in 1882/3, who was famously presented with the urn containing the 'ashes of English cricket'. He was a fine games player, Public Schools and Open Rackets champion and a real tennis champion, too.

Eton fives at this time was a game for Etonians and masters, often Old Etonians themselves. Some were very good players, notably RAH

Freeman Thomas

Freeman Thomas, later 1st Marquess of Willingdon (1866-1941) was at Eton where he won the School Fives with RH Pemberton in 1883 and with C Barclay in 1885, the year that they played Harrow for the first time. Thomas was also in the cricket XI for three years and captain in 1885. He went on to Trinity College, Cambridge, where he gained cricket blues in 1886-89 and played also for Sussex. In 1892 he changed his surname to Freeman-Thomas and married Marie Adelaide, daughter of Lord Brassey (the Brassey family lived at Heythrop Park in Oxfordshire, where they built their own Eton fives court).

Freeman Freeman-Thomas became an MP in 1900 and spent his early life getting himself into the right positions, first as secretary to Prime Minister, Herbert Asquith, and then as Lord-in-Waiting to King George V, with whom he used to play tennis. Thomas was Governor of Bombay from 1913-18 and of Madras 1919-24, having early clashes with Mahatma Gandhi and picking up distinctions and titles along the way. He was appointed Governor-General of Canada in 1926, serving until 1931 when he was appointed Viceroy of India, a post he held until 1936.

Thomas's elder son, the Hon GH Freeman-

Thomas was winner of the School Fives at Eton with RJF Chance in 1912, but was killed in World War I.

After Freeman Thomas's death in 1941, Edward Lyttelton wrote, "Tributes have been paid to Lord Willingdon as a cricketer, but he was supreme as a fives player of the Eton game. He helped to bring to a close the victorious career of two Cheam masters, Tancock and Wilson, who year after year challenged and defeated the Eton Keepers with only one defeat. About 1882 I felt a yearning to efface this stigma, and arranged two matches with the veterans, both of which they won. I ransacked the country, and in about 1887 secured Thomas as a partner, and at last laid the enemy low by six games to one. They had been, it is true, separated for a year, and Tancock was past his prime. But it was a mighty conflict between two traditions of play. The Cheam men evolved a technique of their own; a perfect system of collaboration, mostly 'on-wall' play, whereas the Eton tradition was a free and open game, almost as much 'off-wall' as 'on'. For a combination of gracefulness, agility, and force, I think I should reckon Freeman Thomas the best fives player I have ever seen."

WH Gladstone, winner of the School Fives in 1858; son of WE, Prime Minister

AC Ainger, the 'Father of Eton Fives'

The Hon Charles Lyttelton, winner of the School Fives in 1860; later Viscount Cobham and 5th Baron Lyttelton

RAH Mitchell, Old Etonian and Assistant Master at Eton 1866-1901. He was master in charge of cricket until 1897

Pages 20–22: 19th century fives players who were caught by the pen of Spy and other cartoonists

Mitchell, AC Ainger, EC Austen Leigh, GR Dupuis and JL Joynes. Others were less so. In the latter category fell the Rev JE Yonge, known as Johnny, whom Lubbock described as having "a strong vein of humour". In the heat of a rally, he had a tendency to play a very feeble stroke down the middle of the court, which he claimed was aimed for the edge of the step – a 'shooter' that sometimes happens as a fluke but could never be aimed for. Whenever it did happen, it was known as a 'Johnny Yonge'.

So far the rules of the game had been handed down by word of mouth. Indeed there had been disagreement on some points and proposals for changes. One such, in a letter to the *Chronicle* in 1870, suggests that "the first cut, if taken and hit 'down', should concede a point." 'Carrying' is mentioned for the first time in 1865 and an umpire was appointed for the Final of the School Fives – a sure sign that the match was being competitively contested. In 1875 there appeared a letter in the *Chronicle* from an Old Harrovian, Henry Jackson, in which he refers to the game being played at Cambridge, calling for some official rules of Eton fives to be published. There had been courts at Harrow since 1865 but, by all accounts, the design of these early courts was seriously different from the Eton courts and Jackson also asks for the proper dimensions to be written down. The following year AC Ainger "in conjunction with several clear-headed friends" (EC Austen Leigh, RAH Mitchell, A & E Lubbock, H & EH Hoare, WH Gladstone, EM Young and H Jackson) formulated the first set of rules.

Ainger may have thought that he and his colleagues had produced a clear set of rules, but to a modern reader – even one well versed in the game of Eton fives – they are incomprehensible. This is largely because of the terminology, which was inherited from a well established oral tradition. Who would have thought that the 'on-wall' and 'off-wall' actually referred to the floor of the upper and lower courts? Who would have thought that the player serving had 'holes innings' and that the player cutting was 'in holes'? Most bizarre of all, a shot that fell out of court and therefore lost the point, was called "a good 'un" whereas by any logical interpretation it was a 'bad 'un'! Few of these terms survived the re-drafting in 1933 and no purpose will be served by reproducing this set of rules here.

Fives was going through a period of great popularity at this time: the number of pairs in the

School Fives had climbed to 84 by 1881. "Fives of course will be as popular as ever…" crowed the *Chronicle* in its column, 'Present Times'. Two more distinguished cricketers, both later to play for England, won in 1878 and 1879: the Studd brothers, GB and CT. By 1894 Eton had 50 fives courts "and finds them none too many".

A correspondent to the *Chronicle* proposed the removal of the lower court ledges in 1866 and there is a body of opinion to this day that maintains that the game would be better without them. However this rather esoteric discussion need not detain us here. The request for a set of official rules from Cambridge would have caused no great surprise since there were many Old Etonians in residence and it was natural that they should wish to continue playing one of their school games. That the request should have come from an Old Harrovian might have raised a few eyebrows.

Matches in the School Fives were played up to 15 points but decided on the best of 3 games. The *Chronicle* report of 1882 refers in two places to games where the score had reached 14 all being 'sett' (sic). Whether this is some obscure reference to badgers – Etonians were notably ingenious in devising obscure terms – or just a spelling error is not clear!

AC Ainger claims that the term Keepers came to be used in 1867. The first mention in the *Chronicle* is in 1870 when the Keepers of Fives were authorised to be holders of the fives cups "unless they have left, in which case the responsibility fell to the Captain of the XI and the Captain of the School." The term 'keeper' is used at Eton rather than the more usual word 'captain' except in the two cases above. In fives, where presumably they are Keepers of the Fives Courts or Keepers of the Record Book, the term is extended to both the school pair, who are the Keepers. The 'Fives Book' only seems to have started in 1900 and comprises the Keeper's review of the season, traditionally signed off with the admirable sentiment: "Floreat Etona et hic noster ludus esto perpetuus".

Albert Brassey, a 'wet bob' at Eton but built his own fives court at Heythrop Park in Oxfordshire

Duke of Argyll; as Marquess of Lorne he donated the cup for the Junior Fives at Eton in 1865

The Hon Alfred Lyttelton, Winner of the School Fives in 1873; later played for England at both cricket and football

Arthur, 11th Lord Kinnaird; football international who played in nine FA Cup Finals; father of Kenneth, donor of the challenge cup for the Amateur Championship

It is clear from the above that there was a powerful fives culture among the 'beaks' at Eton, running right through its history at least up to World War II. This ran alongside the School Fives and is one of the reasons why the School Fives was played to such a high standard. Except for a period in the early 1900s when Edward Butler and George Townsend Warner, two Harrow Masters, formed a very strong pair, the Eton Masters set the standards to be matched. When

The Hon FS Jackson, the only non-Etonian of this collection, played in the Harrow pair of 1889; later he captained the England cricket XI that retained the Ashes in 1905

Edward Lyttelton, Winner of the School Fives at Eton 1873, 1874; Master of Haileybury; Head Master of Eton; county cricketer and international footballer

The Hon Ivo Bligh, Winner of the School Fives in 1876, 1877; later captained England cricket XI that regained the Ashes in 1882-3

Edgar Lubbock, a three times Winner of the School Fives in 1882, 1885 and 1886

Lionel Ford left the staff to become Head Master of Repton in 1901, Henry Marten wrote, "Lionel was almost in a class by himself; I don't think he and his partner (for some time George Mount) ever suffered defeat against the School pair, or had any

fear of it except perhaps in the case of Moon and Hely-Hutchison (Keepers 1901) and possibly Macnaghten and Kinnaird (Keepers 1898, 1899). But I think Lionel's greatest feats were in the games he used to play with Broadbent against two other Masters: Broadbent was a safe but rather slow-moving player... My impression is that as a pair they were seldom beaten. Of course, Lionel like all first-class players knew exactly where to stand, namely about two feet to the right of the pepper-box with one foot on the top and one on the lower step. From that position he, with his reach, could take almost anything and owing, in addition, to his big physique he was harder to dislodge than any other player I have ever played against – you had to resign yourself, unless you could remove him by guile, to a permanently inferior position in most rallies. His long left arm enabled him to take the offensive and he generally kept it."

Henry Salt, an Old Etonian who returned to teach at Eton from 1875 to 1884, later wrote:

"My one irreparable loss in leaving Eton was not that of culture or scholarship or social position, but of the game of Fives; for I used to think that the evolution of the Eton Fives court, the original of which was a flagged space between two buttresses of the Chapel ("Tax not the royal Saint with vain expense"*), was the most valuable contribution ever made by the School to the well-being of mankind. Fives is a great game; and to have played it with such master hands as AC Ainger, EC Austen-Leigh, Edward Lyttelton, or CT Studd, was a privilege neither to be forgotten nor replaced. I used afterwards to dream at times that I was again engaged in the game – serving, perhaps, or taking the service, or enjoying a duel of long sweeping strokes on the outer court, or mixed up in one of those close-fought rallies that centred round the 'pepper box', until a perfect shot from one side or the other had sent the ball to its resting place in 'dead man's hole'." Happy days, indeed!

---

* The first line of a sonnet by William Wordsworth, *Inside of King's College Chapel, Cambridge*

Chapter 5

The First Satellites

St Columba's and Uppingham

St Columba's College at Stackallen in County Meath was opened in 1844 to "furnish the gentry of Ireland with a school on the model of Eton". In 1849 the school moved to its present site at Rathfarnham, Co Dublin, with 18 boys. John Beresford, the Anglican archbishop of Armagh and Primate of Ireland, held a formal Visitation that year and in his speech signified his wish that a ball-court should be provided for the recreation of the boys and that he would defray the cost. The ball-court was completed in 1849 as the surviving plaque states. Shortly after the arrival at Rathfarnham, the Warden, who was a terminally sick man although aged only thirty-one, departed and was replaced by the Rev George Williams.

George Williams was born in 1814 in Eton where his father was a bookseller and entered the Fourth Form at the School in 1823. He was elected a King's Scholar in 1827 when he was thirteen, and left in 1832 to go as a scholar to King's College, Cambridge. He held a fellowship there from 1835 to 1870.

Portrait of the Rev. George Wiliams, Warden of St Columba's 1850–56

Williams arrived as Warden at St Columba's in 1850 and, as Gregory White in his *History of St Columba's* describes, "embarked on a confident programme of reform…. There is evidence of a new concern for the life of the boys apart from their studies. Williams introduced Eton fives and the fact that the list of cricket secretaries begins in 1853 suggests some move towards serious organisation of the game." The two Eton fives courts were built in 1850-1 and again Archbishop Beresford (who was also an Old Etonian) helped with the expense. These are thought to be the first Eton fives courts to have been built away from Eton.

The archbishop's patronage was vital for the College as it was running at a financial loss and each year Beresford made up the deficit but, not long after Williams's arrival, the two men had a disagreement over a religious matter. The row rumbled on for several years before Beresford withdrew his patronage from the College in 1853 and Williams resigned as Warden in 1856.

Handball has a long history in Ireland and fives and handball existed happily side by side until in 1865 the father of a boy in the school paid for the conversion of the ball-court into a rackets court. This was probably a political move as, at this time, St Columba's was desperate to attract boys who would otherwise have gone to English Public Schools – a threat that was becoming a reality with ferry links and the expansion of the railways.

Following an inspection in 1879, the Mahaffy report on Irish grammar schools commented on the "excellent racquet court and two Eton Fives courts" to be found at St Columba's but interest in these games seems to have been intermittent. In 1912 *The Columban* welcomed Mr MH Elis-

St. Columba's, Rathfarnham, where the first Eton fives courts away from Eton were built in 1851. This architect's sketch of the college dates from the same year

cher, "formerly of Cheltenham College and Pembroke College, Cambridge. He is an excellent Fives player and has already inspired a small following with his own keenness for the game." The Fives Cup was awarded in 1913 for the first time for ten years. Alas, Elischer left St Columba's a year later.

There was another attempt to revive fives and rackets in 1919 and letters to *The Columban* criticised the school's emphasis on rugby football, proposing that more funds should be diverted into 'minor' games, but it was to no avail. What fives needed was the incentive of inter-school fixtures, which were by then being played by schools in England but, at St Columba's, fives was doomed to be an internal game only. As with so many courts to be built later at locations at long distance from the epicentre of the game, external fixtures were well nigh impossible. The last mention of fives is in the school magazine of 1935 but the game continued to be played up until the 1960s. Surprisingly the courts still stand – albeit without their buttresses – and are currently used as practice walls for lawn tennis.

A much greater influence on the spread of Eton fives occurred at Uppingham under the Headmastership of Edward Thring. In 1841 Thring had been the Senior Colleger and Captain of the School at Eton and he had already established

himself as a fives enthusiast. There is a story that when he was a small boy, a senior boy tried to get him off the fives court. In a dramatic gesture Thring threw himself on the ground, asserting that his right to the court was to 'die for'. The phrase stuck and he was given the sobriquet 'Die-for' by his fellows. He became a useful player: GR Parkin, a contemporary, later described Thring as "a capital fives player...he used to make a good fight on the fives court, with the captain of the cricket club [Emilius Bayley], who had more reach...his pluck and muscle were peerless."

Edward Thring was born on 21 November 1821, at Alford, Somerset, the third son of the rector, the Rev John Gale Dalton Thring and his wife, Sarah; a family of five brothers and two sisters. In 1832 he entered Eton, first as an Oppidan then as a Colleger; he was there for nine years. The fact that he was both an enthusiastic fives player and in an important position in the school at just the time that the building of the first fives courts was being considered, suggests that he must have been involved with the deliberations.

In 1841 Thring went up to King's College, Cambridge, where, as a scholar and then fellow, he was in residence for six years. He was ordained in 1846 and in 1852 he was dispatched to Germany by his father to discourage his brother from marrying Marie Louise Koch, the daughter of a Prussian counsellor of whom his father disapproved. Thring succeeded in the purpose of his visit, but not quite in the way his father had intended: he married Fraulein Koch himself.

A year later he was appointed Headmaster of Uppingham, at that time a school of just 25 boys; within ten years that number would be increased to 300. As well as knowing all his pupils, Thring applied a number of 'principles' to his conduct of the school. He believed that 'every boy was good for something' and it was the task of the teacher to discover what that 'something' was. He was years ahead of his time in this respect: for the next hundred years the philosophy in most schools was to find out which boys were best at something and then to concentrate all energies on making them even better.

Thring's strategy was to expand the Uppingham curriculum to enable boys not only to engage in academic subjects other than the classics, but also to experience subjects that were at that time considered outside the normal school curriculum: woodwork, art, and music. He was particularly concerned that music should be well established in the school, thereby creating a musical tradition that survives at Uppingham to this day. In the 1860s there was no such tradition and, as a way of getting boys to sing, he wrote the lyrics of three songs on subjects that he knew would interest them: The Uppingham Chorus, The Cricket Song and The Fives Song were published in 1864. Malcolm Tozer in *Physical Education at Thring's Uppingham*, writes, "These were probably the first songs written about school games: they were lively and their lyrics exude the joyous boyish pleasure of the games."

Thring's third principle he called the 'Almighty Wall': this was not a reference to fives but meant the importance of fine surroundings to encourage learning. During his headship he converted his modest provincial grammar school into a fine architectural example of a handsome English public school. "A school should have a chapel, a library, a museum, workshops, swimming baths, a gymnasium, fives courts, as well as classrooms," wrote Thring in *Education & School*. One of the first things he did on arriving at Uppingham in 1853 was to build an Eton fives court inside the 'Tectum', a covered area that had been used for cricket and bat fives.

The second half of the 19th century was a period when the English public schools were dominated by 'Muscular Christianity'. Following the lead of Dr Arnold of Rugby, the Chapel

became the centre of school life, but games were equally revered and the school hero did not lag far behind the Almighty. This was all about manliness and playing for the team; shirkers and loafers were to be deplored. Where Thring differed from many of his fellow headmasters of the period was that he used to play cricket, football and fives with the boys. "Games are wondrous, vital powers," he wrote, "and a true school life will deal with them as of the highest educational value." First, they enabled masters and boys to mix. Second, they provided a healthy competitive environment, an opportunity for less intelligent boys to shine, and third, they were a training of character: "Never cheat, never funk, never lose your temper, never brag" were unwritten rules that promoted 'manliness'.

The *School Magazine* of April 1864 contains the announcement: "On Tuesday the 15 March the Headmaster and The Rev F Witts maintained their reputation for Fives by beating the Champi-

Edward Thring (1821-87) Headmaster of Uppingham 1853-87, introduced Eton fives to the school

ons." WF Rawnsley, who was at Uppingham from 1855 to 1864 and became Thring's biographer, later wrote, "Thring himself was a first-rate player in the Eton court, and every year he and another Etonian master, 'Daddy' Witts, played the best school pair, and generally won. On one occasion when I was playing against him, Thring hit, with all his might, a fine low ball which would have taken the back wall just above the line and come back beautifully into the pepper-box, but that Daddy's head was a little too high and received the ball instead. We looked for some word of commiseration, but what we heard was 'Why don't you keep your head out of the light!' Thring's black trousers and braces were a familiar sight on the fives courts – although he would drop the right side of his braces from the shoulder to free his arm for cutting."

By 1869 almost every House at Uppingham had its fives court and the game flourished. Two of these built by WF Earl at Brooklands still stand. Although he gave up playing both cricket and fives in 1871 – "Thring played a fine game till rheumatism seized him by the leg, when he was turned 50" – he never lost his love for the game. "Thring's favourite fives steadily gained new courts," wrote JP Graham in 1883. The rules of fives at Uppingham, which were unsurprisingly very similar to those published at Eton two years later, were printed in the School magazine in 1875.

In spite of Thring's ardent belief in games as a vital part of a boy's education, he did not want to give them undue prominence. He was strongly opposed to the hero worship of the school athlete that he saw appearing in other schools. He refused therefore to allow 'foreign' matches and when his brother

Charles proposed that Uppingham should become a member of the newly founded Football Association in 1863, Edward Thring refused to allow it. The two brothers quarrelled and Charles Thring left the staff at Uppingham.

When Thring died in 1887 the school had risen from a small country grammar school to become a great public school. He had established himself as one of the great reforming headmasters of the Victorian age. On a much smaller scale he had also established Eton fives in a central role among the games at Uppingham, but it would be another ten years before they played a match against another school.

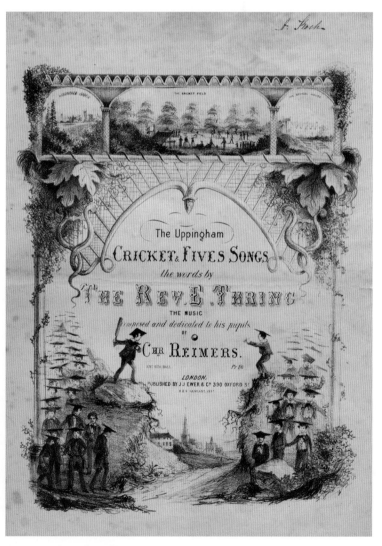

The Uppingham Song Book

The Uppingham Fives Song written by Edward Thring in 1864

Chapter 6

From Eton to the Diaspora

The Spread of Eton Fives Courts

Walls were a feature of most schools and hitting a ball up against them a popular activity. There was usually a space beside the buildings that became a recreational area. The commonest activities were football and fives. For football, it was usual to stuff with material a piece of cloth or leather, appropriately stitched, until the more sophisticated 'pig's bladder' was devised as an inflatable inner lining. For 'hitting' games, a denser consistency was required and balls for most of these games – including cricket – were made by winding string round a piece of cloth, building up a spherical shape. The ball was later covered with a piece of cloth or leather and stitched (see *The Path of the Eton Fives Ball*, Appendix 4).

There is no means of knowing when these 'wall games' started to be played. School histories usually make some references as these extracts show. At Sherborne there was reference to "ye fives place" in 1685 and Winchester claims a 'ball court' dating from 1688, but Eton's Chapel was completed two hundred years before either. At many schools, where the space allowed, they played a form of bat fives: at Shrewsbury two bat fives courts were built in 1798. At Uppingham the 'Tectum' was used "for cricket and fives when the melancholy days are come". When the eastern end of Little Dean's Yard at Westminster was paved in 1838, a "peculiar form of rackets" was played there. At Tonbridge the bat fives wall fell down in 1893; Clifton played bat fives up to 1915 – even employing a 'rackets professional' to teach it. At the original Charterhouse, there were "two open

Influential Headmasters

Henry Montagu Butler, Head Master of Harrow 1860-85. He was responsible for the school adopting Eton fives. His son EM and grandson GM were both fine players

John Bradley Dyne, Headmaster of Highgate 1838-74. "The dynamic Dr Dyne moved into new school buildings in 1866 and included three Eton fives courts"

Henry Whitehead Moss, Headmaster of Shrewsbury 1864-1908 (44 years!) "Moss had been in no way attracted to games, indeed he was frequently the butt of jokes because of his ignorance, but he pressed for provision of facilities."

Steuart Adolphus Pears, Headmaster of Repton 1854–74. "Dr Pears and Mr Johnson and Mr Joe Gould always played Fives in Top-hats". Eton fives courts were not built at Repton until the return of Lionel Ford in 1901

courts which existed in the north-east corner of Green, hard up against Verites [one of the board-

Charterhouse: Eton fives and lawn tennis courts in 1883. Charterhouse was one of the few schools to embrace lawn tennis at this time

ing houses]. One of these had a side wall of a kind, the other had a mere paved court with one wall. These courts had always been used for a kind of bat fives, played with an ordinary rackets ball and a wooden bat of the shape and size of a battledore. It was called tennis having however strangely little resemblance to that ancient game." At Highgate pre-1866, "where the chapel now stands were the remains of the Old Chapel walls, one portion of which was turned into a fives court; the other was overgrown with very thick ivy".... "When Pears [Headmaster] came to Repton [1854] there was one fives court without a roof on the site of the present Marshal's Lodge...." Thomas Churton, a pupil at Rugby, wrote in 1812, "...Our most fashionable game now is Fives, which has been principally brought in by the Quadrangle, where there is good room

to play, and also against the end of the school towards the play-ground and in the Great School. I am fond of it, though not yet very expert. It is very good exercise and makes one warm without putting one out of breath."

By 1860 most of the public schools and many grammar schools had fives courts. Some, where the courts had been in existence for many years, continued to use them; others built new courts based on the rectangular four-wall court that was to become known as Rugby fives; yet others built three-walled courts with a buttress based on the Eton courts, but very few of these new courts paid any attention to detail or dimensions. At Harrow, their form of bat fives, played with cut-down (real) tennis rackets against the walls of the school yard, became the game of rackets. When funds were collected to build a rackets court in

1865, an unusual situation arose whereby more money was subscribed than was necessary and the surplus was used to build two Eton fives courts and four Rugby courts. However the Eton courts were poor replicas, being described some years later as "peculiar rather than pleasing and appeared to have been constructed by a builder who had dreamt of an Eton court and copied his nightmare in bricks and mortar". Moreover the boys did not take to Rugby fives but took in their racquets and a soft ball to invent another game: squash.

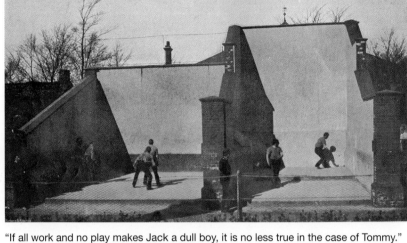

"If all work and no play makes Jack a dull boy, it is no less true in the case of Tommy." The courts at Aldershot military camp, 1899

Ironically Rugby, which lent its name not only to one of the codes of football but also to the four-walled version of fives, acquired Eton courts in 1863, presented by two members of staff. Two more were added later but, for some reason, popularity waned and the last House competition was played in 1913. The courts were only demolished in 1991.

Many of the wall-games were played against just one wall, often with netting on top to restrain wayward shots; some had 'wings' or short side walls as well. A version, sometimes known as Warminster fives, was played in just such a court: one-wall with short wings at 135 degrees at each side. Similar courts were to be found at Marlborough (where it was also played with bats) and Gresham's. The Warminster court still stands. It has been suggested that Thomas Arnold, who had been a pupil at Warminster, played the game there and introduced it to Rugby

when he became Head Master, but that is pure speculation.

The problem with one-walled courts was that there was nothing to stop the ball flying off in any direction – except, of course, boys. Rackets or fives fagging was common (as was cricket fagging before the introduction of nets) and was a boring and time-consuming occupation. Clements Markham, a pupil at Westminster, later wrote: "...the ball-fag had to retrieve all the balls that went out of play and be ready to supply the man serving as required. When ball-fagging you had

The fives courts at Borough Road College, a teacher training college in Isleworth specialising in athletics, 1899

Some more winners of the School Fives at Eton

Hon Charles Lyttelton 1860

CJ Ottaway
1868, 1869

Hon E Lyttelton 1874

the right to call on any boy junior to yourself who came into Little Dean's Yard, and he had to take your place until he could spot some other unfortunate to relieve him. For this cause one was often tied to one's house till school-time if a boy senior to oneself was doing ball-fag...." This sort of practice was common in many other schools.

When, in 1863, the Clarendon Commission was appointed to investigate the affairs of the Nine Great Public Schools, Uppingham was not among them – a slight that stung Thring and led him to invite thirty-seven headmasters of similar schools to a meeting in 1869. Fourteen headmasters accepted and this was the inaugural meeting of the Headmasters' Conference. The 'Clarendon nine' later joined HMC and by 1899 there were 101 members. Membership of HMC (later the Headmasters' and Headmistresses' Conference) has since come to be understood as the defining qualification for a 'public' or 'independent' school.

With the notable exception of George Cotton at Marlborough, who frequently waded into scrummages on the rugby field, and of Thring himself, few of these educationally reforming headmasters were actually interested in games. Both Hawtrey of Eton and Moss of Shrewsbury, for example, were much derided by staff and boys for their total ignorance on the subject. However they were attracted to the idea of team spirit, all working together for the common

good, and what Dr Pears of Repton described as "the healthy exertion of body and spirit together, which is found in the excitement, the emulation and the friendly strife of school games". At the lowest level, boys occupied with games were kept away from destructive activities; a bonus was, some thought, that strenuous exercise lowered their testosterone levels, thereby reducing incidents of sexual proclivity and 'vice'.

The spread of Eton and Rugby fives well beyond their original homes can be attributed to the status and reputation of these two schools and the influence of some distinguished headmasters. After all, if the Battle of Waterloo had been won on the playing fields of Eton, surely there were bright prospects in less important skirmishes on their fives courts. Of the schools that built new courts, there was a three-way split – with some eccentric offshoots. These were the versions played at Eton, Rugby and Winchester and appear to be due to the influences of former pupils or masters from these three schools. The simplest version, with the most numerous courts, is Rugby fives, played in a plain rectangular

The Studd brothers, JEK, GB and CT. CT won the School Fives in 1878, GB in 1879. Both later played cricket for England

"Buns" Thornton, winner of the School Fives in 1867 and 1868, was also "a tremendous hitter of a cricket ball". He played for Kent and Middlesex

court. As at other schools, the original 'courts' at Rugby varied in size and design. There were games played in the Old Quadrangle, and in the porch leading in from the High Street; there was also a bat fives court next to the Birching Tower. Courts without a buttress were preferred and, as elsewhere, the most popular design was adopted for replication.

The origin of the distinctive feature of the Winchester game is unknown. Although called a buttress, it is in fact a narrowing of the left-hand wall in a fashion similar to the tambour in a real tennis court. The nine and three-quarter inch wide end of the buttress, angled at 135 degrees is the only hazard, but it plays a significant part in the game. The court, in other respects rectangular, bears no resemblance to the bat fives court dating back to 1688. Winchester fives courts have been built at Malvern, Bradfield and Radley among other well known schools, but the game has not achieved wider popularity and most Winchester fives players turn to Rugby fives after leaving school.

The courts at Uppingham were, as has been shown, the direct result of the interest of the Headmaster, Edward Thring, an Old Etonian who had played fives at Eton. EM Young, another Old Etonian, is credited with introducing the game to Harrow in 1865, although the Harrow courts were such poor reproductions that they were replaced fifteen years later. Highgate, under the dynamic Dr John Bradley Dyne, moved into new school buildings in 1866 and included three Eton fives courts. When Charterhouse moved out of London to Godalming in 1874, four Eton fives courts were built at the new site. Thomas Page, a master who had formerly taught at Shrewsbury, was credited with the initiative, but again the construction was conspicuously different from the courts at Eton.

The likelihood is that Eton fives came to Shrewsbury through the Thring connection. Edward Thring's two youngest brothers were at school there. Godfrey, later an Anglican clergyman, became a well-known hymn writer. His two

SM Macnaghten and the Hon KF Kinnaird won the School Fives at Eton in 1899. They were 'the best pair for some years'. Kinnaird presented the cup for the Amateur Championship in 1923 thereby making his name part of the vocabulary of all Eton fives players

best known compositions were *The radiant morn has passed away* and *Fierce raged the tempest o'er the deep* – neither with any obvious sporting theme! However Charles, later a master at Uppingham, was a games enthusiast and was responsible, with Henry de Winton, a fellow Old Salopian, for devising the 'Cambridge Rules' of football in 1846, an attempt to find a compromise between all the different sets of rules being played by schools at this time. This was the first step towards the creation of the game of association football. It seems at least possible that the Governors and Headmaster of Shrewsbury would have consulted Charles Thring or his elder brother Edward, founder of the Headmasters' Conference, on a matter of major expenditure such as fives courts.

Freeman Thomas (above) and C Barclay played in the first Eton v Harrow fives match in 1885

Plans for fives courts at Gonville & Caius College, Cambridge, were drawn up as early as 1866 but it seems that they were not converted into bricks and mortar for another 26 years. The first Eton fives court at the university was probably the one built against the side of the real tennis court in Grange Road in 1876. Others followed

Two unidentified Etonians posing in a fives court. Caps were often worn in the days before courts were covered. At Eton 'choices' were awarded caps – until wearing them went out of fashion

at Portugal Place in 1886 and at Emmanuel, Selwyn and Magdalene Colleges in the 1890s. When City of London School moved to Victoria Embankment in 1883, two covered and three open Eton fives courts were built. Westminster also built two courts in 1883, thanks to the help of Sir Walter Phillimore, a Governor and Old Westminster. Also in 1883, Emanuel School took over a site between the railway lines diverging from Clapham Junction, formerly the Royal Patriotic Asylum for the sons of veterans and orphans of the Crimean War. Whether they inherited two Eton fives courts or built them shortly after arriving is not clear. Other schools to have courts dating from this time were King

Edward VI Grammar in Bury St Edmunds (1872), The Leys, Cambridge (1876), Queen Elizabeth's Grammar, Barnet (1880), St Paul's (1884) at its West Kensington site, St Bartholomew's Grammar, Newbury (1885), Chigwell (1889) and Dover College (1895). When the boys' grammar school was built at St Bartholomew's in 1885 the original plans for a "covered playground and latrines had been altered in favour of two fives courts". While fives enthusiasts will admire the prioritisation, one does wonder about the latrines....

There is also a long list of schools that had fives courts at least resembling Eton courts. One of the counties most highly populated with courts was Yorkshire: Aysgarth Prep School, Bedale; Doncaster GS, Heckmondwike GS, Hemsworth GS, Hipperholme GS, Hymers College, Hull; Leeds GS; Queen Elizabeth's GS, Wakefield; and Woodhouse Grove School, Bradford, are all either known or alleged to have possessed courts. In most cases, when these courts were built, they were intended purely for internal use and therefore the odd variation of dimensions or size of the pepper box was of no significance. This second generation of Eton fives courts was therefore a hotchpotch. It was only when schools started to play each other that the differences became apparent.

There are no records of any inter-school Eton fives matches before Eton's first match against Harrow in 1885. It is therefore impossible to judge the standard of play at other schools, although it is very unlikely that they approached the quality at Eton. There were, however, some distinguished games players among those playing at other schools. Charterhouse played no school matches before 1891 but the House ties were keenly fought: WNF Cobbold, who played cricket and tennis for Cambridge, and association football for Cambridge and England, was in the winning Verites pair of 1882; GO Smith, who captained both Cam-

Four Headmasters who did much to promote Eton fives in the schools where they taught.

Arthur Edmund Allcock, Headmaster of Highgate 1893-1908: "a fanatical games player, who listed his recreations in *Who's Who* as cricket, fives and golf". His brother CH was a House Master at Eton and also a fine fives player

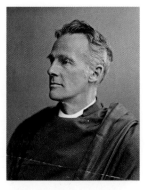

Edward Lyttelton, Head Master of Eton 1905-16; a supremely talented sportsman but no scholar; "a controversial Head Master who won the affection of the boys in spite of some blazing indiscretions"

Cyril Alington, Assistant Master at Eton 1899-1908; Headmaster of Shrewsbury 1908-17, Head Master of Eton 1917-33. "He was an enormous influence for good on Eton fives at these two schools"

Henry Bowlby was an Assistant Master at Eton 1897-1909, Head Master of Lancing 1909-25. The Eton fives courts at Lancing were built to commemorate his headmastership

Two outstanding sportsmen from Charterhouse: WN Cobbold and GO Smith. "Nuts" Cobbold won nine international football caps and played cricket for Kent. "G.O." won 20 England international football caps and later became Joint Headmaster of Ludgrove Preparatory School. Both won the House Fives at Charterhouse in the days before inter-school matches were played

bridge and England at association football, was in the winning Hodgesonites pair of 1892. At Shrewsbury GB Raikes, who went on to represent England at both cricket and football, was captain of fives in 1889.

Chapter 7

A Peek outside the Nest

The First Inter-school Matches

The difficulties of travel before the 1880s meant that 'away' matches against other schools in any game were rare. First XI cricket had been well established since the beginning of the century but the opposition was usually adult club or scratch sides and the matches played at home – except for the Eton, Harrow and Winchester matches at Lord's. Even those had been opposed by the Headmasters in the early days, largely for fear of the behaviour of the crowds, and many were played outside the school term.

By 1885 fives had been enjoyed at Eton for over forty years with hardly an outward glance. Eton's first 'match' against another school was in 1885 when the 3 March issue of *Harrow Notes* reported, "On Thursday the 12th ult., the Hon and Rev E Lyttelton, F Thomas and C Barclay paid a visit to our Fives Court, and showed us the way Fives are played at Eton." It was really more of a missionary expedition than a match: Thomas and Barclay were far too good for EM Butler and BR Warren, the Harrow pair; unsurprisingly they won the return encounter even more convincingly. The correspondent in the *Chronicle* wrote, "The Harrow courts are very dirty in colour but otherwise the same as our own." He continued in a self-congratulatory tone, "The matches, if such they may be termed, between the Keepers and two representatives of Harrow resulted in each case in a most decisive victory for the Keepers and proved that Eton is *facile princeps* with regard to this game, of which we are the founder."

In 1889 Harrow was represented by FS Jack-son, later to be England's cricket captain, and DR Napier. This pair managed to get a game off HR Bromley-Davenport and HW Studd in the Eton courts and it seemed that the lion had been tamed.

Fives at Eton had its ups and downs through the 1890s. For the first time the 'fives half' came

The Eton courts about 1900; there were nearly sixty courts at this time and "found to be none too many".

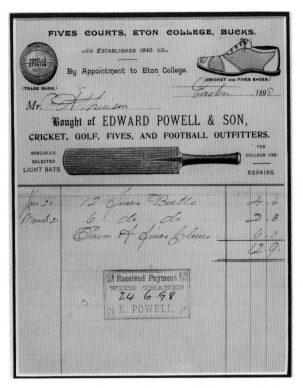

A receipt for fives gloves and balls bought from Powell's, the Eton shop, in 1898

A "FIVES" SONG

(Hard Lines on a Fives Ball)

Words by G. T. ATKINSON
(Assistant Master 1879-1903)

Music by F. CUNNINGHAM WOODS.
(Director of Music 1896-1928)

My skin is as soft as my lady's glove,
  And white as her dainty shoe,
And I've come to sport in the senior court
  With warriors keen and true.
There be four which stand with well gloved hand,
  And they bandy me to and fro,
While each and each they pray and they preach -
  "Pepper him! pepper him! Hard and low!"

"Pepper him! pepper him! Hard and low!"

They may call - "Love all!" as they start to play,
  But there's little love lost on me,
For they smite me hard without any regard
  For a "Prosser" of high degree.
They make me a butt for volley and cut
  With many a "black-guard" blow,
And the kids in a ring all chatter and sing -
  "Pepper him! pepper him! Hard and low!"

I'm not the figure I used to be,
  And my ribs are aching sore;
They've a nasty knack of dealing a whack
  That leaves me dead on the floor.
It is easy to call - "Game ball! game ball!"
  But I'd very much like to know,
If even in play it is fair to say -
  "Pepper him! pepper him! Hard and low!"

Like Wolsey I've lost all my favour at Court,
  And my waistcoat is shewing through;
I would give my head for a needle and thread
  Or a dollop of whole-some glue;
But they hoof me out to the smallboy rout
  With a casual turn of the toe,
And for ever I fly from their mannerless cry -
  "Pepper him! pepper him! Hard and low!"

Highgate's Fives Song

under pressure from other sports. There was a proposal to introduce rugby football in 1897 and soccer was introduced in 1892. The editor of the *Chronicle* commented, "Fives seems hardly so popular this year as last, and it was by no means uncommon to come down 'after 12' to find courts unoccupied. Play of the select few is as good as ever but that of the average majority has slightly deteriorated. Whether this is due to increase in football we cannot say." In 1898: "Fives courts are not nearly as full as is their wont; we are credibly informed that it was necessary to take steps to provide a third game of Association football and over 60 names have been sent in to play Rugby football." A lengthy correspondence ensued: one writer thought that the empty courts were due to the increase in soccer. The answer, he wrote, was for Fives Choices [for whom courts were reserved] to give their courts to others. Another, noting that both beagling and fives had become impossible because of snow, suggested that Eton should

"learn from other schools: a few covered fives courts would be an excellent institution". A long editorial followed and provoked Old Etonian interest. One such, on a visit, was "filled with apprehension" when he found 18 courts unoccupied and at a time when floods prevented activities other than fives. Lower boys were said to be

This postcard of the Shrewsbury courts is undated but there are only six; about 1900?

Harrow for the first time in 1897. In 1900 FB Wilson and RH Crake beat Eton both home and away for the first time and, between 1904 and 1906, EH Crake (brother of RH) and RE Eiloart had the distinguished record of beating both Eton and Charterhouse, home and away, for three years in succession. Crake later wrote, "The two masters of the game when I was at Harrow were George Warner and Teddy Butler and though both were approaching forty at the time, Eiloart and I only managed to beat them twice while we were there, and we used to play them every Friday of each Easter term. George Warner had the best first cut I have seen in the game and

shopping! However the situation had improved by 1901. The *Chronicle* Past Times column: "The serious athletic interests of the half have been divided between fives and beagling. Fives has been an unqualified success. Large sums have been spent getting the courts into good order and the school shop has made playing a good deal more comfortable than in any other year." [A reference to the opening of the little shop selling drinks and snacks, later known as 'Jacks']... "A high standard has been reached throughout the school; courts have been well filled even on whole school days 'after 4'. Lower boys occupied most of the courts.... We are probably not justified in building more courts at present but perhaps when the present generation of lower boys are at the top of the school. House Fives reflect the general revival." 99 pairs entered.

Eton, playing a long-established major game with over fifty courts, remained unbeatable until George Townsend Warner returned to teach at Harrow in 1891. Townsend Warner had learnt his fives at Cambridge where he and Butler were contemporaries of Freeman Thomas (Eton Keeper in 1885). Back at Harrow they became a very good pair: in 1901 the Eton Masters were described in the *Chronicle* as "probably not far from being the best pair of fives players in existence" but they were not good enough to beat Warner and Butler. The Keepers were beaten by

EH Crake and RE Eiloart in 1904; this oustanding Harrow pair beat both Eton and Charterhouse home and away for three years

Fives was a popular game at King Edward VI GS, Bury St Edmunds, until the 1950s. Its final demise came when the school became a Comprehensive in 1972 and moved to a new site. Notice the player on the right flattening himself against the wall in an exaggerated fashion. There are other examples of this. See page 35

EM Butler   G Townsend Warner

Two Harrow Masters who became an outstanding pair in the early 1900s. Butler played for Harrow in the first Eton match of 1885; Warner learnt his fives from Freeman Thomas at Cambridge. Together they were responsible for coaching some very strong Harrow pairs at this time

his reach was tremendous, while Butler was absolutely safe and a genius in the art of placing; we could not have had better teachers of the game." In 1908 a new covered court was built at Harrow with a plaque bearing the inscription:

Hoc saxo
Per triennium uno tenore
Felicissimi consociati
Memoriae traduntur
E H CRAKE, R E EILOART
MCMIV, V, VI

(*Memories of a most happy partnership over three years are borne by this stone*)

In 1899, Eton played Charterhouse for the first time and won both matches with some ease. Charterhouse were perhaps unlucky that the Keepers, SM Macnaghten and KF Kinnaird, were "the strongest pair for some years". There was, however, comment that the match at Charterhouse was played "in a red court!" This was the beginning of an interesting triangular competition between Eton, Harrow and Charterhouse that continued until 1916. Eton generally held the whip hand. In 1909, JC Craigie and EWS Foljambe won all their matches: Craigie was "a

HG Stocker and RSA Straus, the Harrow pair of 1901. At Harrow the first pair were awarded 'flannels', a custom probably derived from cricket. 'Flannels' were entitled to wear long white trousers. This custom persisted into the 1940s by which time shorts had become universal – later to be augmented by the track suit

The Highgate team of 1905. Standing: RL Sharpe, Augustus Barker, PM Taylor; sitting: GR Sayer, MG Ferguson, GD Owen

CM Pitts Tucker and BH Radford, winners of the House Fives at Charterhouse in 1902

player of exceptional merit, who hit the ball very hard" and Foljambe "imparted a lot of cut to his back court strokes". However JSF Marriott and HW Leatham of Charterhouse beat both Eton and Harrow twice in 1911. The Eton pair, JM Bevan and G Hamilton-Fletcher, were all-victorious again in 1913.

With occasional exceptions, as in Harrow's purple patch described above, the Eton pairs' strongest opposition came from the Masters. The talented pair of 1901, JW Hely-Hutchinson and A Moon, was only beaten by the Masters. The departure of Lionel Ford that year (to be Headmaster of his old school, Repton) was a blow: "He has done more than anyone else for Fives and we shall miss him greatly in this branch of Eton life," wrote the *Chronicle*, but that was more than made up for by the arrival of EH Lyttelton as Head Master in 1905. Henry Marten, SG Lubbock, H Macnaghten, Cyril

> ## ON FIVES.
>
> I oft have in amazement gazed
>   At players great and small,
> But never have I managed yet
>   To hit that little ball.
>
> It dances off the plaster walls
>   And lights upon the floor,
> But when I strike with all my might
>   It twists and turns galore.
>
> It bounces back from wall to wall
>   And tumbles in the box,
> Or else it swiftly falls full pitch
>   And gives one sundry knocks.
>
> I've chased that ball about the court
>   With efforts all in vain,
> I've fallen flat upon my back
>   Until I'm racked with pain.
>
> Although I vainly struggle on
>   We'll hope that day arrives,
> When men will say that I can play—
>   That glorious game of fives.
>
> ᕙᐧᗒᐧᑐᕗ

From the Gresham's Magazine 1908

Alington and Henry Bowlby stood out among many enthusiastic masters and more than five pairs were frequently played against the School. Twelve new courts were added in 1903 and two were covered in 1906, which "saved six matches that would otherwise have been lost to the weather". The fixture list expanded significantly: by 1905 there were fifteen matches, two each against Harrow and Charterhouse, the rest against Old Etonian and other Old Boy opposition. Harrow and Charterhouse remained the only school opposition until Alington, who had become Headmaster of Shrewsbury, returned to Eton as Head Master in 1917.

Both Harrow and Charterhouse kept external matches within the triangle with

Sir Francis Stanley Jackson

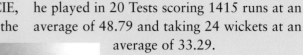

Sir Francis Stanley Jackson, GCSI, GCIE, PC, KStJ (1870-1947), known as the Hon FS Jackson in his earlier life, played with DR Napier for Harrow against Eton in 1889. They were beaten by HR Bromley-Davenport and EG Clifton-Brown 10-15, 15-8, 10-15, 10-15 in the Eton courts. Jackson also played in Harrow's cricket XI between 1887 and 1889, being captain in his last year.

He went on to play cricket for Cambridge, Yorkshire and England and was named a Wisden Cricketer of the Year in 1894. Jackson captained England against Australia when they retained The Ashes in 1905; altogether he played in 20 Tests scoring 1415 runs at an average of 48.79 and taking 24 wickets at an average of 33.29.

Stanley Jackson was a Member of Parliament from 1915-26, Financial Secretary to the War Office 1922-23 and Governor of Bengal from 1927 to 1932. He was President of the MCC in 1921 and President of Yorkshire CCC from 1938 until his death in 1947. Recalling his funeral, the Bishop of Knaresborough remarked, "As I gazed down on the rapt faces of that vast congregation, I could see how they revered him as though he were the Almighty, though, of course, infinitely stronger on the leg side."

Eton, except for a single sortie by Harrow to Uppingham in 1905, when one of the Harrow pair had a brother playing for Uppingham, and an occasional match for Charterhouse against Wellington, whom they had first played in 1891. The standard of play at Charterhouse improved dramatically from 1909. The correspondent in *The Carthusian* noted the contrast of style with that at Eton: "Charterhouse players rely on hard hitting and do not 'make shots' whereas Eton cultivate reserve and finish, only forcing the pace from time to time." This analysis soon bore fruit in practice.

The difficulties of travel and away matches in those days were highlighted when Eton's 1903 visit to Charterhouse involved a four-hour train journey, a hurried lunch at 3pm, play with a different-sized ball in a court "far different from our own – after a few minutes play the ball becomes assimilated to the colour of the walls". And the match had to be completed before darkness descended.

Chapter 8

Crossing the Frontiers

The Spread of Inter-school Fives

As has been shown, for the most part, fives in the 19th century was an internal school game with the House ties and other internal competitions paramount but, as communications became easier and the rail network expanded, schools began to look beyond their own narrow horizons. Charterhouse's first recorded match was against Wellington in 1891; this was repeated spasmodically but Charterhouse began an annual series of home and away fixtures with Eton in 1898 and with Harrow from 1903. Highgate's first external fixture was against City of London in 1894. The first Shrewsbury v Uppingham match was played in 1897. By modern standards this was a leisurely affair: the Uppingham IV travelled by train the day before, and spent the morning knocking up and getting used to the strange courts; the match was played in the afternoon. Westminster did not play another school until they went to Charterhouse in 1901 and they were so traumatised by the experience they did not repeat the venture for another five years – when they met with a similar defeat.

At first these inter-school matches went decisively the way of the home side, which often had its own terminology, played with its own type of ball and, in many cases, had developed its own rules. The protocol was that the visiting pair should accept the home team's rules – which might or might not have been explained to them before the match. This led to some strange, sometimes hilarious, situations. When Harrow went to Uppingham in 1905, they discovered that the courts were covered with a glass roof

and this was 'in play', "so introducing a new element to the game and new way of getting out of difficulties under the line when the ball can be hit up against it". This rule was not changed until 1913. Shrewsbury played their matches as a IV, each pair playing three games and the match being decided by an aggregate of points; one-pair matches were also decided by point aggregate. When Shrewsbury played at Eton in 1921 they lost 2-3 but won more points and, therefore, would have won under their own scoring system.

For both Shrewsbury and Uppingham, their match was the only school fixture until 1909: in *The Salopian* it was titled, 'The Fives Match'. Much of the credit for Shrewsbury's early success at fives must go to FT Prior, who was appointed as an assistant master in 1891; he coached, raised opposition teams and umpired matches. (Umpiring was normal practice at Shrewsbury at the time.) Opposition included regular visits from the Liverpool Racquet Club, often including Etonians and Harrovians, who taught them some useful lessons. In 1899 *The Salopian* wrote, "We were honoured to be opposed by Steel, Stoddart, Medley & Stewart-Brown… Shrewsbury needs to change its style of play: use more wrist in hitting; pay more attention to placing and use greater variety of stroke. " Shrewsbury's best season of this era was 1903 when RD Craig, RS Hall, Carver and Mitchell won all their matches, beating Liverpool by 63 points and Uppingham (away) by 34 points.

Some of this received wisdom was passed on. The Uppingham magazine of 1902 reported, "Shrewsbury players stand up to the return [of

The Rev Lionel Ford

The Rev Lionel Ford (1865-1932) was educated at Repton and King's, Cambridge. He joined the staff at Eton in 1888, became Headmaster of Repton in 1901 and Head Master of Harrow in 1910. From 1926-32 he was Dean of York. With the possible exception of AC Ainger, Ford probably had a greater influence on Eton fives than anyone else of his generation – a strong claim. His colleague at Eton, Canon Bowlby, later wrote, "Out of school, Ford's name will always be honoured in the pre-eminently Eton game of fives. He had been trained in the variety of plain-walled court as a boy at Repton, which largely accounted for the force of his

long strokes, and the readiness and strength of his left hand. But he quickly learnt the wiles of the 'pepper-box' and the 'dead man's hole', and also of the commanding position in the court. When once entrenched there after preliminary jostling, he was practically invincible. A crowd always assembled in front of the court when he was playing with the late Mr George Mount or the Vice-Provost, Mr CHK Marten, against the Keepers, whom they beat almost invariably; or in games with the recently retired Head Master, Dr Alington; or again with a most unflagging but less quick-footed devotee, Mr Broadbent. "

Henry Marten wrote, "Lionel was almost in a class by himself; I don't think he and his partner ever suffered defeat against the School pair, or had any fear of it except perhaps in the case of Moon and Hely-Hutchison [Keepers 1901] and possibly Macnaghten and Kinnaird [Keepers 1898,9]. But I think Lionel's greatest feats were in the games he used to play with Broadbent against two other Masters: Broadbent was a safe but rather slow-moving player and his main contribution was, from his own wish, one of exhortation to, or of praise and sometimes abuse of his partner; "You are the protagonist in this game", he would say to Lionel, who would be expected to shoot out an arm to every corner of the court. My impression is that as a pair they were seldom beaten. Of course, Lionel, like all first-class players, knew exactly where to stand, namely about two feet to the right of the pepper-box with one foot on the top and one on the lower step. From that position he, with his reach, could take almost anything and owing, in addition, to his big physique he was harder to dislodge than any other player I have ever played against – you had to resign yourself, unless you could remove him by guile, to a permanently inferior position in most rallies. His long left arm enabled him to take the offensive and he generally kept it. "

Dr Alington wrote, "He taught me most of what I ever learnt of the game, and it was much to his credit that I was chosen to succeed him as the present Vice-Provost's partner when he left. But I was incapable of reproducing his first cut, or indeed most of his excellencies, as I was (I trust) of shouldering my opponents out of their legitimate stance!"

The Rev JF Carter, a House Master at Repton, wrote, "Up to the end of his time he was the best fives player in the place and he did all he could to encourage that and other 'by-games'... Among his creations were...twelve Eton fives courts..."

cut] in the pepper box... our fellows stand – or grovel or sneak – under the front wall.... " Uppingham seems to have been well supported by masters: the driving force was FW Welldon, although the first Masters' pair was RN Douglas and EWG Saunders. The Masters were able to raise seven pairs.

Lionel Ford, an Old Reptonian who had taught at Eton, returned to Repton as Headmaster in 1900 and immediately set about building courts: there were twelve by the time he moved on to Harrow in 1910. Shrewsbury was given a fillip in 1909 by the arrival from Eton as Headmaster of Cyril Alington, who took a keen interest in the fives. As *The Salopian* reported, "Only four fives courts were roofed in 1908. They were all roofed in 1911; and court number 10, previously fitted as a lavatory, was added in 1912." This was not the first time an

One of the very strong Shrewsbury teams of this era with the inspiring FT Prior

important decision had to be taken between these two usages of a vital space.

Repton played Shrewsbury for the first time in 1909 but, surprisingly, Repton and Uppingham were not to meet on the fives courts until 1933. In 1911 a set of six courts was built at Wellington College, Shropshire – to be renamed Wrekin College in 1920. The courts had all the correct features except standard tops to the buttresses. These were not fitted until a supportive headmaster, Geoffrey Hadden, gave a boost to the game in the 1970s. Most of Wrekin's fives was internal in these early years.

Oakham and Uppingham were both founded in 1584 by Archdeacon Robert Johnson but their fortunes were conspicuously at variance in the latter half of the 19th century. While Uppingham was thriving under the headmastership of Edward Thring, numbers at Oakham had sunk to such a low that by 1875 the school had just enough boys for a single game of fives: two day boys and two boarders. In fact there were no fives courts at Oakham until 1904 when the roll had increased to over a hundred, and three open courts were built. These lack ledges on the sidewalls below the step but are otherwise of the Eton model.

Also in the West Midlands, an Eton court was

The Eton College Officer Training Corps is lined up for inspection in this photograph. It is undated but the uniforms suggest the first decade of the 20th century. The open fives courts behind the parade were domolished to make way for the swimming pool complex in 1978

built at King Edward's, Birmingham in 1903 and a second added two years later. HD Bache, who was captain of fives in 1906 and 1907, was a distinguished games player, as was HL Higgins, captain in 1911. Distinguished as a rugby footballer but also a fives player at that time was JRR Tolkien, later better known as author of *Lord of the Rings*. However, no fixtures against other Eton fives playing schools were ventured for many years, although an annual fives match (with its own rules) had been played against Bromsgrove, traditionally the school's biggest rugby football opponents, since 1896.

In the London area, the most active school was City of London, who had played both Emanuel and Highgate in 1894. The arrival of the Rev AE Allcock as Headmaster at Highgate in 1893 "revolutionised school fives" according to *The Cholmeleian*. He was responsible for the six new courts built in 1899 and "was always ready and

keen to take a hand – those who played with him know what a hand it was". Allcock and his younger brother CH, who was a master at Eton, had been educated at King Edward's, Birmingham, and both played county cricket for Staffordshire. They both had a big influence on the fives at the schools where they taught. When AE Allcock retired from Highgate in 1908, one of his last acts was to appoint as an assistant master the Rev KRG Hunt, an outstanding games player. Hunt had won two full international football caps for England in 1911 and had scored the opening goal in the 1908 Cup Final for Wolverhampton Wanderers. He was also a fine fives player and was largely responsible for the success of Highgate fives in the next twenty years. Four more courts were built in 1913.

Highgate had been playing Aldenham in their old courts since 1901 with a predictable skew of results, but the erection of four Eton courts at

Aldenham in 1916, following the bequest two years earlier of £1000 by EH Mariette, a master and former pupil, redressed the balance. Mill Hill, who had played some form of fives since the 1870s, built two Eton courts in 1908 and also began fixtures with Highgate, Aldenham and Berkhamsted, another school with a long fives tradition. Berkhamsted, who only built their first Eton courts in 1926 to replace older non-Eton courts, had actually started playing Aldenham in 1917. Fixtures among this group of schools soon became regular.

The Rev WC Compton, who had previously taught at Uppingham, introduced Eton fives to Dover College when he became Headmaster in 1895. Geographically it was rather out on a limb and so play in the two courts was restricted to internal games and House matches.

Harrow and Westminster kept largely to themselves. Fifty years earlier, Westminster had been guilty of what the author, Rupert Wilkinson, called a 'comic exclusivity'. There is a well-documented correspondence following Shrewsbury's

request for a cricket fixture with Westminster in 1866; it was refused on the grounds that Westminster played only "Public Schools". Harrow is purported to be guilty of a similar solecism, following a request from a perceived "minor school", with the alleged reply, "Eton we know, Rugby we've heard of, but who are ye?"

Whether or not these anecdotes are true, there is no doubt that, through much of its history, Eton fives has been both elevated and tainted by its name. In 1963, Dr Grundy, Headmaster of Emanuel, insisted on the building of new Eton fives courts, a game for which there was no call, either from staff or from the pupils. His motive was to raise the profile of the school by re-introducing a game that he thought had social status. On the other side of the coin, when City of London moved to its new site in Queen Victoria Street the Headmaster at the time, JA Boyes, and the Corporation deliberately did not include Eton fives courts because they perceived the game to be elitist.

There was a small group of schools in East

Cyril Argentine Alington

Cyril Argentine Alington (1872-1955) was the second son of the Rev. Henry Giles Alington, an inspector of schools, who came from a long line of clerics. He was educated at Marlborough and may well have played Rugby fives while a pupil there. There were no Eton fives courts at Marlborough until much later. Alington had an enormous influence on Eton fives in the first three decades of the twentieth century at the two schools, Eton and Shrewsbury, where he spent most of his teaching life. He was also a very successful cricketer and maintained a high standard as a player of both fives and rackets.

After Marlborough he went up to Oxford where he took two firsts in classics and was elected to a Fellowship of All Souls in 1896. That same year he became Sixth-form Master at Marlborough before moving to Eton in 1899 as an Assistant Master where he remained for nine years, being ordained while there. By the time he was appointed Headmaster of Shrewsbury in 1908 at the age of thirty-five, he was described as a more than ordinarily expert exponent of Eton fives. The previous head had not been a games player and all but two of the staff were older than Alington so the change was striking.

At the end of 1916 he left Shrewsbury to return to Eton as Headmaster where he remained until 1933 when he was appointed Dean of Durham. In a footnote in his book *Things Ancient and Modern*, Alington wrote: "On one occasion it fell to my lot to have a boy to breakfast one morning, to beat him (with his entire consent) an hour or two later for an offence undiscovered when the invitation was issued, and to play fives with him before luncheon. This was an engagement made a day or two before, and neither of us saw the least reason for cancelling it. No one who cannot understand that story has any claim to a knowledge of the English public school boy – or his master. "Alington was chairman of the Headmasters' Conference and later chaplain to the king. He was a prolific writer of religion, biography, history and poetry, and also wrote a series of detective novels as well as composing several hymns and prayers. School buildings at both Shrewsbury and Eton still carry his name.

Anglia with Eton courts: Woodbridge (1898); Gresham's, Holt (1903), Ipswich (1908), King's, Ely, City of Norwich and Framlingham, plus the previously mentioned Leys, Cambridge and King Edward VI, Bury St Edmunds, but they rarely seem to have played against each other. The most significant was the latter, often known as Bury School, which converted a court to Eton design in 1895:

The Bureian wrote, "The new courts were formally opened on Monday 7 October, when Lord Chelsea, MP for Bury, and the Hon Mortimer Tollemache played a series of matches against the Headmaster and Mr Richmond. The two Old Etonians showed they still retained that skill and quickness of eye which characterises the good Fives player, and some most exciting play was witnessed.... Simultaneously a match took place in the Rugby Court between Mr. Faulkner (with Summers as his partner) and Mr Parker (with Groom). The latter pair proved successful after some good games. It is proposed to have a Fives Tournament next term, when the football season is drawing to a close. An Old Boys' Fives match was played on 21 November under Eton rules. The Headmaster and CW Rodwell represented the School and the Mayor, Mr JG Oliver, and Mr JA Rodwell, the Old Boys…. "

Ipswich built two courts in 1908, directly after the arrival of a new Headmaster, AK Watson, an Old Harrovian. "Eton fives," he said at his first Speech Day, "is one of the best open-air games that can be played." He challenged the Headmaster of Bury to come over with one of his assistants to play against himself and Mr James, the science master. The invitation was accepted and Ipswich, in their new courts, won 3-0. This was the beginning of a regular fixture between these two schools – indeed it was Bury's only external fixture – until 1917 when it was discontinued "due to an increase in rail fares". It was never resumed. Both Eton and Rugby fives flourished at Bury, encouraged by a succession of enthusiastic head-

masters, until the beginning of the Second World War. Matches in the Eton court were played against The Leys from time to time, but the major part of the activity was internal.

Ipswich played regular matches at home and away to Woodbridge right up to 1939. After the war, their experiences differed widely: Ipswich was poised for a revival when MJ Shortland-Jones, a Kinnaird Cup champion, arrived on the teaching staff in 1953. He only stayed five years but he built up a club of over fifty players, introduced new competitions, arranged away matches and raised the profile of the game; his legacy has lasted until the present day.

At Woodbridge there was no such saviour: the courts fell into disuse and were finally demolished to make way for a dining hall in 1962. At Bury, fives suffered a different fate but with the same result. Following the demise of the gram-

These four photographs show the Highgate v Old Cholmeleians fives match of 1921 being played in the Upper courts

Percy Chapman was an outstanding Eton fives player at Uppingham. After the Shrewsbury match of 1919 *The Salopian* reported that a feature had been "Chapman's brilliant play"

England cricket captain, Percy Chapman & WM Woodfull, captain of Australia, going out to toss at Trent Bridge in 1930

The Uppingham Fives Team of 1919: WAH Maxwell, WJ Wilkin, CM Hodgkinson, APF Chapman

mar schools, King Edward VI became a mixed comprehensive and moved to a new site in 1972. No fives courts were included.

A pre-1903 photograph shows a foursome playing racket-fives at a 'winged wall' that appears to be identical to the wall at Warminster. This was at the Old School House at Gresham's; the school moved to its present site in 1903 and built three Eton courts. Most of the play seems to have been on a House basis but it certainly thrived up to 1939. After the war there were references to fives in the school magazine and the writer "hoped that matches would be revived owing to its growing popularity". That failed to

materialise and classrooms were built on the site in the 1960s.

The Leys certainly played some matches against Bury in the early years of the 20th century; two new courts were built there in the 1920s and still exist, but are currently used as a climbing wall and a canoe store. Fives has never been really popular at The Leys and, although the courts were renovated in the 1990s and an arrangement was made for the University players to use them, a rather weak attempt to generate interest at the school petered out.

Throughout the reports on inter-school fives of this era, one is struck by the repeated cancellation of matches due to epidemics. Year after year there are outbreaks of mumps, measles, diphtheria and other diseases with one school or both in quarantine for months on end.

'Fives Ties' were being played at Cambridge University as early as 1869, when Arthur Kinnaird was described as 'fives champion'. After that there are few references until 1885 when *The Harrovian* records that L Sanderson and MT Baines beat the previous year's winners of the School Fives at Eton, St John Meyrick and ERB Hall. In the colleges, over a dozen courts were built between 1890 and 1900 and during these years the game was popular with undergraduates, mostly, it seems, Etonians and Harrovians. Lord Kinnaird, FB Wilson, and Ralph Straus were regular players but strangely, considering that rackets had been played since 1855, there was no Varsity Eton fives match until 1928. One reason was that Merton was probably the only Oxford college with a court, although there were public Eton fives courts in St Giles and Holywell. A pewter mug recently discovered in a Nassau mansion and inscribed "Oriel College, Eton Scratch Fives, First Prize, November 8th, 1859: JW Wager, CR Dawson, H Williams, ET Churton" shows that the game was also played among Oxford undergraduates from an early date. The competition for this may well have been played on the Merton courts as Oriel is close by.

Liverpool Racquet Club had a court and

played regularly against schools. When the Borough Road Training College (for teachers) moved to a new site at Isleworth in 1899, a row of three fives courts was built. The centre court was an Eton fives court; the other two had a bar on the front wall, no buttress and no back wall and a contemporary photograph shows singles bat fives being played in these. The college became well known for sport, especially athletics.

An Eton fives court was built, also in 1899, at the London Hospital, Turner Street, Whitechapel, now known as the Royal London Hospital. This was the gift of Mr Fowell Buxton of the brewers, Truman, Hanbury, Buxton & Company, and a Mr McWharrie; it was built in the House Governor's garden. A Fives Club was formed, the first officers being JH Buxton (President), HF Buxton, Munro Scott (Vice-Presidents)

Fives at Aldenham in the 1920s: the first Eton fives court was not built until 1916

and AL Simey (captain). It was a great success: "Such was the demand for courts that a book for names has been found necessary" and the Club immediately attracted forty members; a Handi-

Harold Godfrey Bache

Harold Godfrey Bache (1889-1916) was born in Kidderminster and educated at King Edward's School, Birmingham. He was a pupil when the courts were converted to Eton courts in 1905. In the previous year he had played in both the singles and doubles competitions on the old court, reaching the quarter finals of the doubles although only fourteen years of age. He was subsequently captain of Eton fives in 1906 and 1907 and, playing with GH Alabaster in a match against an Old Edwardian pair, was described as "playing a most brilliant game at the pillar".

He played association football (blues in 1909-10-11), hockey, rugby and tennis for Cambridge University. As a centre forward he scored 87 goals in 39 games for the famous Corinthians and also won seven amateur International caps for England, scoring seven-

teen goals, including seven in a 20-0 victory over France.

Bache also excelled at cricket, representing Worcestershire regularly. In 1914 he joined West Bromwich Albion, whose secretary had travelled all the way to Amiens to secure his signature, and he led the attack at the start of that last pre-war season. He was also preparing to take up a teaching post at Clifton but on the outbreak of war joined the army and was tragically killed in France in 1916 while serving with the Lancashire Fusiliers. Bache is remembered on Panel 33 of the Menin Gate memorial at Ypres.

The "Bache Memorial Award" is presented annually to the best all-round sportsman at King Edward's School, Birmingham, and the honours board lists all winners from its inception in 1920.

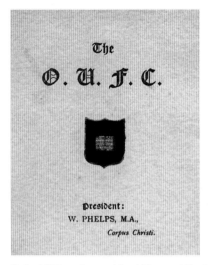

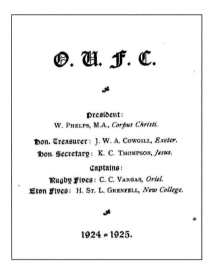

Oxford University combined Eton and Rugby fives fixture card 1924. The first Varsity Eton fives match took place in 1928

cap Tournament was arranged and two matches were played against City of London School in 1900. The following October it was reported that the new court was "in full swing…the only drawback is the lowness of the roof, many shots from the back court being spoilt by striking it".

At about this time a number of enthusiasts, many of them Old Etonians, built themselves courts at their country houses. Examples are Linton Park, Maidstone, Kent (Cornwallis family); Wallsworth Hall, Twigworth, Gloucestershire (de Winter family); Downham Hall, Clitheroe, Lancashire (Assheton family); High Elms, Orpington, Kent (Lubbock family); Joldwynds, Holmbury Hill, Dorking (Sir William Paget Bowman), demolished in 1930; Heythrop Park, Enstone, Oxfordshire (Brassey family) and Glyndebourne Manor (Christie family), now famous for its opera house and where the fives court is part of the organ room. There are also remains of former Eton fives courts at Hawarden Castle in Wales (Sir William Gladstone, Bt); Hardwick House, Whitchurch (probably during the ownership of Philip Powys, later Philip Powys Lybbe) and at Cliveden (probably during the ownership of Hugh Grosvenor, 1st Duke of Westminster, 1868-

93). Further afield in Portugal, George Warre, brother of Edmond, Head Master of Eton (1884-1905), built a court at Quinta do Zimbro near Tua in the Douro, a property he had acquired in 1892. Needless to say, 'family and friends' fives was the extent of the activity in most of these courts.

Fives also seems to have been played extensively in an area that received almost no publicity: the military. The September 1899 issue of *The Navy and Army Illustrated* depicts two courts at Aldershot, one of which is an Eton fives court. The caption reads, "If all work and no play makes Jack a dull boy, it is no less true in the case of Tommy. At almost every military station a fives court is to be found, and every afternoon there are seen in military camps such as Aldershot and Shorncliffe, a number of men joining enthusiastically in the game, which is all the more interesting when teams from different regiments compete."

As these examples show, Eton fives had spread well beyond its heartlands by the end of the 19th century, but perhaps the most unlikely site of all was a school five thousand miles away in the far north of West Bengal. When EA Newaton became the Rector at St Paul's School, Darjeeling, in 1898, one of the first building projects undertaken was Eton fives courts; these were completed in 1899 and were the first to be built outside the British Isles. At seven thousand feet above sea level, the courts are the highest in the world; the thin air and the swirling mists of the Himalayan foothills add an altogether new dimension to the game. The view of the massif of Kangchenjunga from the adjacent cricket field is breathtaking.

Chapter 9

The Beginning of the Golden Age

1919-30

Cleopatra, Anthony
Were introspective you'll agree,
Got in a morbid state because
They lounged about too much indoors.
If they'd gone in for Eton fives,
They wouldn't have gone and lost their lives.

From *Give Up Love* by WH Auden, who was a pupil at
Gresham's, Holt, between 1920 and 1925. Eton fives courts
were built at Gresham's in 1903.

The period between the two World Wars can reasonably be described as "The Golden Age of Eton Fives", as it was then that the game came to be played more widely than ever before – or since. It was a period when all the best school games players played fives and so the list of the leading players reads like a *Who's Who of Sport*. It saw the establishment of the national championships for individual pairs, the Schools' Championships, a national club championship and the formation of the Eton Fives Association. Fives of one code or another was now an important feature in all the leading schools and Eton and Rugby fives courts were springing up abroad too. In 1922 Eton fives was introduced to Nigeria with two mud courts, complete with ledges and buttresses, at Birnin Kebbi. Three courts were built at Zuoz, near St Moritz, in Switzerland in 1923; two courts at Kolej Melayu (Malay College) in Kuala Kangsar, Perak in 1928; two courts at St. Thomas', Mount Lavinia in Sri Lanka in 1931 with two more courts the following year. There was also a court at the British Embassy in Lisbon, known to have

been played on by the then British Ambassador, Sir Lancelot Carnegie, an Old Etonian.

Prior to 1914 there were very few references to Eton fives in the national press, apart from the occasional result of the Eton v Harrow match. After the war the pages of *The Times* regularly reported at length from the championship events, and listed a multitude of results of fives matches between schools and clubs. Although there had been a handful of inter-school fixtures established before the Great War, the number increased rapidly afterwards. From 1919 onwards, results were regularly published in *The Times* and included matches involving the following schools (in chronological order): Eton, Harrow, Shrewsbury, Charterhouse, Uppingham, City of London, Highgate, Westminster, Emanuel, Lancing, Repton, Aldenham, Berkhamsted, Lyceum Alpinum Zuoz, Mill Hill, Stowe, The Leys, Woodbridge, Ipswich, Wellington and Cranleigh. Many of these schools also had masters' teams featuring regularly in the reported results; two examples not in the above list were Bryanston Masters and Seaford Masters (from the prep schools St Peter's and St Wilfrid's and the many others that existed in the town at that time).

The Great War had crept up slowly. At Eton "de Quetteville left at Christmas to go into the Army, so missed the chance of becoming Keeper," reported the *Eton College Chronicle*. The prizes for the School Fives were reduced from £5 to £4 "owing to the war", but an unbeaten pair played a full fixture list of twelve matches. The school seemed to be unaffected; a greater disruption came from flu and German measles. It was not until 1917 that effects really began to bite: early leaving meant that both the Keepers were 16-year-olds and there was a severe shortage of fives balls. In 1918 the number of school fixtures was reduced to eight but the enthusiasm for fives was greater than ever with 97 pairs entering the School Fives and 92 pairs the House Fives. Moreover Mr Marten declared the Keepers, the Marquess of Worcester and T Bevan, to be "as good as they have ever been." The return of Dr Alington to Eton as Head Master immediately produced a fixture with Shrewsbury.

Although a number of other schools had standard Eton fives courts before the war, there was a significant increase in the building of new courts in the subsequent twenty years. Aldenham added a further two courts in 1925 to the four that had been built nine years previously. Eton added another eight covered courts in 1923; by 1934 there were 52 courts in total. Highgate opened a new covered block of eight courts in 1924 to add to the ten open courts already standing. Six new courts were built at Berkhamsted in 1926 – the plans had been for three but "the financial position had improved so the number of courts was doubled" – an unusual sit-

uation. In the same year Lancing constructed four courts to commemorate the headmastership of Canon Bowlby, who had been a devotee of the game when he was on the teaching staff at Eton.

Further new courts followed rapidly. The magnificent Stowe House had formerly been the home of the Duke of Buckingham and Chandos. His daughter, Lady Kinross, inherited the estate in 1889 but when her son was killed in the war, the estate was sold. Stowe School was founded in 1923 under Headmaster JF Roxburgh, a Housemaster from Lancing, with 99 boys mostly aged 13. Within two years two Eton fives courts were ready for use. Moreover "a very beautiful House Cup was presented by Mr and Mrs FRS Balfour of Dawyck for an annual competition....The cup is Viennese work of the 18th century: a single tusk of ivory, with carving showing the Black Prince at the battle of Crecy." It was a generous gift – although the relevance to Eton fives of the depiction is elusive.

At Westminster, fives had long been popular but expansion had been held back by the impossibility of finding a site for new courts. This was resolved in 1928 when the old rackets court was converted into four Eton fives courts, covered and lit.

Also in 1928 a court was built at Wolverhampton Grammar School, a gift of the Mander family. During the opening ceremony Gerald Mander, who was Chairman of the Governors for many years, is recorded as saying that no school was complete without an Eton fives court. Six years later he presented a second court to the school. In 1929 Marlborough built four Eton fives courts to add to their exist-

ZUOZ COLLEGE
LYCEUM IN ZUOZ

ICE HOCKEY,
HOCKEY, CRICKET
& FIVES

Fixture List

1928~1929

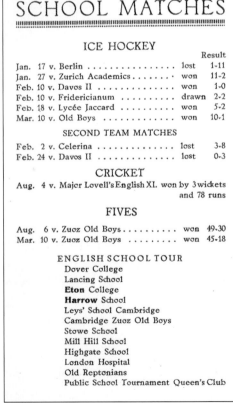

SCHOOL MATCHES

ICE HOCKEY

		Result
Jan. 17 v. Berlin	lost	1-11
Jan. 27 v. Zurich Academics	won	11-2
Feb. 10 v. Davos II	won	1-0
Feb. 10 v. Fridericianum	drawn	2-2
Feb. 18 v. Lycée Jaccard	won	5-2
Mar. 10 v. Old Boys	won	10-1

SECOND TEAM MATCHES

Feb. 2 v. Celerina	lost	3-8
Feb. 24 v. Davos II	lost	0-3

CRICKET

Aug. 4 v. Major Lovell's English XI.	won by 3 wickets and 78 runs	

FIVES

Aug. 6 v. Zuoz Old Boys	won	49-30
Mar. 10 v. Zuoz Old Boys	won	45-18

ENGLISH SCHOOL TOUR
Dover College
Lancing School
Eton College
Harrow School
Leys' School Cambridge
Cambridge Zuoz Old Boys
Stowe School
Mill Hill School
Highgate School
London Hospital
Old Reptonians
Public School Tournament Queen's Club

Regular tours to England were arranged by Gordon Spencer in the 1920s and 1930s

ing Rugby fives courts, and in 1930 three courts were constructed at Bryanston, which had only been open as a school for two years. In that same year Shrewsbury added two more courts to bring their total up to fourteen. A sign that Eton fives really had arrived was shown by an advertisement seeking a property for a house party that appeared in *The Times* in 1931 with the added phrase, "fives courts an asset".

On the other side of the world two Eton fives courts were built at each of two schools in what is now Malaysia. At Kolej Melayu (Malay College) in Kuala Kangsar, as referred to earlier, and at the Penang Free School, which moved to its current site in George Town in the same year. The latter is the oldest anglophone school in Southeast Asia and had English headmasters until 1963. The courts were situated at the western edge of the polo ground but it is likely that they were demolished in one of the many new building programmes.

After the war, fives at the leading schools soon picked up momentum. At Eton, the game was hugely popular with over 600 boys playing regularly, giving rise to more arguments about the allocation of courts. Eight new courts were covered and much more fives began to be played in the 'Michaelmas half'; twelve pairs usually played in the Masters' match and, following the formal constitution of the Old Etonian Fives Club in 1925, the first match against the OEFC ran to nineteen pairs. In 1919 the Keepers, HD Sheldon and WW Hill-Wood, beat the Masters pair, Messrs Marten and Headlam "for the first time ever", but they lost to Charterhouse twice; at Eton by the narrowest of margins: 15-17 in the fifth game of a match in which every game had been 'set'. In 1923 the Keeper, "at Mr Marten's suggestion", introduced team matches – although the number of pairs was unspecified – and there was a call to increase the number of 'choices' (that is 'colours' or 'caps' for fives) from eight.

Fives at Eton was certainly flourishing but they were matched if not bettered by Shrewsbury, which produced a number of extraordinarily tal-

ented players at this time. A flu epidemic at Eton in 1918 reduced their fixture list from twelve matches to just four but the Keepers, RS Hill-Wood and T Bevan, only just squeezed home against Peterson and Hughes, winning 18-13 at Eton, where Shrewsbury had to get used to a "slower court and a larger ball". At Shrewsbury the home pair won 3-0. This was Peterson's first of four years in the Shrewsbury team; he was captain for the following three. A keen student of the game and mature beyond his years, he wrote some hints for Salopians playing at Eton:

> *Play with an Eton ball for at least a week before the match;*
> *Practise the Eton game-ball rule;*
> *Knock up at Eton in the morning;*
> *Note different features of the Eton court: sides, roof, and top of the 'pepper';*
> *Get to know their rules;*
> *Try to find 'length'. Killing the ball is not easy;*
> *'Cut' the ball, especially on slams.*

After a two year lapse, Shrewsbury resumed their big match against Uppingham in 1919; Peterson and Hughes played APF Chapman and CM Hodgkinson, The *Salopian* commenting that a feature of the match was "Chapman's brilliant play". The Uppingham report described Chapman as "a tower of strength...we have not seen many better players," and spoke of "his strong left hand, long reach, good placing, hard hitting...." This was, of course, Percy Chapman, who had achieved a 1st XI batting average of 111 in 1917 and was to go on to captain Cambridge, Kent and England at cricket – a legend in his own lifetime. The scores in the top court were 15-10, 15-5, 6-15 to Shrewsbury.

In 1919 Peterson played also with RS Worth, who was to have both a son and a grandson as Schools' winners. In 1920 he played with EP Hewetson, who "was a worthy partner and excellent all-round sportsman" – this was said at the time to be Shrewsbury's best pair for thirty years – and when he played with JS Stephenson in 1921, they were probably even better. *The*

Lord Dunglass, winner of the School Fives at Eton in 1922. Later he became Sir Alec Douglas-Home and then Lord Home of the Hirsel. He was President of the EFA 1966–71

Salopian wrote: "Stephenson is a very fine player, fit to match, if not slightly better, any previous Shrewsbury player. He has a fine reach, powerful physique, and a good eye...." Stephenson went on to win blues at Oxford for cricket, football and golf and played cricket for Yorkshire. At Oxford he was a cult figure. A contemporary later told this story: "Probably no undergraduate since the War has been known by sight and reputation to so large a proportion of the university. It was not merely his magnificent physique and his fame as an athlete: he was a personality. In those days the game of 'Beaver' was in fashion, the scoring being as in tennis. To see Mr Stephenson in his morning walk up the High was 15; to be honoured with a "Good morning", 30; if he stopped and talked to you it was 40, but if he walked up the street with you, it was game set and match!

"Dining alone in the Grid with the *Evening Standard*, he was pointed out to awestruck freshmen as if he were royalty, and when a well-meaning hostess, meeting him for the first time, sought to terminate an awkward silence by the inquiry, 'Do you play games, too, Mr Stevens?' it seemed to the company that it was only a miraculous suspension of the laws of nature that the ground did not open and swallow her."

In 1921 Stephenson and IM Veitch had an easy victory, 15-10, 15-3, 15-3, over Eton, represented by N Llewelyn-Davies and Lord Dunglass (later Sir Alec Douglas-Home, Lord Home of the Hirsel) in the Eton courts. In 1922, the Shrewsbury IV, JS Stephenson, AED Penn, IM Veitch and HF Robinson, were very strong again, beating Uppingham and Repton easily but losing narrowly to Eton at Eton.

In 1923 Robinson and AT Barber of Shrewsbury beat Eton, Kennerley-Rumford and Bridgeman, where they played in the covered court "which was very fast". At this time the covered court was not popular and was only used in wet weather. "Robinson was the best player on court; Barber is a fighter, a good volleyer with both hands..." Barber was another outstanding Salopian games player, winning blues at Oxford for soccer, golf and cricket and later captaining Yorkshire CCC. His is another name that runs through the story of Eton fives.

It was becoming increasingly apparent at this time that court dimensions differed and that schools were playing with different-sized fives balls to a different scoring system. Hence the comment after the 1922 match that Shrewsbury had to play with a smaller ball in smaller courts at Uppingham. These two schools also still played the 'points system', whereby two pairs each played the best of three games against each of the opposition pairs and the team with the most points was the winner. Thus home and away matches with, for example, Eton, were played under different rules. As an illustration of the confusion with scoring at this time, in 1927 Charterhouse played to three different systems:

the one-pair match against Harrow was decided on the best of five games; against Old Carthusians, three pairs played best of five games each and the match was won by six games to four; against Old Etonians (of all clubs) the Uppingham/Shrewsbury method was used, Charterhouse winning on points 120-113. The time for a ruling was overdue.

Harrow, after their purple patch in the early years of the century, reverted to mediocrity until the later 1920s, although the 1918 pair included GM Butler, who, opined *The Harrovian*, "with more time at his disposal for fives, would become a class player". Butler was Head of the School, captain of cricket, Harrow football and association football and Victor Ludorum – and later an Olympic gold medallist – so fives for him was but a minor diversion. In 1920 another successful Charterhouse pair, FH Barnard and GB Garnett, beat Harrow 3-0, Eton

Tom Longfield was one of the best Eton fives players to come from Aldenham until their successes in the 1950s. He was in the cricket XI for five years and won blues at Cambridge for football and cricket, captaining the cricket XI in 1927-28.

3-2 and Highgate 3-0, all at home.

The popularity of Eton fives at Repton had stemmed from Lionel Ford's headmastership. Their contest with Shrewsbury, dating from 1909, has always been regarded as the most important match of the year, although Repton had not enjoyed much success in these encounters. So the Repton victory by ACJ German and EKM Hilleary in 1923, which marked the end of a long run of defeats, was welcomed ecstatically. JW Buckland and HW Austin, two very good players, represented Repton the following year, but the Shrewsbury match was lost easily, and no further success was achieved until 1934, when DW Foster and LD Hall scraped home 17–14 in the fifth game. Playing for Repton's 2nd pair in 1925 was Bryan Valentine, who won blues for soccer and cricket at Cambridge in 1928 and 1929, captained Kent and won seven England Test caps with a batting average of 64.85.

Aldenham had been rather late-comers to the fives elite, only having built Eton courts in 1916. They had played Highgate for many years in their old courts but had a match against Harrow for the first time in 1924. Their best player of this era was TC Longfield, who was five years in the cricket XI, a soccer blue, captain of Cambridge cricket in 1927 and 1928, and who played cricket for Kent off and on up to 1939. Berkhamsted, who were even later in building Eton courts, played Aldenham regularly during this

The Aldenham courts in about 1935

time and these two schools have been each other's most regular opponents ever since.

In 1919 Highgate had their first fixture at Harrow in which FW Barnes and FG Baddeley lost in three very close games to H Bathurst-Norman and CH Gurney; Barnes was described as "the best player for many years" and had been four years in the first VI. DGA Lowe, who won an Olympic Gold Medal for the 800m in Paris in 1924, was in the 1st VI in 1921 and RWV Robins, later Middlesex and England cricket captain, in the 1st pair of 1924 and 1925.

The 1928 Highgate pair was AH Fabian and J Aguirre, who beat all school and club first pairs with the exception of an Old Etonian pair, the Hill-Wood brothers, and just two years later were to win the Kinnaird Cup together. In many of Highgate's matches at this time, it was the custom for the first pair also to play against the opposition second pair and that year, Highgate's second pair, the brothers EN and ED Portu, were also victorious over these first pairs. The following year Aguirre played with ED Portu, thus forming another all-Basque pair. These Basques had been brought up on pelota and they had a different way of hitting the ball, including a distinctive jab that confounded their opponents.

Aguirre and Portu were a formidable partnership and they beat the current Kinnaird Cup winners twice in that season. In 1929 Highgate, Aguirre and PW Westerby (ED Portu was "unable to be in London"), lost to eventual

winners Harrow in the semi-finals of the Public Schools' Handicaps. Sadly, Aguirre was killed in the Spanish Civil War.

In 1925 Highgate played their first matches against Berkhamsted and Westminster. Up to this point Westminster had seemed perfectly happy to play all their matches in their own courts against club sides, although they also had a full programme of internal competitions. TG Lund of the 1925 pair is the only Old Westminster ever to have played in a Kinnaird Cup Final.

The Keepers at Eton that year, T Mott and DJ Hill-Wood, were only beaten once in 15 matches but they lost the School Fives to TA Pilkington and JPT Boscawen. The following year Pilkington and Mott, playing together, were beaten by NM Ford and KC Gandar Dower of Harrow, who also beat the Old

Three school Eton fives players who later achieved great success in other sports

GM Butler (1899-1981). Guy Butler was the son of EM Butler and educated at Harrow where he was Head of School and captain of cricket, football and fives. At Trinity College, Cambridge, he was President of the CUAC and he was the first athlete to compete in three Olympic Games; he won a gold, a silver and two bronze medals. He taught at Lancing 1922-28 and then became an athletics correspondent and coach.

DGA Lowe (1902-81). Douglas Lowe was captain of fives at Highgate in 1921. He then went up to Pembroke College, Cambridge where he won athletics blues in 1922-24. He went on to win gold medals for the half-mile in the 1924 Olympics in Paris and 1928 Olympics in Amsterdam. He became a distinguished lawyer, appinted a judge in 1964, and Recorder at the Crown Court.

R. W. V. ROBINS

RWV Robins (1906-68). Walter Robins was captain of fives at Highgate in 1924 and was an outstanding all-round sportsman. He played football for Nottingham Forest and cricket for Cambridge, Middlesex and England as a batsman and leg-break bowler. He captained Middlesex 1935-38, 1946-47 and 1950 and led them to the County Championship in 1947. Robins captained England for the three Test series v New Zealand in 1937 and later became Chairman of the England Test Selectors.

Etonian pair, de Quetteville and Redhead, the winners of the first Kinnaird Cup competition. Neville Ford was one of four sons of Lionel Ford, and the most talented as a sportsman; he won the Public Schools Rackets Championship and played in the Oxford cricket XI from 1928-30. This was Gandar Dower's first year in the Harrow pair; he was to become one of the best court games players of his generation.

In 1927 Shrewsbury's 1st pair, PHC Staples and DN Moore, celebrated an unbeaten season, beating Eton twice. Moore won cricket blues at Oxford in 1930 and 1931, when he was captain. The following year Moore and JSO Haslewood inflicted what the *Eton College Chronicle* described as the "severest ever defeat by another school on Eton courts": Shrewsbury won 18-13, 15-5, 15-3. Shrewsbury also played Harrow that year, but rather surprisingly lost to RB Hodgkinson and CG Ford (NM's younger brother) – especially as Hodgkinson's usual partner, WM Welch, did not play.

Probably because of Alington's and Peterson's presence at Eton, relationships between Eton and Shrewsbury were particularly cordial at this time. The correspondent in *The Salopian* in 1927 wrote, "The [Eton] match was, as it always is, the fixture to which all the Fives world looks forward with greatest interest as it is certain that it will be the most pleasant contest for every point of view; in fact it is difficult to persuade our opposition to take advantages to which they are justly entitled."

An important event in the fives world occurred on November 19th 1927: the opening of a covered court at Queen's Club. Queen's, named after its first patron Queen Victoria, had been founded in 1886 as a club offering many different sports, the first of its kind in the world. It had rackets, real tennis, lawn tennis and squash courts and in 1908 had been the hosts for the 'jeu de paume' event – actually real tennis but named thus – in the Summer Olympics. Up to 1922 it had been the main ground for the Corinthians Football Club and the England v Wales International was played there in 1895. It was a highly prestigious club and for Eton fives to be included among its facilities was a real mark of recognition. Up to the beginning of World War II Queen's was to become the centre of Eton fives in the United Kingdom. The court had a glass roof and electric lighting. We have got used to covered and lit courts nowadays and expect nothing less, but in the 1920s they were a rarity and the benefits had to be spelt out. A report of the exhibition matches in *The Times* explained the advantage: "Rain makes an open court unplayable for hours, and so does a muggy day following frost. If the court is wet or the walls are sweating, Eton fives is hopeless. In this climate it is therefore not good enough for four players to make arrangements any distance ahead...." The two exhibition matches played were between the Etonians, RG de Quetteville and RA Redhead, and the Harrovians, NM Ford and KC Gandar Dower, followed by a match between the Aldenham Masters and the Highgate Masters.

The development of Eton fives in the decade following the Great War was remarkable and the press gave it full coverage. An article in *The Times* in 1919 on the history and tradition of fives stated that it "will no doubt remain always chiefly a school game, but it is such splendid exercise and so interesting that it deserves to be played far more widely than it is". In the 1920s Eton fives was being written about at considerable length in the same newspaper but, in those days, articles in *The Times* were unattributed. The following from 1924 – and many others – were probably written by FB Wilson, who was in the Harrow fives pair in 1899 and 1900. He was a talented all round games player and was said to be able to beat anyone at Queen's Club at table tennis using a bread-knife as a bat! One has to add that his talents with the bread-knife do not seem to be extended to verification of facts for his reports: these are studded with errors, not least of the spelling of names [*These have been corrected where they are known*].

The generosity of certain Old Etonians has just provided Eton with eight new covered Eton fives courts, and the school now possesses some 60 courts – 10 covered and the rest open. Other schools, in increasing numbers, have taken to the game. Harrow, for instance, has Eton courts and many of them. Amongst others, Charterhouse, Wellington, Repton, Uppingham, and Shrewsbury have them, and the last named school recently produced one of the best players that the present writer, in his experience of not far short of 40 years, has ever seen [*This probably refers to Stephenson but could be Peterson, Robinson or Barber*]. Quite recently two courts have been built by the Grammar School at High Wycombe; and there is at least one girls' school where Eton fives is provided. Considering, however, what an admirable game Eton fives is, the number of courts in the country is not nearly as numerous as it might be. And yet it is a game which takes little space, is not unduly expensive to provide, and is quite cheap to play; and the game has undeniable attractions. It is in the first place suited to all ages. The present writer began at the age of eight, and sees no reason why he should not, if he is still alive, complete a Jubilee or even a Diamond Jubilee at the game.

Then fives is a game which requires the use of the mind as well as of every muscle of the body; the ledges and the pepper-box and the 'dead man's hole' bring complications which demand more concentration. In fives you always have to be on your toes and be ready for the unexpected, and to be manoeuvring to 'kill' the ball or to make your opponent return a weak shot. You have to be thinking all the time, and unless you do, you are lost. Moreover, fives necessitates the use of both hands. It is the great demerit of most games that they are right-handed, and the great merit of fives that you must be able to use the left hand, especially

for volleying and in the pepper-box, which is on the left side. You cannot avoid, try how you will, the use of that hand; and if you are weak with it your opponents, if they know their job, will provide you with plenty of practice.

A distinguished educationist once put forward a theory that the use of the left hand developed the right side of the brain and of the right hand the left side. If there is any biological truth in this dictum it should lead to the adoption of the game as part of the compulsory syllabus enforced by the new President of the Board of Education – himself a Harrovian [*This was Charles Trevelyan, who was in the Harrow football XI of 1888 but not known to have been a fives player*] – and to a sensible rise in the standard of the nation's intellect. And then fives is a very sociable game. You choose your own partner – and the association between fives partners is often the most abiding of boyish friendships. Not only that, but except in competitions, you can choose your opponents; and in fives between old opponents one can have, towards the end of a close game, the same tense feeling of friendly hostility that occurs in a golfing foursome. You know your opponents' weak points and play to them; they know yours and seem to you to be perhaps a trifle unscrupulous in the way they endeavour to exploit them; and although the games are hard fought, there is an element of chivalry in them. Umpires are rare. In the most difficult of all cases, a 'let', the tradition is that the player who might have been in the way should be scrupulous in offering a 'let' and his opponent should be chary in accepting it.

Covered Fives courts have not the objection of squash racket and rackets courts that the air is stagnant in them. For the back of a fives court is always open, and the courts can so be covered that the air flows freely at the top on the other three sides. But, like rackets and squash rackets, the game of Fives has a supreme advantage – that you can get as much exercise as you want in a short time; an hour and a half's hard game is sufficient for anybody. Mr AC Ainger, a distinguished exponent of the game, once said that Eton fives was the very best game for boys that had ever been invented. We need not enter upon such a controversial topic, but, at any rate, for boys it is certainly a very good game, and for older people it might be called the lawn tennis of the winter. It is to be hoped that Eton fives may some day attain a similar popularity to that great summer game.

This elicited a reply from inside the Eton fives world in the form of a letter to the editor of *The Times* from the Honorary Secretary of the Old Cholmeleian Society:

Sir,

Lovers of the game of Eton fives will endorse every word of the article published in your edition of yesterday. Eton fives is indeed a game of many attractions. I think, however, that the game is rather better known than your correspondent is aware. Since I began looking round for opponents some three years ago, I have been surprised and pleased to find how many schools, colleges, and hospitals in and near London play the game. At Highgate School we have ten open courts, and eight new ones (covered) are about to be completed. Great things are expected from the newly formed Fives Association.

The rapid spread of the game was well illustrated by the Swiss tour of England in 1929, just six years after the first courts were built there. The visiting Lyceum Alpinum team from Zuoz played matches at Eton, Harrow, Lancing and Stowe.

Footnote:

Of all the activities one might encounter in a fives court – and there have been many – one of the least likely would seem to be romance. There is something about the starkness of the grey walls and the draught, so it may come as a surprise to the reader to learn that Bernard Montgomery, later to be Field Marshal Earl Montgomery of Alamein – but not an Eton fives player – proposed to his future wife, Elizabeth Carver, in the fives courts at Charterhouse in 1927. The reason why they were at Charterhouse was that Mrs Carver, widowed in the Great War, had two boys at the school; the reason why he chose the fives courts as the venue to pop the question is less obvious. Maybe he thought that, out of season, it was a place where they would be assured of privacy.

Chapter 10

Tying the Strands Together

The Genesis of the Eton Fives Association

By the beginning of the 1920s, as more Eton fives matches came to be played between schools and clubs, it was becoming clear that there needed to be some sort of central organisation. On Wednesday, 7 November 1923, there appeared in *The Times* a short notice that read, "A Fives Association has been formed to popularise the game and organise the club matches on the lines of the Bath Club Squash Rackets Cup."

The Chairman of this new Fives Association was Sir Lionel Alexander, the Honorary Secretary was CMW Prior and among those on the Committee were Lord Kinnaird and EB Noel. Three weeks later, it was followed by a further notice: "It has been decided to form an Eton Fives Association of Old Boys Clubs and other organisations which play the game. Among its objects will be the increasing of facilities and the arrangement of inter-club matches. The Association has received the approval of the Headmaster (sic) of Eton. Application for representation on the Tennis and Rackets Association will be made later…"

It is clear from this notice that Eton fives had been the only version of the game considered and it seems likely that it prompted some objections from Old Boys' Clubs and individuals interested in either the Rugby or other forms of the game. As a result a small executive committee was formed with Sir Lionel Alexander as Chairman and Dr Cyriax, representing Rugby fives, as Vice Chairman; they decided that the Association should revert to its original name, The Fives Association, and should embrace all forms of fives with Eton, Rugby and Winchester fives each

being responsible for running its own affairs. A general meeting was held at Queen's Club on October 24th 1924, which was again reported in *The Times*. This confirmed the arrangement agreed above and announced that the Association would be affiliated to the Tennis and Rackets Association. It went on to say that "it strengthens the standing of the Fives Committee immensely that the Head Masters of Eton and Harrow have given not only their support but their encouragement to this association". It finished, "At present it is but a baby: but seeing how squash rackets has grown since the first inter-club matches were mooted, one has great faith, without undue optimism, in the future of fives. A good deal more might be said as to the intentions of the association in the matter of championships; but perhaps it is wiser not to attempt to rush the committee into too wonderful promises."

It would not have escaped the notice of readers of *The Times* that the report mentions the support of the Head Masters of Eton and Harrow but there is no reference to the Headmaster of Rugby or of any other Rugby fives-playing school. Three weeks later on November 6th, a committee meeting of the Fives Association was held at the Queen's Club. Again *The Times* reported:

"…The Rugby Fives Clubs seem very well together, and Dr Cyriax collected his committee directly after the meeting. Rugby fives is played in England by a comparatively small number of clubs, but Dr Cyriax, who was, perhaps, the greatest player of this game in the last 70 years – beyond that one can only go by hearsay – has

This sequence of pictures is reprinted from David Egerton's chapter on Eton fives in the *Lonsdale Library of Sports and Games*, published in 1934. In a series of still pictures it gives a good idea of how the game was played. Notice that in the 1930s some players still wore long trousers and others shorts. Caps had ceased to be worn, but were still awarded at Eton and other schools well into the 1950s

Rugby fives very much under control and in being."

This gung-ho, but at the same time patronising, tone smacks of FB Wilson again. The report went on to extol the merits of Eton fives and pilloried an observer who had suggested that Eton fives was to Rugby fives what real tennis was to lawn tennis – not a bad comparison actually! It seems that, rightly or wrongly, the Rugby fives section perceived themselves to be the junior partner in this association – certainly *The Times* correspondent left no doubt as to where his allegiance lay. Three years later, in 1927, the Rugby fives group seceded.

As for Eton fives, *The Times* wrote:

"... Colonel AHC Kearsey has elected to co-opt two other advisers. He was able to persuade Mr CHK Marten [*Lower Master at Eton*] to join his board, and one immediately knew that Eton fives was established... Lord Kinnaird was co-opted to the Fives Committee, and so was Lord Wodehouse. Mr EB Noel [*an Old Wykehamist*] resigned the position of Hon. Secretary. It is impossible to write what immeasurable force he has lent to the propagation of the game of fives by his work, his suggestions, and his personality. Without his gentle persuasion and occasional firmness, fives could not be in the happy position which it now occupies. Mr TS Hankey, who will be remembered as a dogged Etonian at Lord's [*a reference to the Eton v Harrow cricket match of 1914*] at a most critical time, takes over from Mr Noel. His election was not only unanimous, but hailed with great relief."

In spite of the optimistic tone of the reports on the foundation of the Eton Fives Association, it seems that it made a less than happy start. Although no minutes of the early meetings have survived, reports of its activities include emotive words such as "chaos" and "quagmire". The impression is that the Association drifted along in those early years without much impetus or vitality. That may have been the context for the Rugby fives group leaving the Fives Association in 1927 and branching out on its own – although pique at a sense of undervaluation seems a more likely cause. All the same, one must not give the impression that nothing was achieved, as it was during this period that the Public Schools' Handicaps were conceived and the Varsity match was first played.

All seemed relatively quiet until yet another article, this time "concerning the re-organisation of the Eton Fives Association" appeared in *The Times* on 13 March 1931:

To keep alive the interest in Eton fives in the Schools, among Old Boys, and at the Universities a letter has been issued by the Eton Fives Association and the Wyverns Eton Fives Club to all interested in the game. It states that the Eton Fives Association is a representative Committee of Eton fives players, past and present, and has lately been reorganized with a view to making fur-

ther efforts to develop interest in the game of Eton fives. Its work is to be purely executive, and includes the standardization of courts and rules as far as possible, and the promotion and efficient running of competitions. It is also to be the body of appeal in case of any possible dispute. Schools, Old Boys' Clubs, and Universities which play Eton fives are invited to affiliate to the Eton Fives Association, the fee being one guinea a year. The object is to keep players in touch with one another after leaving school, and to keep alive their interest in Eton fives.

This sudden burst of activity was due to the new Hon Secretary of the Association, David Egerton. Egerton, a nineteen-year-old undergraduate in his second year at Magdalene College, Cambridge, had been at Lancing College and left in 1928. He was there when the Eton fives courts were built and played in the College's first Eton fives match against the Masters in 1927. The Masters' team consisted of the Rev FA Woodard, a grandson of the Founder and a Housemaster; Guy Butler, the Olympic athlete and a former captain of fives at Harrow; W Parnell-Smith who had played Eton fives at Hymers, Hull; and AFH Neale, an Old Etonian. The College team was MMcL Symington, GR Taylor, JP Wheeler and DG Egerton. It is also possible that Egerton may have been inspired by John Stephenson, who joined the staff in 1928. Whoever was the catalyst, here was an energetic and enthusiastic young man stepping where his elders had hesitated to tread.

It was while he was an undergraduate at Cambridge that Egerton became Secretary of the EFA, probably in 1930, although, without any 'minutes', the circumstances of his election are unclear. It was certainly a considerable responsibility to give to a nineteen-year-old – especially as he seemed to be receiving little guidance from the Chairman and others.

As a priority Egerton drew the Association's attention to the need for the standardization of

WINNERS OF THE FIVES

Year	Winners	Year	Winners	Year	Winners	Year	Winners	Year	Winners
1917	B.S.HILL WOOD, T.BEVAN	1929	A.G.HAZLERIGG, C.E.W.SHEEPSHANKS	1941	E.H.SPOONER, H.M.CHINNERY	1953	A.M.RANKIN, A.B.GASCOIGNE	1965	S.P.SHERRARD, P.N.H.GIBBS
1918	B.S.HILL WOOD, T.BEVAN	1930	C.E.W.SHEEPSHANKS, M.S.GOSLING	1942	J.H.HALE, A.D.TRENCHARD-COX	1954	P.D.HILL-WOOD, P.M.O.STRAFFORD	1966	P.N.H.GIBBS, N.R.COLQUHOUN
1919	R.A.READHEAD, P.D.LINDSAY	1931	M.S.GOSLING, J.N.HOGG	1943	J.H.HALE, M.D.HOARE	1955	H.S.LANGTON, A.R.B.BURROWS	1967	P.N.H.GIBBS, B.L.H.POWELL
1920	W.F.PRETYMAN, H.R.C.SURTEES	1932	M.A.C.NOBLE, C.M.McLAREN	1944	J.C.L.JENKINSON, P.E.MAUDE	1956	H.S.LANGTON, A.R.B.BURROWS	1968	D.N.HARRIS, D.L.FORBES
1921	G.C.BRIGHT, R.D.SHELDON	1933	R.B.GOSLING, J.W.STRANGE-STEEL	1945	J.D.STEWART-GRAY, P.ASQUITH	1957	A.R.B.BURROWS, J.W.LEONARD	1969	Hon.C.H.R.FORTESCUE, W.R.BURDON
1922	N.LLEWELYN-DAVIES, LORD DUNGLASS	1934	C.S.BRODRICK, J.H.CRIPPS	1946	M.D.CONSTANTINIDI, A.L.CLELAND	1958	D.M.NORMAN, S.M.de ZOETE	1970	M.P.POWELL, R.H.T.HILDYARD
1923	G.S.INGE-WEBBER, J.E.HURLEY	1935	B.M.FISHER, R.V.C.WESTMACOTT	1947	W.J.COLLINS, P.T.LEWIS	1959	D.M.NORMAN, S.M.de ZOETE	1971	R.H.T.HILDYARD, P.G.GREENALL
1924	J.E.TEW, J.A.KING	1936	G.W.WALKER, D.H.MACINDOE	1948	R.A.C.LINZEE, A.J.TENNANT	1960	M.A.ROGERSON, A.C.FARQUHAR	1972	Hon.P.J.REMNANT, M.O.McL.MILLS
1925	J.P.T.BOSCAWEN, T.A.PILKINGTON	1937	J.P.MANN, M.J.ADLER	1949	R.A.C.LINZEE, A.A.W.KIMPTON	1961	G.W.P.BARBER, J.G.M.WALSH	1973	Hon.P.J.REMNANT, M.O.McL.MILLS
1926	C.K.H.HILL-WOOD, ST.J.O.FORBES	1938	R.C.I.de ROUGEMONT, D.L.CURLING	1950	R.T.GARDINER-HILL, J.S.GUTHRIE	1962	T.G.W.BEST, W.D.ROBSON	1974	J.A.HOWARD, H.A.JOHNSEN
1927	C.H.GOSLING, J.M.CARNEGIE	1939	T.TUFNELL, N.T.A.FIENNES	1951	A.C.D.INGLEBY-MACKENZIE, N.F.ROBINSON	1963	T.G.W.BEST, R.A.PILKINGTON	1975	M.I.BEELAERTS, N.J.GOLDSMID
1928	LAKERS-DOUGLAS, I.A.de H.LYLE	1940	A.D.HENDERSON, J.G.MILLN	1952	D.A.C.MARR, D.M.G.BAILEY	1964	A.S.T.NEGRETTI, S.P.SHERRARD	1976	J.A.J.STRAKER, R.H.M.RAISON

Winners of the School Fives at Eton. This board shows the years 1917-76

the laws of the game. These had remained unrevised since the 'Rules of the Games of Fives as Played at Eton' had been drawn up and published by AC Ainger "in conjunction with several clear-headed friends" in 1877. But since that time the only schools that Eton had played were Harrow, Charterhouse and Shrewsbury. There were other groupings of schools, many of which had been playing Eton fives for up to fifty years, that played to their own rules with their own scoring methods and even their own terminology. Some, for example, called the 'first cut' a 'cut', others a 'slam', others a 'swipe', others a 'smite' and yet others a 'smash'. This did not matter very much (and schools continued to use their own names for many years to come) but the rules and scoring did matter. As a result the Laws of the Game were officially drawn up by the Eton Fives Association in 1931. The discussions had clearly involved some disagreements and *The Times* correspondent had this to say:

> The chief importance of the new laws, as now drawn up, is the standardization of the game. Eton have always played the 'set' as in rackets; Harrow have always played 'sudden death' in their own courts[1]. At one time there were players who wished to play, and did play, an extra set of two points at 17 all, which was absurd. Very many schools and some clubs play Eton fives, but not all of them have played by even the Badminton laws[2] or those which obtain at Eton.

---

[1] One of the 'standardisations' was in the way of 'setting', that is what happens when the game reaches 'game ball all'. The accepted procedure was that when the score reached 14 all, the cutting team could elect to play to 17 (set 3) or to 19 (set 5). At Eton setting was the rule, but at Harrow there was no setting. In one particular match between Old Etonians and Old Harrovians in 1928 the former pair won by the score of 18-14, 15-1, 21-18. In the final game the score reached 14 all and was played 'set 5'. At 18 all, it was set for the second time to 'set 3'. Presumably the two teams had agreed this but it was described as "so contrary to the usual method of scoring at any other ball game that it must be recorded".

[2] In badminton scoring at the time, games were played to 15 points; if the score reached 13–13, the player reaching 13 first would have the choice of 'setting' or playing straight through to 15. If they chose to 'set', the score reverted to 0–0 and the first to score five points was the winner of the game. If the score reached 14–14, the player reaching 14 first would again have the option to 'set' or play straight through to 15. This time, however, the winner would be the first to score three points.

There are local rules, sometimes most curious ones, which the players in their own courts refuse to give up. There can be no great game in which there is a diversity of regulations and superstitions. It is the Eton game – and one of the greatest in the world. They have had, very properly, the last word in the drawing up of the present laws, but other schools have been as strongly represented on the Committee as they.

There are those who object very strongly to the change of a custom or a rule – much more of a custom than a rule, as history will show – but, though one may sympathize with them, one cannot but vote against them. A glance at the Laws of Cricket, as amended again and again, will surprise many keen cricketers. New laws have been made for tennis – an old game when Henry of Navarre came to the throne of France – quite recently, as they have been for rackets. Squash rackets, a baby game of only some 80 years' duration, had a most drastic, and profitable, alteration made in the game some six years ago. Lawn tennis has gone through many changes in its short but most important career.

In effect very little is changed in the Laws of Eton Fives: the importance of the new laws is that they standardize the game. It is a game, of course, which cannot possibly be played with the slightest pleasure unless both sides are anxious to give much more than they will take. Once in a year a player may ask to be given a 'let' before his opponents have given him one – with an apology. The American tennis players who have visited Queen's Club lately have been fascinated with the game of Eton fives, and it is likely to become popular in the United States of America, where, one has heard, there are already courts[1]. The Americans have, of course, always had some game of Handball.

It was at about the same time that Egerton founded the Wyverns Club: the first fixtures are reported in November 1930. It seems likely that Egerton was no better than an average fives player, although he did get a 'half blue' in 1932 and, wanting more opportunities for players of his standard, he founded a club. In the March 1931 report in *The Times*, the correspondent wrote:

"The Wyverns Eton Fives Club is to be run as a branch of the Eton Fives Association, and is making it possible for all Eton fives players to put themselves up for election. High standard of play is not essential for would-be members, and players of all standards are welcomed. Fixtures are to be organized in the holidays for those at Public Schools, and a special feature is to be made of the Public Schools membership, for which there is no entrance fee, the seasonal subscription being 10s. 6d. It is hoped to arrange at least 80 fixtures in the season between October, 1931, and April, 1932."

In October 1932 the *Squash Rackets, Fives, Lawn Tennis & Rackets (SRFLTR) Journal* referred to "DG Egerton, the Eton Fives Association and Wyverns energetic Secretary" and later reported that there was a big increase in the number of candidates for election to the Wyverns and that its subscriptions had been reduced for both ordinary members and the school members. There was even a proposal to organise a tournament for the members of the club and to hold an annual dinner in March or April 1933, which presumably came to nothing. The *SRFLTR Journal* of October 1933 provides further intriguing

---

[1] An entry in the *Harrow School Register* for Lewis Henry Morgan (1882-3) has the intriguing subscript: "Went out to America and entered Harvard University; introduced Eton Fives Courts into America". Tom O'Connor, an authority on Irish Handball, declared that "New England private schools set up by expatriate Englishmen in the latter part of the 19th century often had fives courts listed as part of their facilities. The local newspaper in Springfield, Illinois, mentions that Abraham Lincoln played fives after receiving news of his nomination as candidate for President on March 17th, 1860."

insight into the events of those three years of 1930-3 and the activities of Egerton, in an article under the title 'Something Solemn on Eton Fives'. The author, writing under the pseudonym "Sportsman" – it may well have been Egerton himself, as it is written in the same rather facetious style as his later pieces – introduced it by explaining the origin of his article:

The Rackets and fives courts at Rugby. Two Eton fives courts were built in 1863 and two more were added later, but the game never achieved the popularity of the version that took the school's name

Your pompous old ass of an editor (he must be 85 if he's a day) detailed me off to write 'something solemn on Eton fives' as his sources of information on that game are hopelessly unreliable. But in fact there is something solemn to report from the Eton fives world.

It was only two or three years ago, though it seems much longer that a superman arose from the chaos that was Eton fives. Gathering up the tangled threads with deft capable strokes, he quickly placed himself at the helm and brought law and order out of the quagmire. I refer to the amazing, the incredible, the stupendous Secretary of the Eton Fives Association. For three years, the man was in the limelight, the star, the actor manager, the producer.... In one year he founded the Wyverns Eton Fives Club, he casually arranged no less than 80 fixtures for it and roped in heavens knows how many players. At the same time, as secretary of the Eton Fives Association, he affiliates all the existing clubs, revises and standardises the rules of the game, organises the Kinnaird Cup competition, instigates the Queen's Club Competition and generally gives one to think that Eton fives is the 'be all and end all' of his bright young life. Inci-

dentally he invented a new type of fives glove which resounded loudly to his credit every time they struck the ball and also brought out an 'everlasting' fives ball (later to become the direct inspiration of the 'googly' ball).

Egerton followed this up with an article entitled 'Eton fives is looking up', this time signed by himself:

First a weekly journal (*Squash Rackets, Fives, Lawn Tennis and Rackets Journal* started in October 1932) of which the hundredth part is to be devoted exclusively to its sluggardly activities, and now a new competition (Queen's Club Competition). The time is drawing nigh when Eton fives results will displace Association Football and Horse Racing in the 6.15 news bulletin.... Failing this, the Eton Fives Association might establish its own broadcasting station in France – Radio Aiton Feefs (I am full of schemes for the welfare of the Eton Fives Association).... It has often been suggested that Eton fives lacks any means of expansion, and one of the difficulties in the way of expansion has been the obstruction caused by a few first class players who remark that, personally speaking, they consider that there is enough Eton fives played already: that is to say, speaking more personally, they themselves manage to get as much fives as they wish. The less expert players cannot get so much.

The considerable achievements of Egerton can be gauged from an article published at the end of December 1932 on 'The Growth of Eton Fives since the War' written by WE Gerrish, who founded the Old Westminsters Fives Society in 1924. "All these little points (i.e. the variety in the rules before September 1931) emphasise the enormous good done to the game by the formation of the Wyverns and through them the revivification of the Eton Fives Association. During the last two or three years great strides have been made – more courts built or covered in, matches are easy to arrange, players demanding selection rather than bribed to appear by a promise of dinner after the game as was sometimes the case ten years ago."

The initial success of the Queen's Club Competition for Old Boys' Clubs echoes these comments. It was reported that this new competition "must be regarded as having been fairly successful in its purpose.... Its popularity with club members would appear to be shown by the increasing demand for evening fives, over 60 players having taken part in the matches." There was even a profit of £2.15s.0d, which had been handed over to the EFA. It was decided to continue the competition for a further year with one or two amendments. It would run from the beginning of October 1933 and finish by mid-December, so as to keep clear of the Kinnaird.

At the beginning of 1933, the prospects for Eton fives were full of promise, but the house of cards suddenly collapsed. 'Sportsman' tells of the denouement:

"Unfortunately for Eton fives, towards the end of last March (1933), David Egerton suddenly 'went out of circulation'. Letters remained unanswered and accumulated. For Eton fives seems to have lost its leader. Just for a handful of silver he

The Harrow pair of 1900, RH Crake and FB Wilson , who beat Eton both at home and away for the first time. Wilson became a journalist and wrote many of the articles on Eton fives that appeared in *The Times* in the 1920s and 1930s

left us for just a handful of miserable prep school boys."

Egerton had been appointed to a teaching post at a preparatory school, Sidcup Place. The school had been founded in 1919 at Sidcup Place, Kent, by the Reverend John Blencowe, but in 1933 he moved it to Brambletye, East Grinstead and it was there that Egerton started teaching. He may have stayed there for two years or so, but then the trail goes dead. Egerton seems to have had nothing more to do with Eton fives. In the following month, November 1933, an article appeared entitled "Mr Egerton Replies to his Critics". "The present state of inactivity is my fault. In bygone days I was able to devote to Eton fives much time that should have been spent in the lecture room or otherwise studying but I have to spend all my days at work and no slack afternoons or free weekends come my way."

The most, he said, he could spend on the administration of the game was one hour a day, but he felt that that would be sufficient "if I had the full and active support of all Eton fives players. Apart from GM Butler and JH Beale, Eton fives players are a lazy race." He goes on to comment on the apathy he faced. Committee meetings of the EFA, with three or more weeks notice, were attended only by the Secretary (himself) and, in the case of the Wyverns, by only himself and the Treasurer. He had found it "one of the world's more complicated tasks" to get players to play their ties in the Kinnaird Cup in time "and last year's Kinnaird (1932-3) is still unfinished". Many of the matches of the Wyverns were scratched, "match managers presumably being too lazy to set about raising the teams early enough." He decided "midway between January and April (1933) to sit on my haunches like Mr Asquith, and wait and see".

So the central direction from the EFA disintegrated for about a year. There is no indication as to who was the President or Chairman, nor when Lionel Alexander resigned or retired. The evidence suggests that JH Beale continued to organise the Queen's Club competition, and other fives matches organised by the Old Boys' Clubs and the schools were maintained. The February 1934 edition of the *SRFLTR Journal* at last had some positive news.

It is splendid news to hear at last that someone in the world of Eton fives has undertaken to do some work in connection with that game. Entries for the Kinnaird Cup have been undertaken by Mr HG Crabtree and it is hoped that he and his supporters will be able to run a thoroughly good competition in which rounds will be played at the proper times. Everyone who has the interests of Eton fives at heart should do all they can to help these new leaders for it appears to be a more difficult task to awake the proper authorities. There has not been a meeting of

the Association for over a year nor any communication issued to its members. Two years ago, with a pilot at the helm, it looked as if the organisation of Eton fives would soon rival that of any other game. New Laws (not Rules) were made and subscriptions demanded from all sides. The Wyverns came into being and then without warning, just as the ship was sailing on an even keel, the pilot was lost at sea and the EFA and the Wyverns disappeared into thin air. The pilot had all his eggs in one basket, invested all power in himself and when the ship went down no one else so much as knew where the bank account was kept. The work of the pilot was of the greatest value if only he had built on some foundations. Now everything will have to be started all over again.

So ended the 'Egerton Episode'. Early in 1934 he resigned as Secretary of the EFA "owing to ill-health". Although it all ended on a sour note, David Egerton's contribution to Eton fives should not be undervalued. He even wrote the chapter on Eton fives in the *Lonsdale Library of Sports, Games & Pastimes*, published in 1934: it is a masterly survey of the history of the game and how it was played. With Townsend Warner's *Hints on Eton Fives* it remained the sole published source material for coaches for over fifty years.

The moral of the tale is surely that responsibility of this sort should never be vested in an undergraduate – however great his enthusiasm – without the support of mature and wiser heads. It leaves unanswered the question of what the President, Chairman and Treasurer were doing through this period.

Postscript: Although the Wyverns Eton Fives Club "disappeared into thin air" in 1934, it may have continued in another guise. Some years later, when a Bursar of Magdalene (Egerton's College) was asked about the Wyverns, he replied, "Do you mean that notorious drinking club?"

Chapter 11

Club Fives Goes National

"And of all easy forms of suicide, I have seen nothing to approach defending the pepperbox. Compared with a fives player in this situation, the average coconut leads a sheltered life".

'Phipps' of the *Daily Mail*, 1934

Although *The Times* correspondent in the 1919 article had suggested that fives would remain a school game, it came increasingly to be played by adults beyond school. Most clubs began as groups of Old Boys, formed to play against their own schools. Now they were beginning to establish themselves formally and to play a wider range of opponents. The exception was the Old Citizens, who claim to have been founded as a club in 1893. There is certainly evidence of secretary/captains from that date and a historical article in the *Old Citizens' Gazette* of 1947 declares that "permission to use the school courts was obtained and so the club followed the school in playing the Eton game". However, activity appears to have been spasmodic: "Apart from an annual fixture against the school and occasional fixtures with Queen's Club and the Old Cholmeleians, little was attempted." The Old Citizens Fives Club was certainly formally founded, if not re-founded, in 1923, just before the Old Etonians in 1924.

In 1926 the Old Westminsters formed a Rackets, Squash, Fives & Tennis Society under the dynamic leadership of their Secretary, WE Gerrish. By 1932 there were 23 fives matches on their fixture list. The Old Salopians and Old Olavians Fives Clubs were formally inaugurated in 1929. There were just two uncovered courts at St

Olave's by Tower Bridge at this time and it says everything for the drive and enthusiasm of Bert Holyoak that not only were there practices every Saturday but also that by 1935-6 they had 33 fixtures. To accommodate some of the extra matches they even hired the Westminster City School courts. It was no exception when six pairs travelled to play at Charterhouse that year.

The Old Etonian Fives Association was formally constituted at a meeting under the chairmanship of the Vice Provost in 1924. Its object was "to provide Old Etonians with a better opportunity of keeping up fives after leaving school". The Committee comprised Mr Marten, Mr Headlam, Capt Burrows (representing the Army), JE Tew (Oxford University), JA King (Cambridge University) and JG King as Hon Secretary. All 'Old Choices' were eligible and life subscription was five shillings. Matches were to be arranged with all Eton fives-playing schools and other clubs.

The creation of these new clubs led to an explosion of fixtures against schools – for, of course, that was where the courts were – although there was no significant increase in the inter-school fixtures. Harrow, for example, who played Eton, Charterhouse, Highgate and Aldenham in 1920 had not added any other schools by 1935, but by then they also played the Old Carthusians, Old Cholmeleians, Old Etonians, Old Westminsters, Old Aldenhamians and Old Reptonians. Matches against the Jesters, Wyverns and Oxford and Cambridge Universities were added the following year.

Perhaps the most important event of all at this

John Stewart Stephenson

John Stewart Stephenson (1903-75) was educated at Shrewsbury where the standard of Eton fives was very high after eight years under the headmastership of Cyril Alington. In 1922, *The Salopian* fives correspondent wrote, "Stephenson is a very fine player, fit to match, if not slightly better, any previous Shrewsbury player" – praise indeed. Stephenson was certainly an outstanding games player. This is an extract from the tribute in the *Lancing College Magazine* when he left the teaching staff there in 1937.

"The ordinary man would be well enough content if he could secure one Blue at the 'Varsity. Mr Stephenson had three and no doubt, if he had wished, could have added to the number. He had the rare distinction of captaining the University in two Varsity soccer matches. He was two years in the cricket side and played regularly for Yorkshire in the vacation: characteristically, his two finest innings were reserved for the two most important occasions of the season, the Australian match at Oxford and the 'Varsity match at Lord's. As a mid-off, he was among the first three in England. Finally, he was for the last two years a member of the golf side, a fine performance for a man most of whose winter was occupied by football.

When he was appointed to Lancing, it was clear that he must if he stayed leave his mark on the place, and few would dispute that he has done so...By his sound knowledge of the games he played so well and his patient inculcation of it he achieved much, by his enthusiasm, his detestation of any form of slackness or softness, and his determination to have everything just as he thought right – perhaps even more. Above all what he taught he could put into practice himself – a priceless asset. It was only necessary to see him playing any game, however trivial the occasion, or however short of practice he might be, to realise that here was one to whom ball games were a kind of second nature. His squash is a good example. He disclaimed all knowledge of the game and seldom played it. Yet in the course of one winter he beat two players who were at the time members of the Sussex County side and in full practice.

Perhaps it is in the fives that his influence can be seen most clearly. When he came, the School had but recently changed from Rugby to the Eton variety, there was no one with any knowledge of the game and such progress as had been made was largely on the wrong lines. Brought up in one of the two leading fives schools, and himself one of that school's outstanding players, he combined with his natural ability an exhaustive knowledge of the game. Always ready to play with anybody however bad, and prepared to give up time as long as there was anyone to play with, he spread an interest in the game and an understanding of its principles which have already borne fruit and will bear more as time goes on.

But it is not primarily as a player or teacher of games that those whose privilege it was to know him well will remember him. Unapproachable to all appearance at first sight, stern (as a schoolmaster should be), it did not take long to discover the kindly and very human person that lay under that Olympian exterior. To many at Lancing of all ages and degrees, and to many who met him only as Old Boys, he has been and always will be a valued and trusted friend."

After the war, John Stephenson became a preparatory school master in Sussex.

time was the setting up of a national championship. It began with the gift of a challenge cup, presented by Lord Kinnaird in 1924, to be competed for annually. "Entries are open to pairs representing any club, association, university, university college, hospital, institution or recognised Service unit. No player shall, during the competition, represent more than one club, association, etc., and the number of pairs from each club, etc., shall be limited to three." The competition was first played in 1925, and though it lapsed for a couple of years after its inception, the building of the covered Eton fives court at Queen's Club in 1927 set it on its feet once more. It was held under the management of the newly formed Fives Association, as it was then known. The draw for the first round of that very first Kinnaird Cup competition held in 1925 is reproduced in full below. The winners were the Etoni-

The Kinnaird Cup Winners in 1930, AH Fabian and J Aguirre

ans, de Quetteville and Redhead.

LONDON HOSPITAL (L.P. Marshall & V.W. Dix) v 2nd BATTALION, 60TH RIFLES (C. Wilson & C.E. Grenville-Grey).

THE CROSS OLD BOYS (B. Jacquet & L.H. Merton) v HARROW DUFFERS (R. Straus & F.O.G. Lloyd).

OLD REPTONIANS "A" (W.W. McLean & M. Shearme) v TORRY HILL (D. Leigh Pemberton & J.R.S. Monckton).

OLD REPTONIANS "C" (L.J. Crook & A.L. Simon) v AVINGTONE (M. Roberts & B.Q.S. Knox).

OLD ALDENHAMIANS "A" (A.J. Conyers & G.C.F. Mead) v IRISH GUARDS (T.E.G. Nugent & W.D. Faulkner).

GILBERTS (J.A. Hartley & A.N. Other) v THE HALF PINKS (T.G.C. Lund & G.L. Oliver-Watts).

HILLBANK (W. Hill-Wood & T.A.L. Brocklebank) v COLDSTREAM GUARDS (G.N. Scott-Chad & C.R. Polhill-Drabble).

OLD CHOLMELEIANS "A" (C.W. Bower & F.W. Barnes) v THE OLD TIMERS (E.B. Noel & Sir L. Alexander).

OLD ETONIANS "B" (A.R. Cook & J.H. Bevan) v THE RANGERS (T.S. Hankey & E.S. Head).

H. BRINTON'S OLD BOYS (R.J.F. Remnant & P.F. Remnant) v OLD REPTONIANS "B" (R.L. Holdsworth & H.M. Morris).

OLD ALDENHAMIANS "B" (P.S. McDougall & D.A. Stanier) v THE TOMBAS (B. Hill-Wood & T. Bevan).

WESTMINSTER BANK (E. Clifton-Brown & Hon. W.D. Gibbs) v ALDENHAM MASTERS (G.H. Vasey & R.C. Clift).

OLD ETONIANS "A" (R.G. de Quetteville & R.A. Redhead) v HIGHGATE MASTERS "B" (M. Miller & T.L. Twidell).

BEAUREPAIRE PARK (J.A. King & J.G. King) v THE GARRYITES (S.R. Gullane & L.F.L. Munro).

HIGHGATE MASTERS "A" (Rev. K.R.G. Hunt & H.J. Gibbon) v ETON CASUALS (G.C. Bright & R.J.F. Burrows).

OLD CHOLMELEIANS "B" (F.G. Baddeley & A.B.B. Valentine) v *CAMBRIDGE UNI-VERSITY* (W.E. Anderson & N.R. Barrett)

It is an intriguing list of Eton fives players active at the time with some pairs representing genuine clubs and others being scratch pairs, who had given themselves the name of a common factor. In 1931 the regulations were revised and the title of the competition was altered to 'The Amateur Championship for the Kinnaird Cup', "thus giving it a larger showing of importance". The final of the first "Kinnaird Cup for the Amateur Championship" in 1932 was fully reported in *The Times* and is reproduced below:

The final match for the Kinnaird Cup, which now carries with it the Amateur Championship of Eton Fives, was played at Queen's Club, West Kensington, during the week-end and resulted in a victory for K. C. Gandar Dower and G. R. McConnell, who defeated the Hon. P. F. Remnant and the Hon. R. J. F. Remnant by three games to one (17-15, 16-17, 15-5, 15-3). Gandar Dower and McConnell won the Kinnaird Cup under its original title and rules three years ago. This year the conditions have been modified to comply with its status as a championship, and the winners become the first amateur champions at the game. Play in the first two games was tremendously fast, and very even. The Remnants both played consistently and supported each other well. It was this pair that showed the initiative in tactics, and they appeared to have the measure of their opponents' play. They were a trifle unlucky to lose the first game and fully deserved the second, which they won, but the loss of the first meant the loss of the match, for whereas their combined ages total over 70, those of their opponents are approximately 45, and youth had to be served in the end. The older pair perhaps made a mistake in the earlier stages of the match through playing too much on

McConnell, the opposing second string, for the latter was in especially good form throughout the match, while Gandar Dower was at that time somewhat erratic. Gandar Dower was thus enabled to take short and necessary rests and, as play progressed, became decidedly the dominating player in the court. The tremendous pace of the first two games perceptibly tired the Remnants, who could score only eight points in the last two games, but these were harder fought than the score suggests, and there was much brilliant volleying and retrieving by all four players. Throughout the competition the standard of play has been far better than in recent years. It culminated in the semi-final match when the present champions met last year's winners, Welch and de Grey Warter, but the standard of the final was but little lower.

Since then the Amateur Championship for the Kinnaird Cup has become the flagship national competition for Eton fives and the list of winners comprises the best players of the game in the last eighty years. In the period up to the Second World War, each of the following pairs won the championship twice: RG de Quetteville & RA Redhead (Etonians); KC Gandar Dower & GR McConnell (Harrovians); WM Welch & HG de Grey Warter (Harrovians); DM Backhouse & AT Barber (Salopians); JM Peterson (Salopian) & CEW Sheepshanks (Etonian); AH Fabian & JKG Webb (Cholmeleians).

The other winning pair was Fabian & J Aguirre (Cholmeleians), thus giving Fabian the distinction of being the most successful Kinnaird competitor of the inter-war period with three wins. Aguirre was only nineteen years old at the time, making him one of the youngest ever winners.

From 1919 onwards the results of club fives matches were regularly published in *The Times*. Clubs for whom reports appeared were, in chronological order: Old Cholmeleians, Old Citizens, Old Etonians, Queen's Club, Old Alden-

KC Gandar Dower

Kenneth Cecil Gandar Dower (1908-1944) was educated at Harrow, where he was captain of fives for two years, playing with NM Ford in 1926 and GR McConnell in 1927. Harrow lost to CNJ Hill-Wood and StJO Forbes of Eton, twice in 1926, and D'A Lambton and MR Norman in 1927, but they were terrific tussles, each match in the Harrow courts being decided 3-2. Gandar Dower and McConnell went on to play for Cambridge in the first Varsity match in 1928 and won the Kinnaird Cup that year and again in 1932.

Gandar Dower was a superb all-round sportsman who became a double international at lawn tennis and squash, and while at Cambridge represented the university at seven different sports. Purists have often described him as having the "wrong technique" for just about every game he played. He had a wonderful eye for a ball and his court craft was unmatched. A report in *The Harrovian* described him (somewhat inelegantly) as "the worst ever good player of Eton fives, rackets, squash, real tennis and lawn tennis". An opponent in a Varsity match was heard to say, "I give up: it's no good playing against a kangaroo." His awkwardness can be traced to a childhood nanny who, appalled at his tendency to left-handedness, had forced him to become a right-hander.

This ambidexterity proved to be to his advantage in Eton fives but he was also light on his feet and remarkably agile despite being quite tall. A set of electric reflexes ensured that he was superb at defending the pepper box.

Gandar Dower also won the Rugby Fives amateur championship singles, a unique achievement at the time and unequalled until recently. When he announced his intention to enter, he was ridiculed with remarks that he did not even know the rules of the game. His rather arrogant response was that he would by the time he reached the semi-finals!

Gandar Dower was obsessed with competitive games: he and his cronies used to frequent the Queen's Club where they would challenge each other to a whole raft of games in a day; these might be lawn tennis, squash, rackets, sticke, ping-pong, real tennis, a quarter-mile, single wicket cricket, throwing the cricket ball, bowls, billiards and so on.

Not the least of Gandar Dower's eccentricities was his failed attempt to popularize cheetah racing at the White City in 1937. He became a war correspondent in Madagascar in the Second World War but was killed in 1944 when the troopship SS Khedive Ishmael was sunk by a Japanese torpedo. 1297 lives were lost, the third highest Allied loss of life in a single action.

hamians, London Hospital, Pembroke College Cambridge, Old Reptonians, Liverpool Racquet Club, Old Westminsters, White Rabbits, Old Harrovians, Old Salopians, Cambridge University, Oxford University, Emmanuel College Cambridge, Old Woodbridgeans, Old Olavians, Jesters, Wyverns, Torry Hill, Old Carthusians, Caius College Cambridge, The Triflers, and Christ's College Cambridge.

Most of these names are by now familiar but it is interesting that four Cambridge Colleges were playing matches in addition to the University team. The only universities with Eton fives courts then, as now, were Oxford and Cambridge, and competition between them was already well established in many sports. The surprise was that it had taken the fives players so long to organise a Varsity match. The first match in fact took place in 1928, the same year as the first Public Schools competition, and it was also described as unofficial. However, it became the first of a series of annual contests. A report on that first Varsity match appeared in *The Times* and is reproduced below. It is interesting to note that there were five Etonians, four Harrovians, two Cholmeleians and an Uppinghamian; except for the absence of a Salopian, this is probably a fair reflection of the balance of strength of club fives at the time.

Cambridge University beat Oxford University in a match at Eton fives at Queen's Club, West Kensington, yesterday by three matches to none. This is the first Eton fives match that has been played between Oxford and Cambridge and was unofficial in so far that no blue or half-blue was awarded to the players on either side. KC Gandar-Dower (Harrow and Trinity) and GR McConnell (Harrow and King's) beat NM Ford (Harrow and Oriel) and CNJ Hill-Wood (Eton and Christ Church) by three games to none (15-3, 17-16, 15-3). Gandar Dower was the best player in the court, and is now definitely in the championship class. It is doubtful whether McConnell ever played so well before. Hill-Wood is a natural player, almost as strong with his right hand as with his left; in the top court he can not only kill the ball in the pepper-box, but can kill it with a cross stroke to the right-hand corner of the court, a stroke which scarcely any player – other than a left-handed player as Hill-Wood, of course, is – has ever been able to do. Ford played in his old form in the second game only. AH Fabian (Highgate and Pembroke) and FK Reeves

(Highgate and Clare) beat CH Gosling (Eton and Magdalen) and JM Carnegie (Eton and Christ Church) by three games to none (15-11, 15-7, 15-8). DS Oscroft (Uppingham and Sidney Sussex) and Lord Dundas (Harrow and Trinity) beat Lord Fourneaux (Eton and Christ Church) and Lord Hyde (Eton and Trinity) by three games to one (4-15, 15-5, 15-8, 15-7). In the second game Oscroft played extremely well, his volleying being well placed and severe, and Dundas was very safe in the lower court. Both came in a little and stooped low to take the first cut – as is correct against an opponent who cuts the ball, besides hitting it hard and near the corner – and took it well. The Oxford pair never played as well again as they did in the first game and they did not combine as well as their opponents.

Cambridge dominated the fixture in the period up to the war, winning nine times to Oxford's three.

Most of the clubs in the list above represent institutions of some sort. The exceptions are Torry Hill at Sittingbourne in Kent, home of the Leigh-Pemberton family, where there is still a court; Queen's Club in Palliser Road near Baron's Court, London, which we have already mentioned; the Wyverns, the Jesters, the Triflers and the White Rabbits. The Wyverns, formed in 1930 was described in *The Times*, 11 November 1931:

At Cambridge a club has recently been formed called the Wyverns Eton Fives Club. They propose to have a court of their own at Cambridge and also, if things can be arranged satisfactorily, to use the two courts in Portugal Street. Thirty years ago a good deal of fives was played in the Portugal Street courts. At that time Lord Kinnaird, Sir Arthur Hazlerigg, and the late G Howard-Smith were all in residence. Sir Arthur Hazlerigg was a really good player; very sound indeed in the lower court, and – he has very big hands – particularly good in taking the first cut, and Howard-Smith, who played with that joy and keenness which characterized everything he did, was more than useful. Lord Kinnaird is the president of the club and Sir Arthur Hazlerigg is a vice president. A G Hazlerigg, a Keeper of Fives at Eton, is, very appropriately, one of the committee. In a season lasting from January 23 to March 23 the Wyverns have a fixture list of 27

Hon RJF Remnant (left) won the School Fives at Eton with FJL Johnstone in 1914; Hon PF Remnant (right) won with NA Pearson in 1916. Together they probably reached the final of the inaugural Kinnaird Cup Competition in 1925 (when proper records were not kept) and they again lost in the final of 1932 to Gandar Dower and McConnell

matches. For the first year this is a remarkable list and one on which the secretary, D Egerton of Magdalene College, is to be congratulated. Matches are arranged with Harrow, Uppingham, Stowe, Aldenham, Charterhouse, Lancing, City of London School and both Oxford and Cambridge. A particularly interesting match will be played against Queen's Club on Saturday, February 7, when both sides will be extremely strong. As at present arranged, the Wyverns first pair will be AH Fabian and WM Welch, who was first string for Harrow last year and one of the best players they ever produced, and their second pair will be AG Hazlerigg and BE Rickett. KC Gandar Dower and GR McConnell, who won the Kinnaird Cup in 1929, will be one of the Queen's Club pairs. RG de Quetteville, who twice won the Kinnaird Cup with RA Redhead, and DM Backhouse, one of the great Shrewsbury players, will be the other.

A report followed on this match between the Wyverns Club and Queen's Club and referred to several of the best players of the day, comparing them to players of an earlier age:

In a match at Eton fives, at Queen's Club, West Kensington, on Saturday, The

Wyverns Club beat Queen's Club by two matches to none. It was unfortunate for Queen's Club that RG de Quetteville, who is one of the best players of Eton fives, was unable to play owing to a chill. AG Hazlerigg and BE Rickett (The Wyverns) beat DM Backhouse and D Egerton (Queen's Club) by three games to none (18-16. 15-9, 15-8). The first game was a very close one, and it is interesting to note that the set is now optional in matches at Eton Fives, as it is at Rackets. AH Fabian and WM Welch (The Wyverns) beat K C Gandar Dower and GR McConnell (Queen's Club) by three games to one (15-8, 15-6, 9-15, 15-4). The play in this match was as good as any that can be seen in England today. Gandar Dower who had played a squash rackets match earlier in the day, was not, perhaps, at his best; his taking of the first cut was not up to his greatest form. It was in the hitting of the first cut, probably, that the Wyverns won the match. Fabian is, according to the best players of the day, the most severe hitter of the first cut now playing. Welch has improved since last year, and then he was probably the best player who has been at Harrow since TO Jameson. GR McConnell is a much more severe player this year than he has ever been, and he was always one who could take a place in any four, however strong, without being below the class. The Queen's court is particularly fast, and the walls are smooth – which makes the taking of the first cut most difficult to the server who does not stand well in and on guard for Dead Man's Hole. In the final game the play of Fabian and Welch was so brilliant that one wishes that Lord Kinnaird, the Dean of York [*Lionel Ford, former Headmaster of Repton and Harrow*], and Mr Marten [*Provost of Eton & former Master*] had been there to see it; only such players could have compared the form with that of 30 years ago when they, G Townsend-Warner, and EM Butler [*former Harrow Masters*] were playing.

The Jesters began in 1928 as a not-very-serious cricket club – as the name suggests. It was founded by Jock Burnet while a boy at St Paul's and quickly led to the idea of a similar wandering club, playing Rugby fives and squash in the winter months. In that first season they played seven Rugby fives matches and one squash match. Burnet went up to Cambridge as a freshman in 1929 and almost immediately 'sold' the idea of the Jesters' Club. Rapid expansion led to 21 Rugby fives matches and 18 squash matches in the second season, and the Club had to be given some structure: a committee was formed. Advice to a young and inexperienced management team came from several sources, none as valuable as that of FB Wilson. In its early days the Club was much assisted by reports of its matches in *The Times* and *Morning Post* written by him. Sadly Wilson died in 1932, aged 55.

When AG Hazlerigg was elected to this committee in 1931, Eton fives was added as a Jesters' game. The club grew like topsy, attracting not only the best court games players at Cambridge but also many of the good and great in the country at large. Lord Wodehouse (later Earl of Kimberley), a famous polo player, became the first President.

At around this time, squash was becoming an increasingly popular game and courts were being built all over the country, in clubs, private houses, hotels, blocks of flats, schools and universities. It was the good fortune of the Jesters that the club had entered a sphere of activity just when there was a high demand for it: the Jesters were able to ride on the wave of the squash phenomenon. In 1934 the Prince of Wales, an active squash player, who played once in the Amateur Championships, became a member. He remained a member all his life and was the Club's Patron during his brief reign as King Edward VIII.

Rather like the Wyverns, the Jesters had been formed to provide light-hearted games for less talented players. Unlike the Wyverns, which had been restricted to Eton fives and which folded after a few seasons, the Jesters survived the war and became more and more prestigious. Top class players were keen to get more matches of a less pressurised nature and schools and clubs were pleased to entertain them. By 1932-3 there were over a hundred matches; by 1934 over 200. The surge of squash left the other games hanging on to its coat tails but the committee controlled the balance of members to ensure that squash was not allowed to dominate and the rise in the number of squash matches was paralleled in both Rugby and Eton fives. Within a few years the Jesters, which had begun life as a club for second-raters, had become **the** court games club, membership being by invitation only.

The Triflers had a short life from 1932 to 1939 – like so many other clubs they were nipped in the bud by the war – but they are worth mentioning, if only because playing for them must have been such fun. They were first and foremost a cricket club, founded by a group of friends from Westminster, who wanted to play cricket together in West Sussex. One of their number, Francis Pagan, wrote a hilarious account of the Triflers Club, unfortunately too long to reproduce here. The name came from an unofficial and irreverent 18th century school magazine called *The Trifler* and the Club's motto was chosen from a line of the poet, William Cowper: "The Solemn Trifler with his Boasted Skill". Rule 4 read: "The Club shall be open to all provided there is always a majority of Westminsters over non-Westminsters in the total membership." A paragraph of the story of the Triflers reads: "There was also a fives section of the club. No records survive but, as Hon Sec, I remember good games and much fun whiling away the winter in the old courts in Great College Street or on visits to Oxford, Cambridge and Charterhouse. Our two pairs usually included Richard Doll and myself but the best player was Tommy Garnett of Charterhouse, who taught at Westminster from 1936-8. A fourth player might be John Rayne, last heard of on tsetse control in East Africa."

The origin of the White Rabbits is not clear but it seems that they were a group of Old Etonians, most of whom were at Oxford together. The driving force came from D'Arcy Lambton and MR Norman, who were contemporaries at Magdalen. This was not unusual: throughout the history of organised games, clubs have begun as a small group of friends – like the Triflers – who enjoyed playing together. It is equally true that whole clubs have been started to avoid playing with certain people, although there is no evidence to suggest that the White Rabbits were born of the urge to exclude some 'black sheep'! Like the Jesters and Wyverns, they probably started by intending not to play too seriously but again, like the others, found the social attractions and the competitiveness of human nature irresistible: they ended up becoming a very strong club. Sadly, that club too failed to survive the war.

In 1932 a new competition, called the 'Queen's Club Competition', was started for nine Old Boys' Clubs and "run as an American style tournament, i.e. one pair from each club played each other club" – what we would today call a league. It was played on set dates before and after Christmas, finishing before the Kinnaird Competition started. The competition was managed by JH Beale, "the very capable secretary of the Old Citizens Fives Club". Results for the inaugural year of 1932-3 are incomplete; the winners in subsequent years were:

1933-4: Old Cholmeleians

1934-5: Old Cholmeleians, Old Harrovians (joint winners)

1935-6: Old Aldenhamians, Old Citizens (joint winners)

1936-7: Old Carthusians.

Immediately after completion of the Queen's Club competition in 1937, a new Inter-Club Competition started with three pairs to represent each club; the final was played in April. This was a knock-out competition but was not restricted to Old Boy clubs; Oxford and Cambridge Universities and the Wyverns all entered. There were eleven entries in the inaugural season, the winners being the Old Harrovians. Because of the outbreak of the Second World War, the competition was only played for a further two years, the winners on both occasions being the Old Carthusians. It seems that this effectively replaced the Queen's Club Competition, of which there was no further mention after March 1937.

In 1938 The Times reported the final, which was won by the Old Carthusians, who beat the Old Aldenhamians by two matches to one, each court playing the best of three games. In the top pair match GS Fletcher and TR Garnett (Carthusians) beat AJ Conyers and AFR Carling (Aldenhamians) 2-1. While it is commendable that the match should have received such exposure in a national newspaper, the report is such a tedious point-by-point account that it will be spared reproduction here.

Chapter 12

Last Act before the Curtain

1930-40

The first Public Schools Competition took place in 1928 but it was described as unofficial, and as yet research has not revealed the winning pair, although Harrow reached the final. Harrow had a fine pair that year, RB Hodgkinson and WM Welch, who lost at home to Eton but beat them 3-1 in their own courts – the first time this had been achieved since 1906.

The Public Schools' Handicaps, as it was known, became an annual competition thereafter. A Junior Public Schools' Handicaps for under-16s started in 1930 and ran alongside the Senior competition. In these competitions pairs were handicapped according to their ability; for example in 1930, Harrow's first pair owed two and Eton's third pair received seven points; games, of course, were still being played up to fifteen points. There was no doubt much discussion about which pair should be handicapped by what amount. There was a small committee charged with the task, but they reserved the right to change the handicaps after the first round when they had actually seen the players in action! Harrow were victors in the first official competition of 1929 and won the trophy on five occasions in total up to the Second World War. Other winners in this period were Eton (twice), Shrewsbury (twice), Uppingham and Charterhouse. Three individual players were in the winning pair on two successive occasions: JFM Lightly and WM Welch of Harrow, and LM Minford of Shrewsbury.

Courts were still being built through the 1930s: Cranleigh had six new courts opened in 1931; Strathallan had three open courts built in 1933; in 1934 four new courts were built on the edge of the playing fields at Chigwell; Rydal built their first two courts in 1935. The two open courts at St Olave's in Tooley Street by Tower Bridge were renovated and ledges were added in 1935; two years later two covered courts were erected, backing onto the old courts. Emmanuel College, Cambridge opened a new court to replace an older one in 1933. The only loss was at Liverpool Racquet Club where the Eton fives court was converted into a squash court in 1936.

In 1931 *The Times* wrote:

The growth of squash rackets in England since 1920 has frequently been termed amazing, and, considering the number of players, courts, championships, handicaps, inter-club and inter-county matches of the present day, even that adjective is not excessive. Eton fives, although its votaries will always maintain that it is a greater game than squash rackets, can never be as widely played as squash rackets, but during the last few years the number of Eton fives players has greatly increased, and the number of matches now played is remarkably satisfactory. The late EB Noel, Sir Lionel Alexander, and others made a big effort some years ago to form an association which would promote the interest of players of the game, but, for a while little progress was made. It seemed very difficult to bring Eton fives players into touch with each other, and even when the very good, electrically lighted, covered court at Queen's Club was built it was doubtful, at first, if it would be a success. With the inception of the Kinnaird Cup, however, things began to move. Lord Kinnaird was the best player in the world of his day, as his father had been the best, or one of the two best, in his time. [*Hon AF Kinnaird was 'Fives Champion' at Cambridge in 1869; Hon KF Kinnaird won the School Fives at Eton in 1888 and 1889*] The cup was only presented a few years ago, but some 40 pairs entered for it last season. There was a remarkably good entry for the Public Schools fives handicaps, including a new one for boys under 16, last year, and

this annual event should be most valuable to the game in that it gets young players from different schools in touch with each other. Eton fives is first and foremost the personal game of Eton. For many years they have played Harrow and Charterhouse at the game, and they have lost – on occasions – to both schools; up till comparatively recently, however, there were at least six players at Eton to every one at Harrow. The extent to which other schools have played the game was realized by very few until five or six years ago. It was news to most people that Rugby had Eton fives courts – as well as their own courts from which the title

Roald Dahl

Roald Dahl (1916-1990) was born in Llandaff to Norwegian parents and was educated at Repton. He was an exceptionally good fives and squash player and was captain of both as well as being in the association football eleven. In his autobiography *Boy: Tales of Childhood* he describes the game of Eton fives as "subtle and crafty, and possibly the fastest ball-game on earth". He won the junior and senior school fives in the same year when only fifteen, and became Captain of Fives. "I would travel with my team to other schools like Shrewsbury and Uppingham to play matches. I loved it." He describes how he awarded fives colours with the magic words 'Graggers on your teamer'. This conferred all manner of privileges, particularly in clothing which made 'the teamer gloriously conspicuous among his fellows'. Dahl did not enjoy much of his time at Repton which shows how important fives was to him then. He did not become a boazer (prefect) because "I was not to be trusted. I did not like rules. I would have

let down the whole principle of Boazerdom by refusing to beat the Fags. I was probably the only Captain of any game who has never become a Boazer at Repton."

After Repton he joined the Shell Petroleum Company and worked in Dar-es-Salaam. In the second world war he became a fighter pilot and took part in the Greek campaign, his record of five aerial victories qualifying him as a 'flying ace'. Dahl began writing in 1942, after he was transferred to Washington as Assistant Air Attaché. His first published work was *Shot Down Over Libya*, which described the crash of his Gloster Gladiator. Dahl went on to create some of the best-loved children's stories of the 20th century, such as *Charlie and the Chocolate Factory*, *Matilda*, *James and the Giant Peach*, *The Witches*, *Charlie and the Great Glass Elevator*, *The BFG*, *George's Marvellous Medicine* and *Fantastic Mr Fox*. The Roald Dahl Museum and Story Centre in Great Missenden commemorates his life and work.

Rugby fives comes – and that some of their best players have preferred Eton to Rugby fives. Shrewsbury were reputed to have the best Public School pair of 1929 in DN Moore and JSO Haslewood, and last year AH Fabian and J Aguirre, the Old Cholmeleians, had the impudence to win the Kinnaird Cup. Aldenham and Highgate are keen rivals at the game.

The school Eton fives scene of the 1930s was dominated by the 'big six': Eton, Shrewsbury, Harrow, Highgate, Charterhouse and Uppingham, although Aldenham and Westminster both reached the Final of the Public Schools' Handicaps once each. Again *The Times* regularly reported the Final in some depth. The report of the 1932 final is reproduced below:

The final match in the Public Schools Eton Fives handicap was played at Queen's Club on Saturday and resulted in the victory of Uppingham I (JV Gillespie and N Knight), who beat Harrow I (GFD Haslewood and JAS Collins), the holders, by three games to two (17-18, 14-16, 15-3, 15-0, 15-1). Harrow were set to owe their opponents two points in each game.

The match was a fine example of snatching victory by grim determination. The Uppingham pair had never played in standard courts before this competition, and to force a win after losing the first two games, a comparatively easy win at the finish, was a fine performance.

Haslewood, second string in last year's winning pair, was expected to set the pace and direct the play, and in the first game he did so. Subsequently, however, his left-handed volley to the right-hand back corner, one of the strongest features of his play, became erratic, and in the last four games he scored three points only with it. The match was played and won from start to finish in the pepper-box. Collins was accurate and retrieved well, but failed to clear the ball into the open part of the court, and when Haslewood was up, Gillespie and Knight kept the ball so low that he had no chance to kill it.

The first two games were very long and even, Uppingham being a bit unlucky to lose the second. By the middle of the third game Collins, who had had to do the major share of the work for his side, tired perceptibly and Haslewood's accuracy deserted him. Uppingham won the third and fourth games easily to square the match at two games all, and then, instead of taking a rest for a few points, tactics to which they might well have been tempted, they wisely pressed home their advantage, increasing the speed of the game. Of the first five points in the final game four were scored actually in the Dead Man's Hole.

Uppingham this year have introduced entirely

Fives on the Wrekin courts: standard buttress tops were not added until the 1970s

Jack Peterson

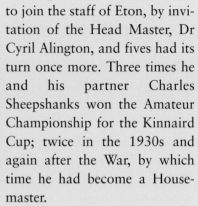

Jack Peterson was in the fives team at Shrewsbury for four years, captain for three, and Head of School for two years. At Oxford, he gained a first in 'Greats', was university football captain in 1925 and a three year fives half-blue. He then became an Assistant Master at Eton, where he stayed until 1950 when he was appointed Headmaster of Shrewsbury. He stayed at Shrewsbury until 1963 and had a great influence on Eton fives at the two schools in which he worked. He was Chairman of the EFA, 1948-50 and a Vice-president from 1948 to 1977. With GW Nickson, another Salopian housemaster at Eton, he was undefeated by the school's first pair for a quarter of a century.

Nickson later wrote, "To his contemporaries at Shrewsbury Jack Peterson became almost a legend during our schooldays together. Every honour, scholastic or athletic, fell to him naturally and was received and worn with humility. Headship of the School, de jure et de facto: pre-eminence in a Classical VIth Form, whose instructor was once overheard complaining to a colleague that the problem in marking Peterson's compositions was to find just cause for varying the sequence of 'alphas' ; caps and captaincies, for cricket, football and fives, with special distinction in the last two. No wonder that we all looked up to him.

"Oxford added its tributes of laurels. A classical scholarship, followed in due course by firsts in Mods and Greats; and a 'blue' for Association Football, with the captaincy of the side the following season. Thence in 1925 to join the staff of Eton, by invitation of the Head Master, Dr Cyril Alington, and fives had its turn once more. Three times he and his partner Charles Sheepshanks won the Amateur Championship for the Kinnaird Cup; twice in the 1930s and again after the War, by which time he had become a Housemaster.

"He ran a notably happy and successful House, whose members, drawn rather than driven, came under the spell of his personality. In 1950 Shrewsbury once again reclaimed him and he left us to take up the Headmastership.

"And a spell it certainly was, woven from a rare combination of qualities: wealth of talents, enhanced by modesty, which at times bordered on diffidence, quiet humour, and wit which was always apposite but never unkind; total sincerity, and a faith which sustained him in the ordeal of personal tragedy caused by the illness and death of his wife, leaving him with a very young family. Such a combination could not fail to influence those who had the good fortune to encounter it, and justifies the summary given to the writer, a few years ago, by one who had been a Governor of Shrewsbury School. He said, 'Every time I met Jack Peterson I came away feeling somehow the better for having been in his company.' There will be many of us who would endorse this tribute."

new tactics to the game, and the success of these tactics depends entirely on their accuracy of touch. They rely on wearing down their opponents within the pepper-box. They are the first players to add any original note to the play since the appearance of J Aguirre, the Highgate player.

In the final round of the Junior Competition Eton (H Legh and M Baring) beat the holders, Aldenham (G.M. Culley and J.

Warwick) by three games to none (15-3, 15-12, 15-5). Eton, the backmarkers in this competition, were set to owe two points to their opponents, and could well have given longer odds. The winning pair play in the true Eton style and hit and volley well with either hand. They were more experienced than their opponents and kept them on the defensive throughout. Aldenham did well to pull up from 3-14 to 12-14 in the second game, but, speaking generally, they were outplayed by a better pair.

In 1929 the Eton pair, AG Hazlerigg and CEW Sheepshanks, won all their school matches; 15 pairs were played against the Old Etonians (17 in 1930) and 12 against the Masters, although there was muttering that there was a "lack of OE Masters who play fives at the moment". The following year Sheepshanks and MS Gosling again won most of their matches but lost at Eton to Harrow, who were entering another purple patch. The left-handed Haslewood of Harrow "hit some devastatingly hard volleys into the corners".

A few lean years at Eton followed. The Keeper in 1932, MAC Noble, poignantly observed, "The standard of fives is not very high at the moment – as masters are fond of remarking. The reason and cure lie largely with them!" 1933 was "a most disastrous season… Fives at Eton is less popular than it was due to increasing rugby and soccer". This happened to coincide with another strong Harrow pair which won the Public Schools Championships. Noble was not pleased: "The Harrow courts are not standard: they are very slow, the lighting is muddling, the ledges are twice as broad, there is no run back and they play with local balls". Although the Masters' match was won 7-3, even the Head Master, Dr Alington, did not escape Noble's criticism: "…he insisted on playing in a moss-covered open court which he knew much better than his young opposition. It was his first game for two years so he was justifiably pleased with his success…."

In spite of this, most schools would have been delighted with the state and status of fives at Eton: a supportive Head Master (who played); coaching from Messrs Headlam (who left in 1935), JM Peterson (who took over) and GW Nickson; flourishing internal competitions (92 entries for the House Fives in 1934) and victory in the Public Schools' Handicaps in 1935.

In 1937, MJ Adler and JP Mann beat the Masters' 1st pair, Nickson and Peterson, and the Old Etonians' 1st pair, Hazlerigg and Sheepshanks, both 3-2, but they lost in a new fixture away at Westminster. Unsurprisingly the Keeper recommended that the experiment should not be repeated, citing as the reason that Westminster courts had "black walls, a red floor and no run back".

Westminster's reluctance to play school matches may have been because of the state of their courts but the conversion of the rackets court in 1928 had given an impetus to the recently formed Old Westminsters Club. By 1926 they were already an active club, playing 16 fixtures in 1928 – increased to 23 by 1932 – and with two pairs entering the Kinnaird Cup in 1930. One of the courts was refurbished in 1934 and the school emerged from the cloisters to play six school fixtures that year, beating Charterhouse and City of London and losing to Aldenham, Lancing and Highgate. The best Westminster pair of this decade, CM O'Brien and DL Wilkinson, were beaten by Harrow in the Public Schools' final of 1936.

Shrewsbury had another talented pair in 1929 when EA Barlow and JJ Adie beat Eton at home and away. Barlow was another outstanding all-round sportsman, gaining blues at Oxford for cricket (three years) and football (two years), and half-blues for Eton fives; he later played cricket, lawn tennis and squash for Lancashire, and lawn tennis for Wales. *The Salopian* gave much credit for the high standard of fives at Shrewsbury at this time to the coaching of two masters, Messrs Sale and Street.

Uppingham played their first match against Repton in 1933-4: four pairs played and the

Uppingham/Shrewsbury scoring method was used, Uppingham winning the 1st IV, 110-108. Roald Dahl was playing for Repton and later wrote about it in his autobiography, *Boy*: "...it was a game I took to right from the beginning.... Soon I bore the splendid title, Captain of Fives, and I would travel with my team to other schools like Shrewsbury and Uppingham to play matches. I loved it. It was a game without physical contact, and the quickness of the eye and the dancing of the feet were all that mattered...." Strangely there are no reports in the Uppingham magazine of the years between 1935 and 1940, maybe because Mr JC Atkins who had been an important influence on fives at Uppingham (and had published tips on playing the game in 1926) retired.

After a dormant spell in the 1920s, fives at King Edward's Birmingham came to life in 1929 with the arrival of Mr ET England as Chief Master. Two new courts were opened and all seven matches were won in 1930. Opponents included Wolverhampton GS, King Charles Kidderminster and King Edward VI Camp Hill; Shrewsbury was added in 1931 and Repton in 1932. In 1935 the school moved to a new site but these successes, the enthusiasm of the Chief Master and the generosity of four particular Old Edwardians ensured that the courts at the new site were even better than before.

Harrow had an excellent spell between 1925 and 1933 producing such players as NM Ford, RV Jenkins, K Gandar Dower, GR McConnell, RB Hodgkinson, WM Welch, HG de Grey Warter, JFM Lightly, GFD Haslewood, JAS Collins and AH Henderson. They won five and were runners-up in two of the first eight Public Schools' Handicaps. Although Harrow's school matches did not extend beyond Eton, Charterhouse, Aldenham (who were very weak until 1934) and Highgate, who were added in 1925, they played an increasing number of club matches. The fixture list topped 20 in 1937-8. Moreover the Masters regularly raised 13 or 14 pairs reaching 18 in 1933; the most influential of these

THE QUEEN'S CLUB
WEST KENSINGTON, W.14

The Second Competition
FOR
ETON FIVES
Public Schools' Handicaps
(SENIOR and JUNIOR)

Monday, April 21st, 1930
TO
Friday, April 25th, 1930

PROGRAMME
SIXPENCE ::

Secretary—
LT.-COL. G. E. BRUCE, M.C.

The Programme for the Public Schools Handicaps played at Queen's in 1930. It was won by Harrow I (W M Welch & J F M Lightly) who beat Charterhouse (C Middleton & A S C Hulton) in the final. Middleton had replaced Wreford Brown in the programme. The entry from Dover College was surprising as its position some distance from other Eton fives schools had prevented them from playing many outside matches. In the event they scratched

were probably RL Holdsworth, an Old Reptonian, who won cricket and football blues at Oxford between 1919 and 1922, and JW Moir, an Old Etonian 'Newcastle Scholar' with a 'first in Greats' from Balliol. Moir actually died in a fives court in 1948.

Fives was becoming very popular at Emanuel in the 1930s and the courts were in regular use. Most of the matches were against clubs: Old Woodbridgeans, Old Olavians, Old Cholmeleians, Old Reptonians, the Wyverns and the Jesters (played at Queen's) were their opponents. Two masters, Messrs Blake and Webber took an interest and 1931 was an unbeaten season for the first pair, FH Capon and C Bradley. Bradley wrote later, "I can

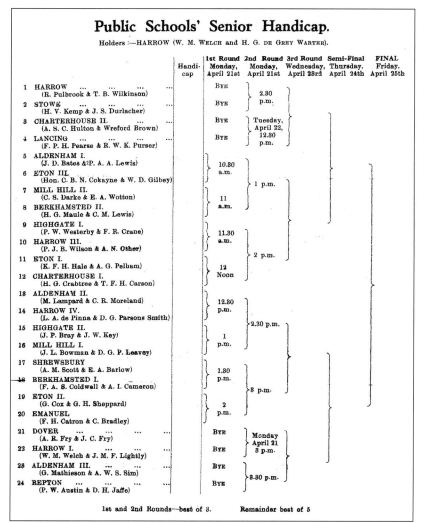

Public Schools' Senior Handicap.

Holders :—HARROW (W. M. WELCH and H. G. DE GREY WARTER).

	Handicap	1st Round Monday, April 21st	2nd Round Monday, April 21st	3rd Round Wednesday, April 23rd	Semi-Final Thursday, April 24th	FINAL Friday. April 25th
1 HARROW ... ... (R. Pulbrook & T. B. Wilkinson)	...	BYE				
2 STOWE ... ... (H. V. Kemp & J. S. Durlacher)	...	BYE	2.30 p.m.			
3 CHARTERHOUSE II. ... ... (A. S. C. Hulton & Wreford Brown)	...	BYE	Tuesday, April 22,			
4 LANCING ... ... (F. P. H. Pearse & R. W. K. Purser)	...	BYE	12.30 p.m.			
5 ALDENHAM I. (J. D. Bates &P. A. A. Lewis)		10.30 a.m.				
6 ETON III. (Hon. C. B. N. Cokayne & W. D. Gilbey)			1 p.m.			
7 MILL HILL II. (C. S. Darke & E. A. Wotton)		11 a.m.				
8 BERKHAMSTED II. (H. G. Maule & C. M. Lewis)						
9 HIGHGATE I. (P. W. Westerby & F. R. Crane)		11.30 a.m.				
10 HARROW III. (P. J. B. Wilson & A. N. Other)			2 p.m.			
11 ETON I. (K. F. H. Hale & A. G. Pelham)		12 Noon				
12 CHARTERHOUSE I. (H. G. Crabtree & T. F. H. Carson)						
13 ALDENHAM II. (M. Lampard & C. R. Moreland)		12.30 p.m.				
14 HARROW IV. (L. A. de Pinna & D. G. Parsons Smith)			2.30 p.m.			
15 HIGHGATE II. (J. P. Bray & J. W. Key)		1 p.m.				
16 MILL HILL I. (J. L. Bowman & D. G. P. Leavey)						
17 SHREWSBURY (A. M. Scott & E. A. Barlow)		1.30 p.m.				
18 BERKHAMSTED I. (F. A. S. Coldwell & A. I. Cameron)			3 p.m.			
19 ETON II. (G. Cox & G. H. Sheppard)		2 p.m.				
20 EMANUEL (F. H. Catron & C. Bradley)						
21 DOVER ... ... (A. R. Fry & J. C. Fry)	...	BYE	Monday April 21			
22 HARROW I. ... ... (W. M. Welch & J. M. F. Lightly)	...	BYE	3 p.m.			
23 ALDENHAM III. ... ... (G. Mathieson & A. W. S. Sim)	...	BYE				
24 REPTON ... ... (P. W. Austin & D. H. Jaffe)	...	BYE	3.30 p.m.			

1st and 2nd Rounds—best of 3.   Remainder best of 5

ter in 1932. Considered to be the best fives player Highgate had ever produced at that time, Fabian was at the top of his game, although still playing football for Derby County. Although Highgate's first fixture with Eton in 1934 ended in defeat, the 1937 pair, JKG Webb and JAA Morton, was described as "the best since Aguirre and Portu" and beat Harrow, Aldenham and Westminster. Sadly, Morton, JKC Scott, Webb's partner in 1936, and Webb's brother, MH, who played in the VI of 1938, were all killed in the Second World War.

At the end of the Great War, an Old Salopian, Donald Boumphrey, joined the teaching staff at Rydal in North Wales. Most of his efforts were directed towards coaching cricket and rugby but he also persuaded them to build two Eton fives courts in 1935. Their most regular school opponents were Shrewsbury, who were usually far too good for them, but they also played matches against St Bees in Cumbria, Wolverhampton and Liverpool College (who have Winchester fives courts). Club teams from Liverpool and Birkenhead made up the fixture list but fives remained a minority sport at Rydal. It was therefore a considerable achievement when JB Hacking and STJ Walker won the Under-16 Public Schools' Competition in 1939.

The re-launching of the Eton Fives Association started on 1 February 1934; this is the date of the first committee meeting recorded in the oldest surviving minute book and the first meeting since 1932. The first business of the first meeting was the election by the five members of Guy Butler as

truthfully say that I have spent no happier hours anywhere than on those two much battered, but much loved, courts in the cobbled yard." Two pairs entered for the Public Schools' Handicaps that year. In 1932 Cranleigh and Mill Hill were added to the traditional opponents, City of London, and the team photograph with the Headmaster seated in the centre was published in the school magazine, *The Portcullis*. By 1937 it was even being suggested that cricket and football were suffering from the rivalry presented by fives and other 'minor games' – a strange inversion of the usual claims.

The success of fives at Highgate in the 1920s had been largely due to the Rev Kenneth Hunt. He then passed the baton to one of his most talented pupils, AH Fabian, who returned as a mas-

Secretary in place of Egerton, GR McConnell continuing as Treasurer. There was a discussion on the functions and composition of the Association and it was unanimously decided that the Association and the Wyverns or any other club should be separate. That decision did not stop

Butler being Secretary of both the EFA and the Wyverns, precisely as Egerton had been!

Until the Annual General Meeting in November 1934, the composition of the committee seems to have been very fluid, apart from de Quetteville (President and Chairman) and Guy Butler (Secretary). J Burnet (founder of The Jesters) and R Straus (one of the founders of the EFA) resigned early on. Gandar Dower and Hazlerigg were "unable to attend" the first meeting and never appeared again in Committee. JM Peterson attended the first two meetings, but no more, and JH Beale, who was running the Queen's Club Competition, attended only the March meeting.

In November 1934 five new committee members were elected to replace Egerton, Burnet, McConnell, Peterson and Straus. TGC Lund became Treasurer and remained in office until the first Annual General Meeting after the war in November 1947. The striking feature from 1934 onwards was the use of special committees, as they were called, usually comprising three people, to run the various affairs of the Association, a reaction no doubt to the period of enlightened autocracy of Egerton. Eight such committees were set up over four years. The most important sub-committee was that set up in March 1934 to consider the whole function, com-

ETON FIVES

A SECOND COURT

During the summer months a second Eton Fives court at Queen's Club, which has stood unused and exposed to the elements for some years, has been repaired, roofed in, and fitted with electric light. To mark the official opening of the court a series of invitation matches were played at Queen's Club on Saturday, in which many great players of the game took part.

In the first match in the new court J. M. Peterson and C. E. W. Sheepshanks, who won the Kinnaird Cup in 1935, met R. A. Redhead, himself a Kinnaird Cup winner with R. G. de Quetteville in the past, and A. J. Conyers. This match produced, as did all the games, a very high standard of Fives, particularly at so early a stage in the season. Peterson and Sheepshanks won by 15—12, 15—7. The new court, which proved to be very fast, played very well.

Meanwhile in the old court the Old Carthusians, G. S. Fletcher and C. G. Fletcher, were playing against Captain R. H. V. Cavendish and R. A. Blair. Cavendish and Blair took the lead from the start of the first game and held it up to 13—10, but the Carthusians went ahead to 3—0 in the set 5 and eventually

won the game at 18—14. The next game was won easily, 15—1, by Cavendish and Blair, who were helped by a run of nine points in one hand, but the Fletchers won the next, 15—12, and the match. The standard of play was high, Blair being in particularly good form.

This game was succeeded in the old court by a match between four Old Harrovians—W. M. Welch and H. G. de Grey Warter, former holders of the Kinnaird Cup, and G. R. McConnell and N. M. Ford. Welch and de Grey Warter took a game to settle down, but in spite of some good play by McConnell and Ford won the match by 12—15, 15—7, 15—11, largely by a superiority in the first cut. In the second match in the new court J. Buckland and T. Turnbull beat G. M. Butler and T. R. Garnett 15—11, 15—11.

The opening of this second court at Queen's is a recognition of the increasing demand for more Eton Fives courts. The Queen's Club, who have always given great assistance to the game by allowing clubs to play their matches in the court there, have now extended this privilege to individual members of all clubs who belong to the Eton Fives Association. Any member of such a club, who has had his name submitted to Queen's, may thus arrange a four among his friends and play at Queen's Club on payment of the ordinary court fees.

The inaugural match at the opening of the new Eton Fives Court at Queen's Club. J. M. Peterson, C. E. W. Sheepshanks, R. H. Redhead, and A. J. Conyers in play.

A cutting from *The Times* reporting the opening of the new court at the Queen's Club in 1937

1936
OPEN FIVES TEAM

C. M. Kraay. J.A. Heath. A.C.J. Burton.
I. G. Stewart. P.H. Rubie (Capt.). A.J. Du Sautoy.

The Lancing Team of 1936. Mr Du Sautoy looks as if he might have been a formidable opponent on the top step. The advance of Lancing fives in the 1930s was largely due to JS Stephenson

position and finances of the Eton Fives Association. It comprised Beale (who had been running the Kinnaird Cup), HG Crabtree (who took over from him), Lund (later to become Treasurer) and Butler (the new Secretary). It was responsible for the new draft of the Rules of the Eton Fives Association, which were approved at the AGM in November 1934 and a copy inserted into the new minute book. As a result of their recommendation, it was agreed to have the accounts for 1934-5 audited by Lionel K. Lund who was retained as the auditor for the Association. Only Butler was a member of the Committee at the time that this first special committee was established, and over the next few years the EFA Committee recruited the services of non-committee members to assist

on these special committees. It seems that eighteen different people took part in these groups, half of whom were not currently on the General Committee. In this way, the responsibilities for running the Association became more widely dispersed. The Egerton lesson had been well and truly learned.

The main concerns of the EFA at this time were the organisation of the Kinnaird or Open Championship Competition as it was called, the Queen's Club competition and the handicapping for the Public Schools Competition. In 1936 another similar special committee was set up to organise a new Inter-Club Knock Out competition, which attracted 11 entries and was considered well worth continuing. Other special committees had a more temporary status. At the beginning of 1937, there was one appointed to carry through the negotiations for the use of the courts at Queen's Club, leading to a formal agreement between the Club and the Association, in which de Quetteville himself took part. Another organised an exhibition match for the opening of the newly reconditioned, covered and lit second court at Queen's in October 1937. A third group was asked to consider methods of publicity to attract more people to fives. Other matters dealt with in these years included the printing and dispatch of the Rules of the Association and Laws of the Game to schools, with a printed card to display at the courts. A few months later in February 1936, each member of the EFA received a copy. Before each season, an allocation of the use of the Queen's Club courts in the evenings was discussed and agreed.

Throughout this period from 1934 to 1938, de Quetteville as President, Lund as Treasurer and Butler as Secretary had provided an overall stability of the administration of the Association. The last pre-war Committee meeting took place on Tuesday 25 October 1938 and the final pre-war meeting of the Association, the Annual General Meeting, was held, perhaps appropriately, at the War Office, on Wednesday 23 November 1938. The President reported on the successful organisation of the four competitions, but the proposal to hold another Public Schools Championship, without any handicapping, had been dropped in the face of opposition from the Headmasters' Conference.

A resolution to reduce the length of a game from 15 points to 12 was passed by

seven votes to four and the Secretary was instructed to write to clubs and schools to report back to him at the end of the 1938-9 season on how the change had worked. Meanwhile *The Times* reported:

> An interesting experimental Eton fives match was played in December 1938 at Charterhouse between the School and Old Carthusians, in which games were played to 12 and not 15 points. The Eton Fives Association was to adopt this method of scoring if the experiment was successful.

All the existing officers and committee were re-elected for the coming season. After the AGM, a brief Committee meeting voted that £10 should be paid to the Secretary, GM Butler, for 'secretarial assistance for the ensuing year'. Nine years were to elapse before the next recorded meeting.

In 1937 the second court at Queen's, which had originally been built before the Great War

The Uppingham team of 1941, including GA Wheatley (sitting left). Wheatley represented Oxford at cricket and fives, and later returned to teach at Uppingham. He was for many years Master i/c cricket and fives

but had stood unused and exposed to the elements for some years, was repaired, roofed, and fitted with electric light. The cost of £175 was partly defrayed by the Eton Fives Association, which paid £30. The terms of the subsequent agreement between the EFA and Queen's Club were that the EFA could use both courts on an annual payment of £25. Queen's Club would ensure that they were properly lit and "maintained in first class condition", and provide changing facilities (including use of bath or shower at the "usual fee of 6d"). EFA members could play at the cost of 1s.8d per hour in daylight or 3s. per hour when the lights were used. The agreement was binding for ten years as from 1 October 1937. The courts were subsequently booked for the Kinnaird Cup and the 1939 Final may well have been the last match ever played at Queen's.

The opening of the second court at Queen's Club was described in *The Times* as "recognition of the increasing demand for more Eton Fives courts. The Queen's Club, who have always given great assistance to the game by allowing clubs to play their matches in the court there, have now extended this privilege to individual members of all clubs who belong to the Eton Fives Association. Any member of such a club, who has had his name submitted to Queen's, may thus arrange a four among his friends and play at Queen's Club on payment of the ordinary court fees."

One cannot emphasise sufficiently the crucial role that Queen's Club was beginning to play in the world of Eton fives. It was a well established club in the capital; there were already facilities for rackets, real tennis, lawn tennis and squash and it carried the kudos that fives needed to mark its position as a national game with a profile and social standing equal to the others. The accident of fate that dashed these hopes will be told in the next chapter.

This ringing endorsement of the flourishing state of Eton fives was the final clarion. Within three years England, and London in particular, would be under aerial bombardment and the only clarion would be the air raid siren. Life would never be the same again.

Chapter 13
World War II and Recovery

1945-60

The Second World War had a serious effect on many sporting activities, and Eton fives was no exception. All the national competitions – the Kinnaird Cup, the Queen's Club Cup and the Public Schools' Handicaps – were suspended. The main London courts had been the two at Queen's Club and these were destroyed by a bomb early in the war; as Queen's had become the Eton fives centre for club players, this loss was a serious blow. At the beginning of the war, the Air Ministry requisitioned the real tennis court at Cambridge and demolished the fives court next to it to make way for a car park. Then two of the courts at St Olave's by Tower Bridge were damaged in the blitz – and not repaired until 1949; the other two were used as temporary storage for wrought-iron railings and gates and ARP equipment. The City of London courts also suffered some damage; the remainder became a coal store. The court at St Mary's Hospital, Sidcup, was bomb-damaged and not rebuilt and in 1944 a flying bomb left the glass roof of the High-gate courts in a dangerous state: play was "limited to a few" – one wonders how that made it safer. There was damage at Eton too, but less serious: court number 59 was hit by an incendiary

bomb – an inconvenience rather than a disaster. Incidentally, play at Eton had been forbidden during air raid alarms, except for the Keepers – a strange regulation that no doubt has some simple explanation.

During the war a number of fives-playing schools, particularly those on the south coast and in the major cities, were evacuated to the countryside, causing disruption of one sort or another. King Edward's, Birmingham, was evacuated to Repton in 1939 but succeeded in playing several matches on the Repton courts. When the school returned to Birmingham the following year it was to the new suburban site at Edgbaston,

The Cambridge University Team of 1951: T Hare (Eton & Magdalene), MJ Shortland-Jones (Harrow & Caius), JS Guthrie (Eton & Queens'), PBH May (Charterhouse & Pembroke), ARB Moulsdale (Shrewsbury & Emmanuel), RGL Taylor (Harrow & Trinity)

Aubrey Howard Fabian

Aubrey Howard Fabian (1909-1984) was educated at Highgate where he was captain of all three major sports – cricket, association football and Eton fives, having already been in the cricket eleven and fives six for three years and the football eleven for four. At Cambridge Fabian played in three Varsity fives matches including the first one in 1928 when he partnered Frank Reeves, a fellow Cholmeleian, to victory. He also won three blues each for cricket and football and was captain of both football and

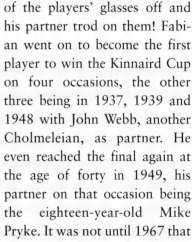

fives. After Cambridge he returned to Highgate as an assistant master, later becoming a Housemaster and then Second Master, and was responsible for the school's success at Eton fives during his forty years there. With Javier Aguirre, who had only left Highgate the previous year, he had "the impudence to win the Kinnaird Cup" in 1930, the only non-Etonian or Harrovian pair to do so in the first seven years of competition. In a 1932 report of a match between the Wyverns and Queen's Club, Fabian was described as "the most severe hitter of the first cut now playing".

Strangely, however, he was never able to get the better of a Cholmeleian pair, Barnes and Bower, until one match when he knocked one of the players' glasses off and his partner trod on them! Fabian went on to become the first player to win the Kinnaird Cup on four occasions, the other three being in 1937, 1939 and 1948 with John Webb, another Cholmeleian, as partner. He even reached the final again at the age of forty in 1949, his partner on that occasion being the eighteen-year-old Mike Pryke. It was not until 1967 that his record number of victories was surpassed.

Fabian was a renowned footballer for Derby County and scored their first goal in the 1933 FA Cup semi-final against Manchester City at Huddersfield, which Derby lost 2-3. He also gained six amateur international caps for England and won an amateur cup final medal with Casuals. He was co-author with Geoffrey Green of the *Book of Association Football* and with Tom Whittaker of *Constructive Football*. His daughter Jenny Fabian wrote the novel *Groupie* in 1969 about life with sixties rock stars.

where the fives courts had been such a priority that they had been up and running for two years! Westminster was also evacuated in 1939, first to Lancing and then to Hurstpierpoint, when Lancing College itself was evacuated to Denstone and then to Ellesmere. Emanuel was evacuated from Wandsworth in 1940 to Petersfield in Hampshire where, it was reported, pupils managed to play some Rugby fives on the Churcher's College courts. Highgate went to Westward Ho! in Devon – although a hundred pupils remained behind in London. Unsurprisingly Dover College disappeared from their front line position to

deepest Devon.

Not much equipment is needed for a game of fives: a ball, preferably gloves and a pair of suitable shoes. But even these meagre requirements were not met in these difficult times; clothes rationing began in 1941 and continued until 1949. In 1940 the Jefferies Malings factory in Woolwich was destroyed by a bomb and with it went the most important source of fives balls. Berkhamsted's fives reports repeatedly complained that balls and gym shoes were difficult to obtain and even in 1947, fully two years after the end of the war, they had to cancel all matches for lack of fives balls. In 1944 Wolverhampton sent a plea to Old Wulfrunians for old Eton fives balls. Two years later Bryanston had managed to acquire sufficient equipment for 12 players and the game had progressed "as far as the present shortage of balls has allowed". A senior Old Bureian remembers playing bare-handed during these war years. At more than one school they even resorted to stitching the covers onto used balls themselves.

Apart from equipment shortages, schools also lost key members of staff to military service. Numerous young masters were called up for military service: among them was 'Bertie' Owen, who had been recruited by Berkhamsted in 1937 especially to run the fives. Roger Pulbrook, master-in-charge at Bryanston, was a Quaker and a pacifist but that did not prevent his services being required in the Friends' Ambulance Unit. Inevitably, not all these young men returned on cessation of hostilities.

Many schools had no external fixtures during the war years and at Ipswich even the House competition was stopped in 1939. Some managed to keep fixtures of some sort going throughout the war: Harrow, rather surprisingly, considering its exposed North London location, was not evacuated but instead provided a temporary home for Malvern, who had been evicted by the Royal Radar Establishment. A reduced fixture list was played and Eton, although they had to cancel some away matches for fuel shortages in 1940, played about a dozen matches each year, many of them against scratch pairs. For them dress problems seemed to be more a matter of protocol than shortage: their opponents from Oxford in 1941 said they were very short of practice and asked if the match could be unofficial. Therefore "we didn't play in 'whites'," reported the *College Chronicle*.

Although they had been forced to play their school fives on a restricted stage, some talented fives players emerged during the war years: ROI Borradaile of Westminster, later to be a master at Wellington; MLY Ainsworth, captain of fives at Shrewsbury; GA Wheatley, captain of Uppingham, 1941-2, later to return there as a master; JH Hale, who won the School Fives at Eton in 1942 and 1943, and GC Willes and B Boobyer, the Uppingham pair of 1945-6, stood out. The Oxford–Cambridge Varsity match struggled on through the war years with Cambridge generally victorious.

The speed of post-war recovery varied enormously from school to school and club to club. The return of school matches was equally haphazard. Aldenham had resumed a full fixture list by 1944; Highgate had matches with Aldenham and City of London in 1945 and introduced new fixtures with Cranleigh and Shrewsbury in the subsequent two years. Bryanston, an isolated Eton fives outpost in the south-west, played two

Jack Peterson (extreme left) and Michael Charlesworth (cutting) playing for the Old Salopians against the School, CD St Johnston and RB Wild (serving), in 1952. At the age of 51, Peterson was still a fine player

matches against Canford in 1946, even though the schools had different types of courts. Lancing and Ipswich only re-started the game in 1949; some never did re-start.

At Eton there was a different sort of celebration: on 4 March 1945 the new Provost, Henry Marten, was knighted by His Majesty King George VI on the steps of the College Chapel. This was not for services to fives, which he had long championed, but for instructing Princess Elizabeth in constitutional history. It was some consolation that the ceremony was conducted on the 'run-out area' of the original fives court.

The evacuated schools had particular regeneration problems. Disused fives courts present an

Peter Barker Howard May CBE

Peter May (1929-94). Of all the great games players who have become famous for their achievements on the cricket field but have also included Eton fives in their curriculum vitae, the greatest is Peter May. May learned his fives at Charterhouse, where his team of 1947 included Simon Kimmins, Peter Nathan, both cricketers, and his brother, John. He went up to Pembroke College, Cambridge in 1949, where he won blues for each of the next three years for cricket and football, for which he captained the university, as well as half blues for Eton fives. As a cricketer he made his Test match debut against the South Africans at Headingley in 1951, scoring 138. He was widely regarded as the best post-war batsman England produced, tall, strong and disciplined with a near-perfect technique, a straight bat and a complete range of strokes.

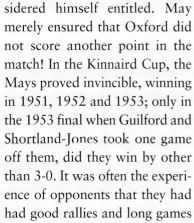

He was equally impressive on the smaller stage of Eton fives. When playing as a pair, PBH and JWH were never defeated. In fact, only once were the May brothers taken to five games and that was by David Guilford and Tom Hare in a Jesters match against Cambridge in 1952. With perfect manners both on and off court, Peter May exuded a modesty and consideration for other people that made him a delight to play with – and even against, so long as you did not expect to win. In spite of his courtesy and charm, there was a ruthlessness about May that, coupled with his superb talent, made him a very difficult player to beat. Robin Mouls-

dale, captain of the Cambridge team of 1951, recalls an incident when May's Oxford opponent refused to give him a let to which he considered himself entitled. May merely ensured that Oxford did not score another point in the match! In the Kinnaird Cup, the Mays proved invincible, winning in 1951, 1952 and 1953; only in the 1953 final when Guilford and Shortland-Jones took one game off them, did they win by other than 3-0. It was often the experience of opponents that they had had good rallies and long games but they usually came off court having won very few points. The Mays' secret was that the good rallies were only when they were serving; their cuts were mostly irretrievable, they seldom failed to return cuts themselves and they rarely made mistakes.

Peter May served on the EFA committee while his other commitments permitted and there is a committee minute in 1956 when the Chairman offered May and his team good wishes for retaining the Ashes against the Australian challenge.

When May died of a brain tumour at the young age of 65, Wisden wrote, "Peter May will be remembered best as a batsman, upright in everything he did, especially the on-drive which, famously, he perfected as a schoolboy... His gifts were sublime, indeed mysterious, and he bore them with honour, modesty and distinction. The fear that we will never see his like again meant his early death was felt all the more keenly."

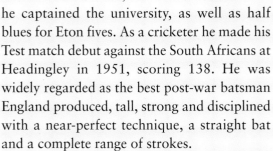

irresistible temptation for 'putting things in'. Fives courts are ideal for all manner of purposes: groundsmen's machinery, stage scenery, bicycles, boats and canoes; a more recent usage is conversion to climbing walls. During the war there were

different needs: storage space for coal and coke was the most popular, although a more macabre use was found at Mill Hill. The school had been used as a military hospital and the fives courts housed the morgue. One imagines that a certain amount of disinfecting was required before the courts were restored to their original purpose. Another bizarre use of a fives court was at Bryanston where it was the meeting place of the witches in the 1947 production of *Macbeth*, but at least the courts were available for use afterwards – until, that is, they became a "temporary" brick store a few years later. Two years after the end of the war, City of Norwich courts were still storing coke. It sometimes seemed as if one only had to stop playing fives in a court for five minutes before someone would arrive with a load of coal or to park a tractor in it.

Open air courts quickly fall victim to the ravages of weather if left unattended. Raymond Harley, a keen botanist at Harrow but a less than enthusiastic fives player, found himself one afternoon a reluctant player in one of the little-used open courts. To his delight – and the bewilderment of the other three players – he spotted a specimen of *hieracium exotericum*, a rare variety of hawkweed, sprouting up between the cracks in the floor. Professor Harley, as he now is, never became a great fives player but it could be said that the Harrow courts played a significant role in his education!

When Westminster returned home in 1945, both boys and masters picked up fives again with gusto: "...the courts are filled with players," reported the school paper; "the old guard of

Investiture of Henry Marten KCVO in 1945. In this picture Henry Marten, Assistant Master, Vice-Provost then Provost of Eton, is being dubbed by King George VI on the Chapel steps, within yards of the pepper pot of the original fives court. Alas, he is not being honoured for his services to Eton fives – of which there were many – but for tutoring the then Princess Elizabeth in British Constitutional History

fives-playing masters, reinforced by new recruits, is on hand...." However they did not re-start fixtures until 1948.

It was 1947 before the EFA Committee called a general meeting at the Law Society's Hall. It was the first meeting for nine years and it must have been an extraordinary occasion. The pre-war officers had all survived and 23 other individuals and representatives attended. RG de Quetteville, as President, took the chair. There was no sign of the Secretary, Guy Butler, but he must have sent along the minutes of the last meeting because everyone pretended they remembered what had happened and they were duly signed as a true record. TGC Lund, the Treasurer, by judicious investment of the Association's finances, had managed almost to double the Association's capital holdings over the war years from £59 14s 8d to £119 3s 0d – "a better financial position than the Association had ever known". He wisely resigned while he was winning and was succeeded by PC Curtis; H Le Bas became Honorary Secretary and the new Chairman was JM Peterson.

Jack Peterson was outrageously talented. At Shrewsbury he had been a Classical scholar, Head of School and "captain of everything": football, cricket and fives. At Oxford he had gained firsts in 'Mods' and in 'Greats', won blues for football, captain in his last year, and half blues for Eton fives. Before the ink was dry on his graduation certificate, CA Alington, the Head Master of Eton, had *invited* him to take up a teaching post there; he later became a House Master. While they were teaching together at Eton, Peterson and Charles Sheepshanks won the Kinnaird three times, twice in the 1930s and once again after the war. The EFA was fortunate to be able to claim his services.

The first agenda item was to put the house in order and that meant tabulating Rules of the Association and agreeing the Laws of Eton Fives. As had been foreseen, it was the latter that was to cause the greater difficulty and two AGMs were allocated for discussion of them. This forum is much beloved of the fives anorak, who finds an irresistible fascination in fiddling with the minutiae of the game. Various proposals were made, some sillier than others, but in the end the only significant change followed the experiment begun before the war: to reduce the number of points in a game from 15 to 12.

In 1947 the EFA was but a fledgling – a fledgling that had suffered a nasty fall – and Peterson's job was to revive the corpse. There were two major issues to be resolved: the first was the courts at Queen's Club that had been seriously damaged by enemy action. Part of the cost of restoration was expected from the War Damage Commission. When the war ended, the EFA and the Jesters' Club offered to pay half the cost until the war damage claim was settled, but Lord Aberdare, chairman of the Club's Board of Directors and holder of the purse strings, refused to consider rebuilding the courts until the claim was settled. Nothing was done and the arguments dragged on for many years with the compensation not being forthcoming and Queen's being intransigent about picking up the remainder of the bill. In the end a licence to rebuild the court and the adjacent tennis court never was issued and the courts never were restored. The matter became even more complicated when the Lawn Tennis Association acquired the club in 1953. They had no interest in the refurbishment of two derelict Eton fives courts and they had development plans of their own. The remains were finally removed in preparation for a building development in the 1980s.

The problems with Queen's meant that the Association had no London base – indeed no base at all. The two covered courts at St Olave's, Tooley Street, had been bombed and the derelict remains used as a store, the Westminster courts were "considered unsafe" for an unexplained reason, and the City of London courts were either still full of coke – a widely encountered situation in the immediate post-war years – or used as a carpenter's store. The first competitions after the war were played out at Highgate and meet-

The Charterhouse Team of 1947: JWH May, MJ Perkins, TRH Savill, PG Nathan, PBH May, SEA Kimmins

ings that had been held at Queen's were held at the Sports Club, the Public Schools Club and various other London venues.

Difficulties over access to the City of London courts persisted for some time to the frustration of the Old Citizens, although that was not their only problem. Their revival was due to the hospitality of the Old Olavians, themselves struggling to re-form using the two surviving uncovered courts at Tooley Street. It did not help that the first few months of 1947 brought the severest weather of the century with snow and ice preventing play in open courts. Once repaired, the courts at St Olave's were used throughout the 1950s for club matches – the EFA paid fees to the school – while Highgate was used for the Public Schools competition; a list of eleven venues acceptable for the Kinnaird matches was issued by the EFA.

The second issue revolved around fives balls.

The 1947 *Old Citizens Gazette* reported, "The suspension of manufacture of fives balls has made it impossible for playing activities of the club to be resumed for the present." The full story is told in the Appendix of this history; it will suffice to say that the war had wrought its havoc here too – although it could be argued that there was a certain predictability about events leading up to the crisis.

The austere years following the end of the war were not a time for building – or even renovation of – such frivolous diversions as fives courts. However there were some further developments in the 1950s. There must have been an enthusiast among the King Edward's foundation trustees in Birmingham as three Eton courts were built in unplastered brick at King Edward VI Camp Hill when it moved to its present site at King's Heath in 1956 and, two years later, three black-surfaced courts were built at King Edward VI Five Ways

The Berkhamsted VI of 1949. In the centre, seated, is Bertie Owens, a popular Master in Charge for 30 years. On his left is Derek Whitehead, one of the great devotees of Eton fives who founded the OBEFC and has served in numerous capacities from 'Keeper of the Fives Balls' to Secretary of the Charitable Trust and has continued to play fives well into his late seventies

at its new green field site. The building seems to have been carried out without much forethought as no more than the occasional burst of interest was shown at either school and both demolished their courts subsequently. Among other schools whose courts did not survive long after the war were Portsmouth Grammar School, where three war-damaged courts were pulled down for a new science block in 1953, and Gresham's, Holt, also victims of demolition to make way for a classroom block in the early 1960s. It is strange that in both these cases there were mutterings of fives regaining popularity with pupils and staff immediately preceding the demise. Rydal did however build two new courts to add to the existing pair, and Queen Elizabeth's, Barnet, who had lost

their courts when they moved site in 1930, used part of a bequest from GWA Harrison to build a single court in 1954. A roof and lights were added ten years later.

With matches in open courts liable to disruption by bad weather, schools and clubs were reluctant to travel to such venues until the courts were roofed. Roofs and lighting became a priority and improvements were made at King Edward's, Birmingham in 1953, at Berkhamsted in 1954, and at Ipswich and Wrekin in 1955. The Wrekin courts still lacked standard buttress caps – a design omission that had never been put right; these were finally added in the 1970s.

The Kinnaird Cup and Public Schools' Handicaps that had been suspended in 1940 were finally re-started in 1948, although there was no longer an Under-16 tournament. The Committee favoured the dropping of the "handicap" element but the Headmasters' Conference objected to the introduction of another representative competition in the Easter holidays. Seventy years later it seems extraordinary that HMC had a view on the matter – or indeed were even consulted. Nor is it obvious why retaining handicapping made the competition any more acceptable. The handicapper's job must have been a nightmare with a gang of headmasters looking over his shoulder and, perhaps predictably, by 1954, HMC agreed to a straight knock-out championship.

The Queen's Club Competition failed to reappear at all after the war, and the Old Boys' clubs now had to arrange their fixtures at their schools or elsewhere rather than at Queen's.

The immediate post-war years witnessed the appearance of more exceptional players. The May brothers, PBH and JWH from Charter-

house, were certainly the pick of the bunch. As a contemporary said, their speed, accuracy and volleying were devastating and they were virtually unbeatable because they never made a mistake. Close behind were ARB Moulsdale and AR Kittermaster of Shrewsbury, beaten by them in the Kinnaird Finals of 1951 and 1952. Dick Kittermaster thought that he and Robin Moulsdale had held their own in the rallies but that the Mays cut and volleyed better. Robin Moulsdale and Dick Kittermaster went on to win for the next three years. Two other talented pairs were PC Curtis and JW Biggs, and the Harrovians, DJS Guilford and MJ Shortland-Jones. And there were two notable pairs from before the war, still strong contenders: AH Fabian and JKG Webb of Highgate and Peterson and Sheepshanks, who were not yet finished. When Jack Peterson was appointed Headmaster of Shrewsbury in 1950 and resigned as Chairman of the EFA, he was to mark his departure in a rather remarkable way:

City of London team, 1959. L to R, back row: M Duschinsky, NR Ponsford, IA Rudolf, AA Salem, PA Hall, TE Manning Esq; front row : PF Lacamp, ALB Sacks, RGF Thatcher, JM Brearley, WW Pantzer. The first pair, Thatcher and Brearley, reached the semifinals of the Public Schools' Competition

he and Charles Sheepshanks won the Kinnaird together for the third time. Jack Peterson was aged 48.

There was no great change in the game itself in the immediate post-war years, apart from the reduction of the game score from 15 to 12 points, but some further standardisation of how the result of a match should be decided was needed. At Uppingham for example, the result had continued to be decided by the tally of points in the top two courts – the method used in Rugby fives. Matches were now to be decided by the number of winning pairs in the top three courts, each pair playing the best of five games, although this was not necessarily followed by all. Generally a school match is decided by the best of the top three courts and it is therefore possible for a team to win the match, even if its first pair has lost. This sort of paradox has allowed masters-in-charge, even in recent times, to employ some 'flexibility' in the interpretation of results. After all a multi-paired match could be considered to have been decided variously by (i) the most winning pairs overall; (ii) the most winning pairs from the first three pairs only; or (iii) the winner of the first pair contest only. The very ingenious could decide by "most individual games won" or even "most points won overall"; there is a large number of possibilities and of course there have indeed been occasions when both teams have considered themselves winners. Headmasters like to crow about sporting successes at their Monday morning assemblies. When schools and clubs listed their end of season results, there were often more wins than losses recorded overall!

Jack Peterson's successor

The Times photographer was present for the Varsity match of 1960. The players are Peter Reynolds (left) and Guy Vine of Cambridge and James Leonard and David Curtis (cutting) of Oxford. The lower picture is clearly 'staged'

OLD CITIZENS

FIVES CLUB

Founded 1893

Affiliated to the Eton Fives
Association

SEASON 1960-61

OLD CITIZENS FIVES CLUB

FIXTURES 1960-61

Date	Opponents	Courts
JUNE		
Wed., 1	Zuoz College	Zuoz
SEPTEMBER		
Sat., 24	Eton College	Eton
Tues., 27	Lancing Old Boys	Blackfriars
Tues., 27	Old Berkhamstedians	Blackfriars
Thurs., 29	Eton Fives Association Committee	Blackfriars
OCTOBER		
Sat., 1	Old Marlburians	Blackfriars
Sat., 1	Old Chigwellians	Blackfriars
Sat., 1	St. Peter's, Seaford	Blackfriars
Sat., 1	Stoke House, Seaford	Blackfriars
Sat., 8	Old Aldenhamians	Aldenham
Sun., 9	St. Peter's Court	Broadstairs
Thurs., 13	Old Carthusians	Blackfriars
Sat., 15	Old Cholmeleians	Blackfriars
Sun., 16	Ipswich School	Ipswich
Tues., 18	Old Millhillians	Blackfriars
Sat., 22	Old Harrovians	Harrow
Sun., 23	Stowe School	Stowe
Tues., 25	St. Olave's School	Tower Bridge
Sat., 29	Cambridge University	Cambridge
Sat., 29	Cambridge University Penguins	Blackfriars
Sun., 30	Oxford University	Oxford
NOVEMBER		
Tues., 1	Old Cranleighans	Blackfriars
Sat., 5	Old Olavians	Blackfriars
Tues., 8	Chigwell School	Blackfriars
Sat., 12	Lancing College	Lancing
Sun., 13	Dover College	Dover
Tues., 15	Westminster School	Blackfriars
Sat., 19	King Edward's Five Ways School	Birmingham
Sat., 19	King Edward's Camp Hill School	Birmingham
Sun., 20	Repton School	Repton
Tues., 22	Old Salopians	Blackfriars
Sat., 26	Old Uppinghamians	Blackfriars
Sat., 26	Old Berkhamstedians	Blackfriars
Tues., 29	Old Reptonians	Blackfriars
DECEMBER		
Sat., 3	Marlborough College	Marlborough
Sat., 3	Old Marlburians	Marlborough
Tues., 6	Old Etonians	Blackfriars
Thurs., 8	City of London School	Blackfriars
Sat., 10	Harrow School	Harrow
Sat., 10	Mill Hill School	Mill Hill
Sun., 11	R. O. I. Borradaile's IV	Wellington
Tues., 13	Westminster City School	Blackfriars
Thurs., 15	Oxford and Cambridge Old Citizens	Blackfriars
Sat., 31	Old Westminsters	Blackfriars
Sat., 31	Old Stoics	Blackfriars
Sat., 31	Ipswich School	Blackfriars

as Chairman in 1950 was Alan Barber, who was to occupy the position for 23 years, the longest reign in the EFA's history. Alan Barber was another colossus of the sporting world: footballer for Oxford and the Corinthians, golf 'blue', captain of cricket at Oxford and later for Yorkshire. He was only captain at Yorkshire for one year but it was long enough for him to build a reputation for leadership and an excellent relationship with the Yorkshire pros – a renownedly difficult bunch, who were innately suspicious of "jazz 'ats from t'university". The great Herbert Sutcliffe later wrote "A great captain was AT Barber, one of those rare men with the power of inspiring confidence." As a fives player, Alan Barber had won the Kinnaird Cup with Desmond Backhouse in 1934 and in 1936. His Secretary up to 1960 was Philip Curtis and

The fixture list of the Old Citizens Fives Club of 1960-61 with a programme of 94 matches (continued opposite). There were two fatalities from cardiac arrest on court; the number of marriage breakdowns was never disclosed

JANUARY							
Tues.,	3	Highgate School	..	..	..	..	Highgate
Sat.,	7	Old Cholmeleians		..	..	..	Highgate
Tues.,	10	King Edward's School	..	..	..	..	Blackfriars
Sat.,	14	Old Harrovians	..	..	..	..	Blackfriars
Tues.,	17	Old Chigwellians		..	..	..	Blackfriars
Sat.,	21	Berkhamsted School		..	..	..	Berkhamsted
Tues.,	24	Lancing Old Boys		..	..	..	Blackfriars
Sat.,	28	Shrewsbury School		..	..	..	Shrewsbury
Sun.,	29	Oxford University		..	..	..	Oxford
Sun.,	29	Old Edwardians	..	..	..	..	Birmingham
Tues.,	31	Jesters	..	..	..	..	Blackfriars
FEBRUARY							
Sat.,	4	Eton College	..	..	..	..	Eton
Sun.,	5	Cambridge University	..	..	..	..	Cambridge
Tues.,	7	Old Uppinghamians		..	..	..	Blackfriars
Sat.,	11	Uppingham School		..	..	..	Uppingham
Sun.,	12	Oakham School	..	..	..	..	Oakham
Sun.,	12	Lincoln School	..	..	..	..	Lincoln
Tues.,	14	St. Olave's School		..	..	..	Blackfriars
Sat.,	18	Charterhouse	..	..	..	..	Charterhouse
Sat.,	18	Cranleigh School		..	..	..	Cranleigh
Sat.,	18	Mill Hill School	..	..	..	..	Mill Hill
Sat.,	18	The Leys School		..	..	..	Cambridge
Tues.,	21	Emanuel School	..	..	..	..	Blackfriars
Sat.,	25	King Edward's School	..	..	..	..	Birmingham
Sat.,	25	Wolverhampton Grammar School		..	..	Wolverhampton
Sun.,	26	St. Peter's School		..	..	..	Seaford
Tues.,	28	Old Millhillians	..	..	..	..	Blackfriars
MARCH							
Thurs.,	2	Old Reptonians	..	..	..	..	Blackfriars
Sat.,	4	Old Aldenhamians		..	..	..	Blackfriars
Sat.,	4	Old Edwardians	..	..	..	..	Blackfriars
Thurs.,	9	Old Carthusians	..	..	..	..	Blackfriars
Sat.,	11	City of London School	..	..	..	..	Blackfriars
Sun.,	12	St. Andrew's School		..	..	..	Eastbourne
Tues.,	14	Westminster School	..	..	..	..	Blackfriars
Tues.,	14	Queen Elizabeth's School		..	..	..	Blackfriars
Sat.,	18	Old Olavians	..	..	..	..	Blackfriars
Sun.,	19	Stoke House	..	..	..	..	Seaford
Sun.,	19	St. Wilfrid's School		..	..	..	Seaford
Tues.,	21	Old Cholmeleians		..	..	..	Highgate
Thurs.,	23	Eton Fives Association Committee		..	..	Blackfriars
Sat.,	25	Old Westminsters		..	..	..	Blackfriars
Sat.,	25	Old Berkhamstedians		..	..	..	Blackfriars
Tues.,	28	Old Etonians	..	..	..	..	Blackfriars
APRIL							
Tues.,	4	Old Salopians	..	..	..	..	Blackfriars
Thurs.,	6	Old Marlburians		..	..	..	Blackfriars
Thurs.,	6	Lancing Old Boys		..	..	..	Blackfriars
Thurs.,	6	Old Stoics	..	..	..	..	Blackfriars
Sat.,	8	Jesters	..	..	..	..	Blackfriars

from 1961-8, David Guilford.

In the 1950s there was no immediate cause for alarm in the Committee room: the depressing aftermath of the war had been negotiated – except for the Queen's Club problem. Eton fives was still being played by all the best school games players and Old Boy Club fives had re-established itself; the Varsity match, now played at Eton, was played to as high a standard as ever and the Jesters were flourishing. The results of matches at all levels were regularly recorded in

The Times and *Daily Telegraph* and the game seemed to be regaining some of its pre-war status.

Eton were still very strong and produced some excellent pairs in the 1950s: HS Langton and ARB Burrows, ACD Ingleby-Mackenzie and NF Robinson, DR Maclean and JH Illingworth, and DAC Marr and DMG Bailey were perhaps the most outstanding but DMG Norman and SM de Zoete, WGA Clegg and TC Pilkington, Pilkington and JR Smithers, and NF Peterson and AR Wagg were all top class. It was also the beginning of a long run of success led by Geoffrey Bolt, master-in-charge at Aldenham: PE Reynolds and EJ Dyson, GB Vine and DR Barker, Barker and U Mohammadu, and AG Irwin and CA Sloan were all Public Schools winners.

Repton had for many years played second fiddle in the Midlands to Shrewsbury but in 1955 they were represented by what was probably the best team they had ever had. In the space of eleven days they beat Highgate, Uppingham, and Shrewsbury. The first pair, RC Nelson-Jones and CP Dollery, reached the semi-final of the Public Schools Competition where they lost to Aldenham 2-3, thus going further than any previous Repton entrants. Their success was credited to Richard Nelson-Jones's keen captaincy and fine play, and also to the coaching of Dick Sale.

Over the years there has been a conspicuous connection between talent for cricket and fives and it is interesting to note that JM Brearley, who

A four in the King Edward's courts in the 1960s. The adults seem to have adopted an unusual code of head wear

mar School, Melbourne, in 1953. He found that a type of handball had been played there in a court "with side walls and an end wall with two curved ledges only". The Headmaster of Geelong at the time, Sir James Darling, had been educated at Repton so at least he knew what an Eton fives court looked like. The school had moved out of Geelong to Corio in 1927 and the December 1943 issue of the *Corian* had reported "a generous gift of £100 by the parent of a boy who is leaving this term, with the wish that this money be used after the war for the establishment of an Eton fives court." Charlesworth was the catalyst and it was only a matter of weeks before a standard Eton fives court was up and running.

was in the City of London pair of 1959, would become the sixth England cricket captain to have been a first-class Eton fives player. The others were the Hon Ivo Bligh, the Hon FS Jackson, APF Chapman, RWV Robins and PBH May*.

This period also marked the emergence of a school hitherto unknown in the top echelons: King Edward's, Birmingham produced two successful pairs, AJG Campbell and NC Brown, and A Hughes and JC Green. Campbell and Hughes were to make a big impact on Eton fives in the next two decades.

During its most fertile period, the game of Eton fives had migrated to some unlikely places in the world but a continent it had never penetrated was Australia and so it was with missionary zeal that Michael Charlesworth arrived from Shrewsbury on a teacher exchange at Geelong Gram-

Colin Ingleby-Mackenzie won the School Fives at Eton and the Public Schools Championships with NF Robinson in 1951. In 1961 he captained Hampshire to the County Cricket Championship. Later he became Chairman of Holmwoods Insurance, sponsors of the Schools Fives

Charlesworth's enthusiasm was infectious and a club of around fifty players was soon built up but, as has been seen in the UK time after time, the difficulty of maintaining the momentum beyond his departure became only too obvious. There was a short boost when TR Garnett, a former winner of the Kinnaird Cup and Master of Marlborough, took over as Headmaster from 1961 to 1973 but without external opposition Eton fives was unlikely to gain wide popularity at the school.

Although some losses of courts were never to be recovered, by 1960 the bruises suffered by the War had largely been healed. School, university and club fives were re-established but there were more problems looming – and one that has never really been solved right up to the present day: after school, for the large majority of players, Eton fives remained a very inconvenient game to play.

---

*Footnote (and this is really a foot note)
It is quite possible that WR Hammond should be added to this list. Between 1914 and 1918, he attended Portsmouth Grammar School where there were Eton fives courts, before moving as a boarder to Cirencester Grammar School after his father had been killed. Information from Portsmouth is sparse as the school was taken over by the Royal Navy in the War and enemy action accounted, not just for the fives courts but also the school's records. However, reminiscences by a contemporary, ES Wilson, published in *The Portsmuthian*, the school magazine, comment on Hammond's love of games, cricket and football in particular, "whilst in the fives court he would astonish us with spectacular overhead kicking". It was not a style of play that won a universal following!

Chapter 14

The Squeeze

1960-80

If World War II was a body blow to Eton fives with the loss of the main match courts at Queen's Club and the destruction of the ball manufacturer's premises, it was followed by a sequence of combination punches in the 1960s. The arrival of the 'sports hall games', the rise of hockey with the universal availability of artificial pitches, and the advance of squash combined to present serious competition to fives as a school game. Ominously, as early as 1948 Uppingham noted a threat to Eton fives from hockey, and four years later, Geoffrey Bolt, master-in-charge at Aldenham, was making a plea for boys to give Eton fives priority over hockey. Although squash had been around since the 19th century, it was now becoming fashionable and new courts were springing up all over the country. The irony, of course, was that squash had begun as the poor relation of rackets and fives, but it had three distinct advantages over its seniors: the courts were cheaper to construct than Eton fives and rackets courts; the game was primarily played as 'singles'; and that it was essentially a simple game. One has only to witness the annual lawn tennis championships at Wimbledon to see the contrasting appeal of the singles competitions over the doubles, although many would argue that doubles is the better spectacle. The attraction of the one-to-one gladiatorial combat led to investment in

Philip Curtis. Hon Treasurer of the EFA 1947-51; Hon Secretary 1952-60; President 1985-91; Founder Chairman of the EFCT

glass-walled courts to accommodate spectators, and allowed the game to become professional. Some aggressive marketing, with particular emphasis on squash as an aid to fitness – the ideal activity for the middle class businessman and a colleague on their way home from the office via the pub – enabled the game to gain astonishing popularity during this decade.

Fives was relatively unprepared for this revolution and, although the appeal of squash has receded, fives has never really recovered its pre-eminence as the Spring term school sport. The golden age when football, cricket and fives were the three main games in the Public Schools was over.

By 1960 the fives ball crisis had come to a head. Following the demise of Jefferies Malings and the failure to find another manufacturer, various attempts were made to find an alternative way of covering the balls. The solution finally adopted was for a completely different design of ball. The invention, by Tony Baden-Fuller, a young chemistry graduate from Cambridge, was a ball of the same size, weight and bounce, consisting of a composition of rubber and cork with a coating of paint. Although initially greeted suspiciously by some of the players, it was soon accepted and the differences such as the greater bounce that occurred by mistake in some cases were actually applauded and adopted. The

Baden-Fuller ball has been in play for nearly fifty years now and only real veterans know of any other. Its effect was to change the game, subtly but decisively. Rallies became faster and longer; the new ball took less 'cut' on the front wall and was rarely 'killed' in the 'pepper'. Eton fives became a different game – neither better nor worse, but different.

Competitive Eton fives in England in the 1960s was essentially a school sport with internal and inter-school matches, culminating in the Public Schools Championships in the Easter holidays. Supplementary to this was a network of Old Boy clubs and the Jesters, playing each other and the schools. The only adult competition was the Kinnaird Cup, the national open championship.

Some of the clubs were more active than others: in the vanguard was the Old Citizens led by a dynamic young secretary, Gordon Stringer, who took over in 1958. At the same time, the master

Alan Theodore Barber

Alan Theodore Barber (1905-1985) was educated at Shrewsbury and Queen's College, Oxford. At Oxford he won blues for cricket, football and golf, captaining the University XIs for both cricket and football. In 1930 he also captained Yorkshire, scoring a century against an England XI; altogether he appeared in a total of seventy first-class cricket matches, scoring 2,261 runs, at an average of 23.30.

When Alan Barber became Headmaster of Ludgrove in 1937, a preparatory school with a long tradition of preparing boys for Eton – and with its own Eton fives courts – he took over from Frank Henley, also an Oxford cricket blue and a fives player. Previous headmasters had been WJ Oakley (up to 1934), GO Smith (up to 1922), both outstanding sportsmen and fine fives players – and originally the legendary Arthur Dunn. It was quite a succession.

Alan Barber had been a distinguished fives player at Shrewsbury, partnering at different times HF Robinson, LT Vyvyan and RL Howland. *The Salopian* described him as "a fighter...he volleys well with both hands." He won the Kinnaird Cup with Desmond Backhouse in 1934 and 1936, and after the war he played briefly with Charlie Sheepshanks in a

partnership which displayed, more than any other perhaps, the skills and beauty of the game.

It was not surprising that fives flourished at Ludgrove both among the boys and in the form of AT Barber's IV. Among the excellent fives players on the teaching staff during his headmastership were Alan Ellis, an Old Salopian, Peter Borgnis and John Rickards, an Old Etonian, who all played regularly. Later there were Mike Ainsworth, Duncan Beardmore-Grey and Micky Burton-Brown.

When Jack Peterson became Headmaster of Shrewsbury in 1950, Alan Barber took over the Chairmanship of the EFA, a post which he filled with no little skill and enthusiasm for the next 23 years. In 1973 he succeeded Lord Home as President and he maintained a lively interest in all aspects of the Association's business. For some years the final of the Kinnaird Cup was played in the Ludgrove courts and it is fitting that the competition for Old Boys' fives teams, bears his name. The fives tradition at Ludgrove has been continued by his son, Gerald, Keeper of Fives at Eton and Oxford captain in 1965, and more recently by his grandson Simon, School Fives winner at Eton for three years with Simon Stephens.

Two successful Masters i/c Fives

Geoffrey Bolt: Aldenham and Cranleigh

Tom Manning: City of London

in charge at City of London, TE Manning, managed to achieve a change of attitude at the school: all six courts were brought back into play and made available to the club. Car parking in the playground, changing and showering facilities on site and team teas after the match made Blackfriars an attractive venue for a Saturday afternoon fixture in the 1960s. By this time the school was beginning to feed some talented players into the club. In the 1960-1 season Stringer arranged no fewer than 94 fixtures, including forays to uncharted territory such as Lincoln and Dover where the game had not recovered after the war, exhibition games at prep schools and annual trips to Switzerland and Germany. Inevitably there were some who thought that resources were being over-stretched and that too much was being asked of older players – an argument that gained some credence when the club suffered two unfortunate fatalities from cardiac arrests on court.

The antidote to the threats from other games was perceived by the EFA committee to be an injection of new competitions: the first to be introduced was the Midland Championships in 1960, similar in format to the Kinnaird Cup but based at the Birmingham courts. This was an important move because, although there were many fives centres in the Midlands, nearly all the matches were played in the south-east; it proved a success and continued until 1988. A one-off London Tournament was held in April 1972 but the annual London Tournament was not to start for another ten years.

In 1964 it was decided to restart the inter-club knockout competition that had taken place at Queen's Club before the war. The entry was limited to Old Boys' Clubs and so was the Eton fives equivalent of the Arthur Dunn Cup for football and the Cricketer Cup, which began two years later. The Alan Barber Cup, as the competition was named, soon became established as the major team competition in Eton fives. In the first four years it was won by the Old Edwardians; then Old Berkhamstedians and Old Etonians were each winners twice and Old Olavians once, before Old Cholmeleians began a fourteen-year run of dominance from 1977-90.

In 1971 a league was inaugurated and Douglas Keeble, a keen Old Olavian fives player, donated a trophy for the winners. Five clubs, Old Berkhamstedians, Old Olavians, Old Cholmeleians, Old Edwardians, and Old Citizens, entered in the first season. Old Olavians won in 1972 but all the entrants succeeded in winning at some time in its first decade.

The introduction of the league was a success in that it provided competitive fives for the leading players; it was a welcome and, at the time, probably necessary addition to the calendar. Perhaps predictably, there were also negative effects: league matches gradually assumed a priority in the eyes of many players. The list of friendly fixtures declined rapidly, and to try to ensure the strongest line-up, league teams tended to be selected from a relatively small pool of players; many of the less talented players became almost disenfranchised. What the league achieved was to produce more fives for fewer players. The less skilful were partly catered for by the introduction of a second division of the League in 1976 with Old Berkhamstedians II winning the initial championship. In the following year the Club was victorious in both divisions, a feat not to be repeated for thirty years. However the problem of providing fives for the great mass of ordinary fives players had yet to be addressed.

Following a trend in other sports, there came a change in the pattern of fives played at the schools. No longer was there the long list of fix-tures against Old Boy club teams; instead these were replaced by matches against other schools, and the arrival of the transit van/minibus enabled up to seven pairs to travel. Another development was the introduction of a Preparatory Schools Competition, held for the first time in 1968 on Semi-finals day of the Public Schools Competition at Highgate; entries, limited to boys under 14 at preparatory schools, were by invitation. Six schools took part: Sunningdale; Ludgrove; Berkhamsted Junior; Highgate Junior; Stoney-gate, Leicester; and St. Andrew's, Eastbourne. The first four of these schools each secured a win in the initial four years. In subsequent years Bel-mont (Mill Hill), Cranleigh Junior, St Peter's, and St Wilfrid's, both of Seaford, Eagle House and Aysgarth joined the entrants.

In 1974 pairs from six schools – City of Lon-don, Eton, Highgate, Shrewsbury, Wolverhamp-ton Grammar and St Wilfrid's, Seaford – partici-pated in the first Under-14 Competition, which was held at Highgate. This competition was quickly absorbed into the main Schools Champi-onships and has gone from strength to strength. Wolverhampton, with an 11+ entry, won five of the first seven tournaments, a clear demonstra-tion that it is possible to reach a high standard of play in just two years.

The success of this venture led to the re-intro-duction of the Public Schools Under-16 Competi-tion in 1977 as an incentive to the middle age group to continue playing the game in their sec-ond and third years at school when the pressure from other games was beginning to build up. A surprisingly large entry of thirty-one pairs meant

The Eton Fives Association Touring Party to Northern Nigeria in 1965: AST Negretti, MJ Shortland-Jones; MG Moss; DJS Guilford; AT Baden-Fuller; BD Barton; GD Stringer

Visitors		Fixtures		
Mallam Mamuda Lagos	The ETON FIVES ASSOCIATION	October		
Mallam Abubakar Udu		6th	Thurs.	Harrow School
Mallam Hamisu Ibrahim		7th	Fri.	Highgate School
Alhaji Abdu Sambo		9th	Sun.	Old Edwardians
Mallam Yahaya Abba	Tour of NIGERIAN FIVES ASSOCIATION	10th	Mon.	King Edward's School
Mallam Sani Musa		11th	Tues.	Shrewsbury School
Mallam Micah Gayya	October 5th - 19th 1966	13th	Thurs.	Eton College
		14th	Fri.	Old Citizens
		15th	Sat.	Jesters Club
		16th	Sun.	Lancing College
		18th	Tues.	Eton Fives Association
		19th	Wed.	Westminster School

Fixture card for the return visit when the Nigerians toured UK in 1966

that the schedule had to be hastily revised to cover two days. Wolverhampton built on their earlier success with three straight wins before Highgate interrupted their dominance with wins in both competitions in 1980.

In 1963 three new courts were opened at Emanuel. The initiative for these had come five years earlier from the Headmaster, Dr Grundy, and they were erected as a memorial to AE 'Titus' Titley, a former pupil. The courts, which stand close to the Victoria to Brighton railway line and are clearly visible from a passing train, were built in the splendidly named "Gag's Corner" so called after "a wonderful hit for seven by Mr Garrington ended up in this far corner of the field in 1897". In 1968 four new indoor fives courts were opened at Orpington, following the move of St Olave's School from Tooley Street near Tower Bridge to the leafy suburbs. At Oxford University a new Sports Centre was opened in 1974 in Iffley Road, scene of Roger Bannister's famous sub-four minute mile twenty years earlier, and two Eton fives courts were incorporated. The old courts, bizarrely situated in the middle of a row of houses off the Abingdon Road, were demolished the following year. Harrow built a fives changing room as an extension of their new rackets court complex and subsequently made improvements to the roofing of the fives courts. Lancing's courts were

given a facelift and those at Chigwell were repaired and in use again by 1979.

All this news of upgrades and improvements gave at least superficial evidence to support the impression of a game, confident in itself, proud of its past, and assured of its future. With hindsight, there was more than a whiff of complacency among the establishment. The loss of the courts at Woodbridge, demolished in 1962 to make way for a new dining hall, was thought to be but an irritating pin prick.

Alan Barber continued as Chairman of the EFA until 1973; Gordon Stringer had taken over as Hon Secretary in 1969 and the Treasurer up to 1971 was David Barton. Later David Guilford wrote, "Alan guided the Association with firmness and fairness at a time when the game was expanding: at more schools the game was thriving, and Eton fives was no longer the preserve of a few bastions. While recognising that wider interest was beneficial, even vital, to the game, he, conservative to some, was determined that Eton fives should avoid the pitfalls into which so many other sports had fallen and that the spirit of the game should far outweigh the confines of petty legislation. Fives should be a game which was entertaining and fun for all.... Meetings at the Sports Club were notable for the good humour of the committee members and for the generosity of their host." It was a great compliment to Alan Barber and the game of Eton fives that, in 1966, Sir Alec Douglas-Home agreed to become President of the Association. He had two important qualifications for the position: first, he had been a good player, having won the School Fives at Eton with N Llewellyn Davies in 1922, and second, he had been Prime Minister. But Alec Douglas-Home did much more than add gravitas to the letter heading; he took an active interest in the game, which continued when he took a step upstairs to become Patron from 1972-95.

What David Guilford meant by "fun for all" and "avoiding pitfalls" was Alan Barber's strongly held belief that Eton fives was an amateur game to be played by those fortunate enough to go to schools where it was played – not everyone would agree about it no longer being a preserve. Alan Barber had not only played football for the Corinthians; he *was* a Corinthian. The pitfalls were popularisation, professionalism and sponsorship. Since the war the two running sores had been "the Queen's Club problem" and "the fives ball problem". The first had been written off as an irredeemable loss; the second had been solved. So superficially this was a serene period for the Association and Eton fives, with the buffeting from the threat of squash, hockey and the sports hall games largely ignored.

But there were some further hazards lurking round the corner. Almost unrecognised as a blow to Eton fives was the reorganisation of secondary education along comprehensive lines during the 1960s and 1970s. Both the direct grant grammar schools, which were finally abolished in 1976, and the voluntary aided grammar schools had to decide whether to join the comprehensive system or to become independent. Many of the old grammar

Tony Hughes, nine times winner of the Amateur Championship for the Kinnaird Cup, playing with Richard Lambert. An amazing enthusiast for fives, he drove a car with registration plate: TON1 4 5S

schools had been fives-playing, with courts on site. Some of those that became independent such as Wolverhampton Grammar retained their site and their fives courts while others such as King Edward VI Grammar, Bury St Edmunds, moved site and the courts were lost. There were also the exceptions, such as St Olave's Grammar, Queen Elizabeth's Grammar, Barnet, and the Royal Grammar, High Wycombe, that were allowed to retain their grammar school status – and so kept their fives courts.

If little notice had been taken of these losses and threats, the warning lights certainly began to flash in 1978 when Eton demolished no fewer than 36 courts (three roofed, the rest open) to make way for a swimming pool. Until that time it had been possible to play all 32 first round matches in the Kinnaird Cup simultaneously; now only 15 courts remained. This was less convenient but not devastating. The greater impact was the message that this decision sent to Etonians, the players of Eton fives and the world: that the game no longer had the importance it had previously been given. The writing was, at least metaphorically, on the wall: '*Hic noster ludus non iam floret*' (This our game flourishes no longer) at the spiritual home of the game.

However, throughout this period, school fives was played as keenly and competitively as ever. Aldenham was coming to the end of its successful run, having won the Schools' Competition five times in eight years under the tutelage of the charismatic Geoffrey Bolt, and Eton maintained its position as top school of the 1960s with four wins. At Highgate Roger Beament took over as master-in-charge and achieved six wins in the ten years from 1965. City of London was also successful in the 1960s with two championship wins.

Cambridge University Eton Fives First Team
1977 1978

Eaden Lilley   Cambridge

C.D.Brant   A.W.Richards   J.P.Batting   K.W.Turnbull
Queens'   St John's   Peterhouse   Trinity

J.L.Hartstone   J.P.Asquith   B.C.Matthews   E.W.F.W.Alton   J.G.M.Pulsford
Queens'   Trinity Hall   Emmanuel   Jesus   Jesus
Hon.Secretary   Captain

Varsity Match Winners 6–0

Although caps ceased to be worn when courts became roofed, the fashion for long hair in the 1970s brought a need for restraint – in both senses. Bandanas and baseball caps (which allowed ponytails to be passed through the loop at the back) became a common sight. Mercifully they were usually removed for photographs

Success was more widely spread in the 1970s when pairs from ten different schools appeared in the Final. Highgate won four times but Shrewsbury were victors in 1970, their first Final since 1939. Michael Charlesworth later wrote in his autobiography that when he came back from Pakistan, "I found myself in charge of fives again for a spell – a good time to be so, as the powerful pair of Nick Pocock and Peter Worth won the Schools Championship. Peter was, I think, the most able ball games player I can recollect." Nick Pocock later captained the Hampshire cricket side for a few years. Two years later Shrewsbury were less strong and the Rydal pair, JR Kaye and DRL

Owen, had the rare satisfaction of being twice victorious in the first pair. Harrow reached the Schools' Final in 1977 for the first time since 1950, and Wolverhampton burst onto the scene in 1980, achieving the first win in what was to be a remarkable fifteen-year period of success under David Pedley.

The Kinnaird Cup was dominated in the 1960s by four pairs: the Old Olavians, JW Biggs and JC Wallis; the Old Edwardians, A Hughes and AJG Campbell; the Old Citizens, CSH Hampton and SH Courtney; and the Old Berkhamstedians, DC Firth and MR Keeling. Prior to 1960 only Howard Fabian had won the Kinnaird Cup on

The Shrewsbury pair, Peter Worth and Nick Pocock, won the Public Schools Competition in 1970. Geoffrey Bolt presented the trophy

great pleasure in ensuring that all his team had the opportunity to play a part and created an atmosphere in which everyone wanted to do their best to please him. Any success that followed would be a shared pride in the achievement. Frank Hooper transferred these leadership qualities off the cricket field and the fives court into vigorous promotion of those causes that were dear to him."

Frank Hooper was essentially a third pair fives player, but after his superstar predecessors, this was no bad thing; he appreciated the game as seen through the eyes of the ordinary club player. He was a publisher printer by trade, working for the family business, Argus Press, and ending up as its managing director for twelve years before he retired. Frank Hooper was a practised board and committee man, being Chairman of the Elizabethan Club (the Old Westminsters), a member of the Council of the Westminster School Society and Chairman of the Governors of Orley Farm School. As Chairman of the EFA Committee, he put the practices of the Committee on a sure footing. He was not however an innovator and his efficiency, ebullience and perception tend-

more than three occasions. Tony Hughes now proceeded to win the trophy on no fewer than nine occasions, eight of them in partnership with fellow Old Edwardian, Gordon Campbell. The other win was with David Guilford, who himself won three Kinnairds, two partnered by a fellow Harrovian, Martin Shortland-Jones.

With the increased dominance by a handful of pairs, in 1968 the organisers decided to introduce a 'plate competition' for first round losers. Its purpose was to offer an incentive to more players and to raise the number of entries. A new trophy, the 'Pepper Pot', was awarded to the winners.

In 1972 Alan Barber stood down as Chairman of the Eton Fives Association to become President; his successor was Frank Hooper, a sharp contrast. Martin Shortland-Jones later wrote of how he had first met Frank Hooper when he (Hooper) was captaining the Harrow Town Cricket Club 3rd XI. He could not have picked a more typical scenario: Hooper of bluff demeanour and bellicose appearance, captaining a side of modest ability in a match of no importance with enthusiasm and seriousness. "He took

Gordon Stringer. Hon Secretary of the EFA 1969–74

David Barton. Hon Treasurer of the EFA 1952–71

ed to work within the existing framework.

Although Eton fives in its homeland was beginning to be squeezed, there stood out one very important cause for encouragement: during this decade many of the traditional all-boy Eton fives schools had begun to take girls. Bryanston, Charterhouse, Lancing, Marlborough, Mill Hill and Westminster were among those and there was scope for the introduction of the game to a whole new pool of players. In 1978 Debbie Till became the first woman to enter the Kinnaird Cup.

Alec Douglas-Home

Alec Douglas-Home (1903–1995), later Lord Home of The Hirsel, learnt his fives at Ludgrove. Under the name of Lord Dunglass, he was winner of the School Fives at Eton with N Llewelyn-Davies in 1922. His contemporary Cyril Connolly later wrote, "He was a votary of the esoteric Eton religion, the kind of graceful tolerant sleepy boy who is showered with favours and crowned with all the laurels, who is liked by the masters and admired by the boys without any apparent exertion on his part, without experiencing the ill effect of success himself or arousing the pangs of envy in others. In the eighteenth century he would have become Prime Minister before he was thirty; as it was he appeared honourably ineligible for the struggle of life."

Alec Douglas-Home went on to Christ Church Oxford, where he gained a cricket blue at Oxford as a fast-medium bowler, and joined a long line of successful graduates with a third in history. His later career in politics led to his becoming Foreign Secretary 1960-63, 1970-74 and Prime Minister 1963-64. Harold Macmillan, when assessing the various candidates as his successor in 1963, wrote, "Lord Home is clearly a man who represents the old governing class at its best ... He is not ambitious in the sense of wanting to scheme for power, although not foolish enough to resist honour when it comes to him ... He gives that impression by a curious mixture of great courtesy, and even if yielding to pressure, with underlying rigidity on matters of principle ... This is exactly the quality that the class to which he belongs have at their best because they think about the question under discussion and not about themselves."

In 1936 Douglas-Home married Elizabeth, second daughter of Cyril Alington (see page 46). Cricket and fives remained an important part of his life: he was President of MCC in 1966; Governor of I Zingari 1977-89; President of the Eton Fives Association from 1966-71 and Patron from 1975-96. His continuing interest in and loyalty to Eton fives, when he had so many more important matters to wrestle with, was remarkable. When the details of the EFA tour to Nigeria were being arranged in 1965, it was his enthusiasm and inspired intervention that cleared away all obstacles and delays, and encouraged the Commonwealth Relations Office to take up the cause. He attended Committee meetings from time to time and was generous with his time when consulted. It was no surprise that he accepted with alacrity the invitation to be Guest of Honour at the Jesters Annual Dinner in 1963, and at the age of 82 he travelled down from Scotland for the Centenary Fives Dinner at Harrow in 1985 to commemorate the first recorded match against Eton. On both occasions, the wise, witty and winning observations of a speaker in whom there was always an infectious sense of fun, added greatly to the enjoyment of the evening.

Chapter 15

Money Matters

1980-2000

Slowly – very slowly – the Eton Fives Association Committee realised that it was presiding over a game that was under threat of its very existence; it was not surprising therefore that politics should enter the committee room. One of the leading protagonists for sweeping changes was Tony Hughes, an energetic but controversial young man, who challenged as many of the administrators in the committee room as he did his opponents on the fives court. He was a very good player, whose name had first come to attention when he was a runner-up in the Public Schools Championships of 1957; he was to go on to win the Kinnaird Cup on nine occasions and to play in nineteen finals, both records at the time. Tony Hughes was passionate about Eton fives; he even drove a car with registration plate TON1 4 5S. He played in every competition he set eyes on and he and Richard Tyler claimed to have played fives in each of six continents. (They claimed they were only prevented from playing in a seventh because of building restrictions in Antarctica!)

Tony Hughes had plenty of ideas too. A game as small as Eton fives was only too pleased to have volunteers to share the load of organisation and Hughes was eager to help. The trouble was that he was not only a very competitive player; Hughes also wanted to jog those in the committee room, whom he perceived as conservative diehards, out of their complacency. He wanted to change the name of Eton fives to remove its elitist image; he was instrumental in getting the word 'public' removed from the schools' competition in 1980. He wanted to introduce sponsorship –

and succeeded – and he wanted to allow Eton fives players to become professional, led by himself. His energy and drive for change undoubtedly rattled the establishment cage but, as one of the leading players, he clearly had a conflict of interests.

In many ways Tony Hughes was right: the comfortable cocoon in which Eton fives was operating at a time when other games were roaring ahead, needed to be opened up. Schools were coming under pressure to improve and expand their facilities, and bursars were looking avariciously at anything under-used. Was the EFA committee going to sit discussing the format of the Kinnaird Cup and the niceties of the 'game ball' rule while the walls of courts were crumbling around them? Hughes was asking the right questions, but his over-combative way of asking them served to divide rather than unite in rea-

Winners of the 1978 Public Schools' Trophy, John Reynolds & Richard Matthews. Tony Hughes may be seen in the background

soned debate.

On Tony Hughes's initiative, Tetrad, a new company from Preston which manufactured up-market sofas, was invited to sponsor the Midland Tournament in 1977, and in 1980 an arrangement was reached with the motor manufacturer Saab for sponsorship of the Kinnaird at Eton, the Midland in Birmingham and two tournaments specially arranged for the sponsors, the London Tournament at Harrow and the Northern Tournament at Shrewsbury. Ballantine's Whisky, a subsidiary of Hiram Walker, took over the sponsorship of the Kinnaird in 1984, 1985 and 1986 until they also were taken over and fell under new management. It may have been the prospect of a whisky-fuelled reception that produced an entry of 72 pairs in 1985. Certainly players and spectators were sumptuously entertained after the Final by the Managing Director, David Evans.

However this toe-dipping into the world of commercial sponsorship was not to everyone's taste. Indeed some of the old guard were appalled. It even forced a very sick Alan Barber, the President of the EFA, to drag himself along to a committee meeting to voice his objections to what he saw as the destruction of the amateur game as he knew it.

In 1964 Graham Turnbull, who had been Honorary Secretary of the Old Etonian Fives Club for two years, had joined the EFA Committee. From that time on he had been an increasingly influential figure in the administration of the game. In 1972 he became Honorary Treasurer, a job he carried out with tact and efficiency. His keen

John Reynolds, Kinnaird Cup Champion for a record 11 successive years 1981-91

interest in fives, his trenchant views and his diplomatic skills, made it almost inevitable that he should be elected Chairman in November 1980. Turnbull favoured a more rational approach. He realised the need for an injection of money into the game but saw that these commercial companies were likely to be little more than one-day wonders. So it proved. However, two more lasting relationships were established with more compatible partners. Holmwoods was an insurance company specialising in schools; it was perfectly logical for the company to associate itself more closely with many of the schools with whom it did business – and some more with which it would like to do business. It may also have helped that the Chairman was Colin Ingleby-Mackenzie, winner of the School Fives at Eton in 1951. In addition to their sponsorship, which has lasted for nearly thirty years and has survived its subsumption by HSBC, and more recently by Marsh Insurance, Holmwoods have given an annual dinner at the host school to which the Chairman has invited headmasters, bursars, fives masters and officers of the EFA, all with spouses. Hosted by Colin Ingleby-Mackenzie's successors, David Godfray, who initiated the event, and Peter Newnham, these have been the most genial of occasions.

Another genial event took place in 1985 when Eton and Harrow celebrated the centenary of the first inter-school match. The 12-pair school match in the afternoon was followed by a six-pair Old Etonian v Old Harrovian match and a dinner in the evening. Lord Home was the guest of honour and he and

In 1982 Wolverhampton won the Open, Under-16 and Under-14 sections of the Schools Championships. The Open Champions were Andrew Stephenson (left) and Gary Baker

the two Head Masters gave speeches.

At National Westminster Bank there was also an Etonian Chairman, Robin Leigh-Pemberton, later Lord Kingsdown, who has his own Eton fives court at his home, Torry Hill in Kent. NatWest were willing to support Eton fives but did not wish to be associated with a competition that was as clearly elitist as the Alan Barber Cup. A new competition was therefore constructed with the intention of breaking down the old school divisions and qualifying players by county of birth or residence. So the NatWest Eton Fives County Championship was born in 1981. The Semi-finals and Finals were played at Eton, NatWest hosted a reception afterwards and a dignitary from the Bank was on hand to present trophies and medals. As well as a much needed income source, the sponsorships added some style to these events.

During the next five years Graham Turnbull guided the Committee through a period of continuing expansion and some necessary innovation. In addition to the annual booklet he produced a newsletter. He introduced an 'extra-ordinary general meeting' at Eton on the first day of the Kinnaird Championships, believing that this was a way of finding out from the best and most enthusiastic players what changes they thought

there should be in the running of the game. After his term as Chairman, Turnbull reverted to being Treasurer; a widely respected counsellor, his untimely death in 1995 was a great loss to Eton fives. A man of great charm, Graham Turnbull was also a 'third pair player' but a delight to play both with and against, and it was appropriate that the Committee should instigate a competition for pairs consisting of a pupil and former pupil in his memory. Graham's widow, Kitty, took a great deal of trouble in getting Theo Fennel to design and produce a suitable trophy.

Meanwhile, inside the cocoon, schools fives was being played as keenly as ever. Forty-four pairs from fifteen schools entered the Schools Championships at Shrewsbury in 1981; this was the first time that they had been played outside the home counties and led to Shrewsbury being regularly included as a host school. In 1991 there were forty pairs but taking all the age groups together, there were 151 pairs from 17 schools. By 1999 this figure had grown to 245 pairs from twenty-three schools. The Open Championships were dominated by Wolverhampton, who were winners on six occasions between 1980 and 1993 and runners-up in three further years. Highgate and Shrewsbury, two schools where the fives has retained major game status, have always played to a high standard and Shrewsbury had the frustration of losing six finals between 1983 and 2000. Berkhamsted won in 1981, although it was to be their last success for many years, and the talented King Edward's pair, Jonathan Mole and Robin Mason in 1986. In 1988 Harrow won for the first time since 1936 and had three more wins in the 1990s, and a new name appeared on the honours board in 1997, that of St Olave's Grammar School, now in Orpington.

The arrival of girls at the traditionally boys' boarding schools did not signal a headlong rush for the fives courts. The boundaries of teenage culture can take some breaking down and fives was seen to be a boys' game. Although there were some early recruits, for the most part the girls stuck to squash, tennis and netball. In fact the involvement of girls and women in fives came along another route.

After the introduction of the leagues, there had been much criticism that there was little scope for the less competitive (and perhaps less talented) players. There was a call for friendly fives and a number of such clubs sprang up: The Hill at Harrow, The Monday Club at Shrewsbury, The Heath at Aldenham, The Village at Highgate, The Brigands at Charterhouse, and the first company team, Thorn EMI, to name but a few. The most successful and adventurous of these was The Hill, which claimed nearly forty members plus a ladies' section at one stage. They held men's and women's evenings during the week and a mixed session on Sunday morning; they played in the fourth division of the league; and they went on numerous tours, including two to Switzerland and Germany. The interesting feature of the membership was that about half had played at school – in some cases many years earlier and with no expectation of ever playing again – while the remainder were newcomers to the game, most of whom quickly became good enough to enjoy it.

It was the women's sections of these clubs that made up the nucleus of the first Ladies Tournament played at Eton in 1984. Fifteen pairs entered; four Hill pairs won through to the Semifinals and the winners were Veronica Hothersall and Krystyna Vargas. The outstanding female player was Karen Runnacles who won the tournament with various partners for eleven years in succession from 1988-98. Anyone who had thought that fives was not a game for women, that they might steer away from bruised hands and damaged nails, was soon disabused of this idea. There had also long been a myth that women could not throw a ball properly and by implication that they would not be able to cut a fives ball. This proved equally untrue and the standard of women's and girls' fives has risen steadily. Sadly the Hill Eton Fives Club came and went like a shooting star. By 1990 most of its members had retired, sustained injuries or left

the area and there was no succession. However it remains the model for 'friendly fives'.

It seems that, in the Kinnaird Cup, once a top pair has become established, it is extremely difficult to topple and so it was with Brian Matthews and John Reynolds, the Old Citizen pair who were runners-up in 1980 and then winners for the next ten years – a record which may never be repeated. They were an outstanding pair whose success was at least partly due to perfecting a style of play that suited the faster ball, which by then was being used in all Eton fives. As the ball became harder to kill in the buttress, volleying was increasingly rewarded and Matthews and Reynolds developed a style that combined a lot of volleying from the back of the court with heavily spun shots. Their strongest challengers were the Old Berkhamstedians, Dennis Firth and Malcolm Keeling, combinations of the Old

RMG Turnbull. Chairman of the EFA 1980–85

Rodney Knight. Hon Secretary of the EFA 1979–89, Chairman of the EFCT

Dale Vargas. Chairman of the EFA 1986–90, President 2001–06

Tony Hughes. Nine times Kinnaird Cup winner, administrator and ambassador for fives

Cholmeleians, Doug Wainwright, Andy Gibson and Mark Williams, and the Old Edwardians, Tony Hughes and Richard Tyler, who all took games off them, even though they remained unbeaten for more than a decade. They deserved their long run of successes, but this sort of dominance can be frustrating for aspiring challengers. Fortunately, there was a more even struggle through the 1990s when the leading Old Edwardian pair, Robin Mason and Jonathan Mole, had five wins but they were strongly challenged by the Old Cholmeleians, Eddie Wass and Jamie Halstead, who won in 1996 and 1997.

NatWest continued their sponsorship of the County Championship until 1991 but they did not leave without a parting gift. *The Eton Fives Coaching Manual*, which had been grinding to completion for several years, was finally ready for production and NatWest contributed generously to this expense. This publication edited by Richard Black was largely the work of John Reynolds. Such a manual is an essential part of any self-respecting game and its arrival was received with approval and applause. It remains the standard book of reference for all Eton fives players, more than twenty years later.

There were more losses of courts in the 1980s. In 1985 Chigwell knocked down their courts, which were right beside the playing fields, to make way for a new pavilion. Although they had a young Oxford Eton fives half-blue on the staff and they had recently spent money on refurbishment, there seemed to be little enthusiasm for the game and so this decision was not altogether surprising. A more serious loss occurred in 1986 when the City of London School moved sites from its home for over a hundred years at Blackfriars on the Victoria Embankment to nearby Queen Victoria Street. At the time this was one of the leading Eton fives-playing schools in the country with a successful school team and a flourishing Old Boys' club whose courts were the focus of Eton fives in the City. Their top pair, Brian Matthews and John Reynolds, had been the Kinnaird Cup champions for the previous

five years and would continue to hold the title for the next five; they would rank with the very best pairs of the modern era. So this was an extraordinary decision by the Headmaster, JA Boyes, and the City of London Corporation, showing what appeared to be a strange lack of awareness of the needs of their pupils. Thomas Hinde in his history of the school, *Carpenter's Children*, wrote, "It was also in keeping with his [the Headmaster's] philosophy – described by his critics as anti-elitist – that squash courts but no fives courts were included in the new building, a decision which outraged some Old Citizens." As a conciliatory gesture, space was identified for fives courts to be built at a future date (unspecified), but this has never occurred. It says much for the resilience of the Old Citizens, pupils and staff that Eton fives continues to be played on Westminster and Westway courts twenty-five years later.

Also under threat in the 1970s and 1980s was the traditional all-boy, all-boarding, privately owned preparatory school. The pressures here were largely economic: long overdue fire and safety regulations called for capital expenditure, the need to pay staff properly, provide contracts of employment, pension rights and a whole raft of bureaucratic regulations made it impossible for such schools of under 100 pupils to balance the books. So under the developer's bulldozer went St Peter's and St Wilfrid's, Seaford. Equally precarious are isolated overseas courts: the only Eton fives court in Greece, at the Anargyrios and Korgialenios School on Spetses Island, was converted into a squash court in 1980 and at the same time the court at the English School in Colombo was converted to classrooms.

King Edward VI Camp Hill modernised its courts in 1982, adding roofs and lights. The first opponents were the Swiss team, preparing for the second International Tournament; Camp Hill won the match and the Headmaster celebrated the occasion by inviting the overseas guests to a cheese and wine party. Yet only five years later the courts were demolished – fickle indeed are the whims of headmasters and governors. Three schools, Hymers Hull, Newcastle-under-Lyme High, and Rydal, decided to suspend Eton fives as a school sport – usually an ominous sign and a preliminary to the revving up of the bulldozer. Westminster City School which, like Hymers and Newcastle-under-Lyme, had shown signs of revival of interest in the 1960s also ceased playing and their two courts were lost.

Little comfort was to be drawn from the news in 1989 that Bromley County Council was renovating the court at High Elms – by then part of a public park – for a "Victorian Picnic". This court had originally been built by Sir John Lubbock for the use of his Etonian sons – who were all very good players – but the estate had since been broken up. A tournament was played on Bank Holiday Monday but the 'Punch and Judy' show drew a bigger crowd.

Jonathan Mole and Robin Mason won the Kinnaird Cup together eight times between 1993 and 2004

There were some flickers of encouragement in the general gloom: lighting was fitted in the courts at Highgate, a third court was completed at Ipswich and the other two refurbished; the courts at Lancing were renovated, as were the two courts at the Kolej Melayu in Perak, Malaysia – where the benefits were less obvious. By 1995 the new courts at Summer Fields, Oxford, came into full use and there was a strange occurrence in Norwich. For some years, since the reorganisation of the education system, City of Norwich School had been in possession of a peculiar edifice the purpose of which they could not explain, so they wrote to a sports historian for advice. He was able to inform them that they were the proud owners of two Eton fives courts – which probably left them none the wiser. Since then much work has been done to bring the courts back into use and to show the pupils what to do in them.

Perhaps the most disastrous demolition of what was a disastrous decade for Eton fives came just three years later when the lease ran out on the Cambridge courts at Portugal Place, a complex of Eton fives, Rugby fives and squash courts, and a rackets court (also used for badminton), owned by St John's College. The proposed annual rent for its continued usage was an increase from £18 to £20,000, a figure that the University authorities did not even deign to consider. At a stroke, the University was reduced to a single court, that at Magdalene College. Temporary relief was provided by The Leys School but this turned out to be just that: temporary. Money was needed more than ever and this was the trigger.

No new sponsors had been found for the Kinnaird and it was becoming clear that commercial sponsorship was not really the best way of attracting financial support for Eton fives. In 1993 the Eton Fives Charitable Trust was set up after some eighteen months of discussions with the Charity Commissioners. The founder trustee and moving force behind the Trust was Philip Curtis, a Kinnaird Cup winner (with Jimmy Biggs) in 1957, Hon Sec of the EFA Committee 1952-60 and President 1985-91, who personally covered all the legal costs of the set-up. Initially his fellow trustees were John Rimer, who became Treasurer, Dale Vargas, Rodney Knight and Derek Whitehead, who became Secretary; the Chairman, and Secretary of the EFA were ex-officio members. Although there were some restrictions imposed by the Commissioners, the broad purpose of the Trust is to enable and encourage young people to play Eton fives.

While the Trust has been unable to unlock the problem of replacing the Cambridge courts, a continuing saga that could occupy a chapter of this book on its own, its modest resources have been able to support fives in the two areas where

Eton Harrow centenary
at Harrow in February 1985

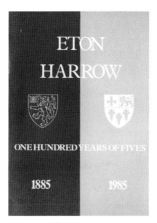

Clockwise from top left: The commemorative programme; the first pairs match in progress; the Old Etonian and Old Harrovian teams gather in sub-zero temperatures before their match; Lord Home in conversation with Dale Vargas before the celebration dinner

it could be most effective: courts and coaching.

It stretches the imagination to describe Eton fives as an international game, although the game flourishes at the Lyceum Alpinum at Zuoz, Switzerland, and among the Lyceum's former pupils, and is widely played in Northern Nigeria. There are also courts at St Paul's, Darjeeling and at Kolej Melayu, Kuala Kangsar in Asia; at Geelong Grammar School in Melbourne; at Quadra Terravista in Brazil and at Buenos Aires, Argentina. The standard of play at these centres varies from "high" to "recreational" to "occasional" and the idea of a truly international competition is fanciful. However, this did not prevent the indefatigable Tony Hughes from devising an 'international' tournament in 1981. It was later sponsored by Rolflex Doors, which certainly gave rise to a few jokes: "open and shut?"; "pre-

sumably sliding?"; "on the way out?" etc. Unfortunately the competing teams of the tournament underlined how misleading a title this was: England, England Under-21, Wales, Scotland (where there are no Eton fives courts) and The Rest of the World were supplemented by Switzerland and West Germany for two years, but then the last two failed to enter and the international flavour was lost. However it seemed to give much pleasure to the players taking part and was played six times in all, the last occasion being in 1988.

New tournaments that *have* lasted are the Mixed Doubles (men and women) and the Veterans (over-40s) both from 1985, the Fathers & Sons Tournament for the Aberconway Cup from 1991 and the Graham Turnbull Trophy for pupil and former pupil school pairings. In 2010,

Richard Black added another trophy to the collection with a cup for the Ladies Team Championships. In addition many centres such as Ipswich (1980), Aldenham (1990) and Rossall (2000) have instituted annual tournaments, largely for their own pupils, staff and alumni, but often including guest players.

In 1984 Alan Barber retired from the Presidency to be replaced by Philip Curtis. Dale Vargas, an Old Harrovian, who had played for Cambridge in 1961 and had been master-in-charge of fives at Harrow, was elected Turnbull's successor as Chairman. As he is one of the authors of this history, an objective character sketch is impossible. Let it suffice to say that under his Chairmanship a regional organisation was begun whereby established administrators were given responsibility for fives centres in different parts of the country and encouraged to organise fives activity with school, former pupil and local resident involvement. Often these were the masters-in-charge. This initiative met with mixed success: it gave rise to such clubs as The Hill and the Shrewsbury Monday Club but failed to touch some of the more remote and unsupported centres. Dale Vargas had also been responsible for attracting the two long-term sponsors, Holmwoods and NatWest, and these relationships flourished bringing long-term benefit to the game. He was less successful in managing some dissidents in the Committee and outside, who were determined to manipulate the competition rules to their own advantage, and who had a narrow view of the function of the Committee. In a bigger game these players would not have been allowed near the administration of competitions. Both Turnbull and Vargas were well served by the Old Reptonian Secretary from 1979-89, Rodney Knight, who provided much wise counsel.

In 1991 Richard Black, a graduate of Lancing College and Oxford University, became Chairman, followed, a year later, by a new President, Martin Shortland-Jones. Lancing had been a comparatively recent recruit to Eton fives (1927) and the College had not been represented on the Committee since the heady days of David Egerton in the 1930s. As Lancing is the most southerly English centre, Richard Black's election also sent a message of positive inclusion. At the time he was the Human Resources Director for Veolia Water Europe. Black's chairmanship will be remembered for finishing off the long-awaited Coaching Manual, for initiating the idea of an Eton Fives Charitable Trust, for improving the administration by the appointment of a professional Administrative Officer, for putting wind in the sails of the slowly emerging coaching agency and for encouraging the revival of a more meaningful international tournament at Zuoz in Switzerland. Perhaps most of all Richard Black will be remembered for starting the Ladies' and Mixed Championships, which he personally organised for many years. He was assisted as Hon Secretary by another devoted servant of the game, Martin Powell, who was to give many more years as the Association's Hon Treasurer.

Chapter 16
The Digital Revolution

Eton fives is not accustomed to revolutions: the change in the composition of the fives ball in 1960 was enough of an upheaval for one century, so how was it going to cope with the information technology revolution? Surprisingly, the answer is "rather well". Increased ease of communication by mobile phone, text and email and later use of social networking sites were a godsend to the long put-upon administrators, match managers and tournament organisers. In short, the new technology was embraced with enthusiasm. The Eton Fives Association website, set up by Jon Wallis and painstakingly assembled by Mike Fenn, has been able to store and allow access to a huge amount of information without one having to rifle through reams of paper. Not least of its uses has been as an invaluable resource for the writing of this history. It was later expanded to include Rugby fives and one-wall fives.

But there was another rapier thrust that was to strike at the heart of the organisation of Eton fives and it arose over the matter of the succession of the Chairman. Traditionally a smooth transfer of power had been achieved by the long tried and tested method of patronage: as the time for passing the baton

approached, the departing Chairman would have a chat with the President and any other interested parties, the candidate himself would confirm that he was willing to do the job and the proposal was carried on the nod at the next Annual General Meeting, attended by a handful of members. Not so in 1996.

Tony Hughes had decided that he would like to be the next Chairman and mounted a powerful campaign to be elected. The outgoing Chairman's nominee withdrew under pressure and as the date of the AGM drew closer there was a serious possibility that Hughes would be unopposed. Although Hughes had his supporters, many of those who had been instrumental in the develop-

The Preparatory Schools Championships began in 1968. This picture shows Gerald Barber, Headmaster of Ludgrove, the organiser, who took over from Nick Dawson of Sunningdale

ment of Eton fives thought that his election would be a disaster; it certainly would not have been uncontentious. With no obvious alternative the atmosphere verged on panic. At this point the Old Etonian Fives Club, a group not accustomed to involvement in the politics of the game, stepped in and nominated Michael Constantinidi, a long-standing and well respected member, for Chairman. Each candidate was asked to write a manifesto and there was much canvassing and lobbying before a postal ballot was conducted. Constantinidi was elected but there was ill feeling between the two camps. Some felt that Hughes had been badly treated; there were murmurings of a conspiracy and a threat to set up a rival body. Fortunately good sense prevailed and equilibrium was restored.

Michael Constantinidi became Chairman of the EFA in 1996. A winner of the School Fives at Eton in 1946 and an Oxford 'half-blue'1949-51, he had been a regular player with the Old Etonian Fives Club for many years. His election broke the mould and exposed the stagnating effect of the linear succession. His Chairmanship certainly drew the Association and the Old Etonians more closely together, to mutual benefit, but it also brought some fresh and stimulating ideas to discussions that had become moribund. Constantinidi's career in the world of advertising had taught him many lessons in business practice and one of his first steps was to arrange for the Association to be incorporated as a limited company, thereby protecting its officers and members from avoidable litigation. It was not a glamorous move but without it, should a disaster have occurred, the implications could have been huge. Thereafter, in keeping with common nomenclature, the Committee became a Board and the Committee members became Directors.

By this time the involvement of the Association in the game of Eton fives had increased multi-fold since its post-war reconvention, with two competitions and two Board meetings a year in 1948. That is not to say that there was more fives being played than in, say, 1930 but that

increasingly competitions had been drawn under the EFA umbrella. In 1997 there were a four-division league, twelve adult competitions, nine schools' competitions and an EFA fixture list of 25 matches. This was clearly stretching volunteer organisers and amateur helpers to the limit. With the creation of the website, the expansion of the *Annual Review* both in size and format to include illustrations, and increased activity in playing and coaching, the need for professional help became pressing and the decision was taken to employ a part-time Administrative Officer. Fortunately Mike Fenn, Association Secretary and founder of the Old Ipswichian Fives Club, who had been steeped in the game since before players wore short trousers, agreed to take on the job. His first task was to do some rallying of supporters. For generations, fives players had taken the arrangements made for them for granted: they played in their school courts for free and expected to enter competitions without cost too. Fenn's first job was to recruit as many as he could of the freeloaders to become members of the EFA, paying a realistic subscription.

The first decade of the twenty-first century was dogged by Government diktats and bureaucratic prescriptions and, as the culture of litigation spread from across the Atlantic, necessary precautions had to be taken. Many of these were sensible and in some cases overdue; others were either irrelevant or unnecessary. The Association was obliged to formulate policies for racial, sexual and religious equality in 2002; for child protection in 2003; and for health and safety on court in 2007 and 2008. There were petty arguments with the insurers about whether the wearing of goggles should be obligatory or voluntary – fortunately the 'voluntary lobby' got their way. In one notorious case Ofsted inspectors insisted on players in a school's courts, where the route to the courts passes through a pupils' play area, having individual Criminal Records Bureau checks. Dealing with all this took the time and energy of volunteers, who would probably have preferred to be directing their efforts to a more

In these pictures two Sunningdale pairs are playing a practice game: Above Christopher Carrelet, Musa Daura (lower step); Aaron Hanif, Toby Weatherall (top step)

obvious promotion of Eton fives.

One of the problems that has beset fives since the golden age between the wars has been that, however strong the game has been at the centre, there has been a continuous leakage at the margins. This has been compounded by the fact that all the courts belong to someone else and are beyond the control of the Association. Moreover, since the demise of the courts at the Liverpool Racquet Club, the courts at hospitals and other institutions that had been allowed to become derelict after the war, and the Queen's Club debacle, all the courts have been in schools and at Oxford and Cambridge. The Liverpool court had been converted into a squash court in 1936 and was destroyed in the Toxteth riots of 1981. While the citizens of Toxteth may have been understandably angry at losing their Eton fives court, their reaction might be considered unnecessarily extreme!

This loss of club courts has made the broadening of the game very difficult. There had been no Eton fives courts built outside schools and universities since those at Queen's Club in the 1930s and never at a centre open to the general public. It was therefore a major breakthrough when four courts were built at the Westway Sports Centre in Notting Dale, West London. This achievement was attributed by the Chairman to "an extraordinary series of coincidences and good fortune". However there is little doubt that much of the

credit must go to him personally, to Roger Matland, Director of the Westway Trust, and to Jim Cogan, Second Master at Westminster, who had for some time been advocating the idea of Eton fives as an inner city game.

The aim was to attract local schools and residents, and a development officer was appointed to generate interest. This proved to be more difficult than anticipated and two appointments and two Chairmen later, a satisfactory working programme had yet to be achieved. It was one thing to build the courts at Westway; it was quite another to attract people to play in them. Not surprisingly the old guard of Old Boys' clubs jumped at the opportunity to use another centre in London but they were not able to fill the courts all the time, nor were the courts intended for them. The purpose of Westway was to introduce a whole new cohort of players to the game, to break the mould of a game largely confined to pupils of independent schools and their alumni. This required an energetic development officer to attract these new players and coaches to teach

The opening of the new court at Ipswich in September 2009; Left to right: Gary Baker, Richard Black, Peter Boughton, Malcolm Keeling (behind), Jimmy Biggs, Mark Moore (partly obscured), Mike Fenn, Martin Shortland-Jones, Brian Matthews.

them how to play. The first two appointments made only limited progress and in 2012 this remains the single most important challenge faced by the EFA. And there still remained a second requirement: coaching.

Up to the 1950s at least, young pupils in schools were taught to play fives by senior boys and interested House Masters; there was usually some silverware on offer as a lure. This had stopped by the mid-1960s and the responsibility for recruiting and coaching fell on the master who had been designated master-in-charge of fives. This worked well if the designated master was a fives player or at least interested in learning about the game. There were also some spectacular examples of successful and devoted masters, who did not have a history of playing but who enabled fives to thrive under their direction. Sadly there were further cases, especially when neither the Headmaster nor the designated master was interested, where the game simply died.

In fact it has been proved that the single most important factor in the success of fives in a school has been the visible support of the Headmaster.

As time has gone by, there have been fewer masters with experience of Eton fives teaching in Eton fives-playing schools, and outside help has been sought. Ian Hutchinson, a talented fives player from Shrewsbury and former Middlesex cricketer, began his itinerant coaching role in 1986, before taking a long-term job at Mill Hill. His skill and enthusiasm has been crucial to the support of fives in at least eight schools but more was needed. In 1996 the Rugby and Eton Fives Coaching Agency was set up by Howard Wiseman, with the purpose of providing coaching in schools where it was needed. Early placements were at Lancing, Wellington, St Olave's and Emanuel; City of Norwich and The Leys were added the following year. By the third year, fifteen schools were being serviced by the agency, several of them playing Rugby fives. Often it has been necessary for the EFA and the Charitable Trust to provide financial support. Sometimes this has been to get a coaching scheme started; at other times it has been to help with the cost of necessary court maintenance and improvements to enable the game to be played properly. In the case of City of Norwich, a comprehensive school, financial help has also been given towards travelling to matches and tournaments.

Howard Wiseman's contribution to Eton fives has been enormous and has significantly improved the health of the game. By the early years of the 1990s the need for external coaches had become urgent: by the mid-2000s the agency was providing Eton fives coaches at about twenty schools, and the total overall has been greater than that. Howard Wiseman's agency can be said to have saved the game at, or re-introduced it to,

many of these schools; these constitute such a large proportion of fives-playing schools that it probably would not be an exaggeration to say he has single-handedly caused a revival in the game's fortunes. Many schools now playing the game have brought their courts back into use thanks to Wiseman's encouragement and support; these include Emanuel, City of Norwich, Rydal Penrhos, St Bartholomew's Newbury and Uppingham. His enlightened and measured approach has been to realise that schools need the guarantee of consistent coaching over a period of several years and other schools to play against. It is this guarantee that has encouraged schools with unused or disused courts to invest in their repair and to restore the game to their schools' activities.

Howard Wiseman's contribution has not been restricted to coaching and court restoration; he

The Westminster courts: a wonderful situation under the walls of the Abbey

Richard Black. Chairman of the EFA 1991–95; Chairman of the EFCT

Roger Beament. Hon Secretary of the EFA 1996–98. Master in Charge Fives at Highgate 1959–75

Mark Powell. Hon Secretary of the EFA 1990–95; Hon Treasurer 1995-

David Pedley. Master in Charge Fives at Wolverhampton 1978–97

ment. In 1990, Wiseman designed some well pro-portioned gloves and arranged for their manu-facture; it is these high-quality, good value, easily obtainable, Velcro-wristed gloves that almost all players now use.

On top of all this, Wiseman has improved international and inter-school relations by organ-ising trips, in which groups of sixteen or so 12-18 year-olds from as many as half a dozen schools travel to play fives at Zuoz in Switzer-land. And it was to Wiseman that the EFA and the Westway turned when they needed a fives manager for the new courts in 2003. Wiseman's energy and vision filled the courts from morning to late evening four days a week, proving the project could work with the right guidance. Without Howard Wiseman, the game would be in immeasurably poorer shape.

Little mention in this story has been made of Eton fives' sister game, Rugby fives. Since the secession of the Rugby fives section from the Fives Association in 1927, and the formation of the Rugby Fives Association, the two codes have been administered separately but there has always been a link between them. It is strange that two games so obviously similar have such a fundamental difference as the way in which the ball is hit. In the Eton game the ball is volleyed – for preference – or hit with 'cut' or 'under-spin'; in the Rugby game such shots rise from the back wall presenting an easy 'kill' and so the ball is driven with over-spin. The service is also differ-ent in Rugby fives: whereas the ball was original-ly thrown up by one of the opposition as in Eton fives, now the 'cutter' throws it up for himself. To confuse matters further, the 'cutter' has become the 'server' and scores points on his serve. Thus Rugby fives is more akin to rackets or squash, in that it is possible to serve an 'ace'. The two games have developed along their own, but parallel, lines. Several Eton fives schools have had Rugby fives-playing masters-in-charge and vice versa, while several of the best Eton players such as Kenneth Gandar Dower, David Guilford, Tony Hughes and James Toop have played

has also taken over the running of tournaments such as the Kinnaird Cup Competition, which had become so poorly attended in the mid-1990s that it attracted as few as a dozen pairs, whereas in the mid-1980s it had attracted more than seventy. Recruitment was improved to the point where a full entry of sixty-four pairs was nearly achieved in 2010. Wiseman's agency also revived the Lon-don and Midland tournaments, which had fallen out of the fives calendar completely, and initiated tournaments for under-12s and under-13s that can attract as many as eighty children.

The supply of fives gloves is another area in which Wiseman has made a major contribution. Since Slazenger stopped making gloves in the 1970s, it had been very hard to buy good-quality gloves; those available had poor proportions and bad padding. By the late 1980s, there was a sin-gle glove manufacturer for Eton fives but supply was poor and players were left using sub-stan-dard and ageing gloves. The situation was becoming critical as young players were being put off the game by the lack of proper equip-

Rugby fives to a very high level. Although the actual courts and the playing of the two games are different, there are clearly many areas of similarity and common interest. The coaching agency had provided one such example.

So in 2003 a discussion group was set up, at which three representatives from the EFA and three from the RFA met; it was known as the Fives Forum. It soon became apparent that there was much common ground and the joint production of the *Annual Review*, shared information about such matters as 'health and safety', insurance and coaching certificates, were examples where a pooling of resources made economic and time-managerial sense. Two years later the Fives Federation, a body to further the interests of all forms of British fives, was formed. It would be tempting to say that the two codes now work together hand in glove.

By this time the idea of 'one-wall fives' had been hatched – or more accurately imported from the United States. This game, popular in the inner cities, had been explored by James Toop on his 'gap year' and he came back full of enthusiasm. He saw one-wall fives, a simple game that needs no explanation here, as both an ideal inner-city playground activity and an introduction to three- and four-wall fives. So 'one-wall fives' was included as the third code to be embraced by the Fives Federation.

Most of the coaches supplied by the Agency have been young school leavers. Usually, they have been good fives players and they have been trained as coaches by Howard Wiseman, but this has been an informal arrangement and it soon became clear that a nationally recognised formal qualification as an Eton fives coach was necessary. Apart from ensuring consistency of standards, this would mean that funding agencies would take the game seriously. It is often a prerequisite that a game has to have an officially recognised coaching system in place before state or official bodies will invest in it. Mark Yates, a member of the EFA Board took a vigorous lead. With advice and guidance from Jennifer Green, who had had experience of coaching qualifications with the England and Wales Cricket Board, Yates worked with 1st4Sport (a part of Sports Coach UK) to devise a UK Coaching Certificate. This enables fives players to become coaches, and school teachers and sports coaches to become fives coaches, and has raised Eton and Rugby fives to a level of coaching qualification equal to that for cricket, football and other more widely played games. Financial support for this development was given by John Lyon's Charity, which had also contributed generously to the costs of the Westway fives courts.

By the end of the century there were real signs that Eton fives was not the anachronism that some had predicted. There were still huge challenges to be faced but there was confidence that they would be met with intelligent, ambitious and courageous responses.

Chapter 17

The Spiky Graph

2000-12

The exciting news of the birth of Eton fives at Westway was offset by disappointments elsewhere. Aysgarth Preparatory School in North Yorkshire, whose Headmasters trace back through John Hodgkinson, formerly master-in-charge of fives at Uppingham, and Simon Reynolds, an Old Etonian, to "Tommy" Thompson, an Old Harrovian, had for generations sent boys to these three schools. The two Eton and two Winchester fives courts dated back to 1890 and the 'plate' trophy in the Preparatory Schools Championships was named in memory of Jeremy Marston, who taught and coached fives there for many years. Since the retirement of John Hodgkinson, and without a fives player on the staff, Aysgarth had been playing less and less. They also considered themselves to be on the northern fringe of the Eton fives-playing world and increasingly out of touch. When pressure came to find a site for a new classroom block, the decision was predictable. The courts were demolished in 2009.

The first two Eton fives courts at Wellington were built in 1881. Three more were added in 1929 and the old ones demolished in 1946. Fives at Wellington, a school dominated by the major team games, had long lived with a low profile. Patrick Mileham, who was at the College from 1959 to 1963, recalls that it was "used as a compulsory game for defaulters". Apparently his Housemaster would often challenge "the odd boy who couldn't think of anything else to do, thinking he was offering unalloyed enjoyment as well as exercise. One learnt quickly to avoid some activities...." Giles Reynolds, who went on

to win half-blues at Oxford in 1987 and 1988, as well as a cricket blue, had a slightly more positive experience. "Fives at Wellington was very much an add-on sport. I remember playing it on Tuesdays and Thursdays after hockey and then 'sevens'. Would that I still had such energy! I found fives incredibly useful for hand-eye coordination and the angles provided an added fascination. There was a pretty small but enthusiastic core of

Richard Barber. Chairman of the EFA 2004–10; President 2010–

Mike Fenn. Hon Secretary of the EFA 1999–2009. Vice President 2010–

John Rimer. Hon Treasurer of the EFCT 1993–2010

Derek Whitehead. Hon Secretary of the EFCT 1993–2012; Vice-President EFA 2004-

players when I played and we met with reasonable success on the circuit." It appears that Giles Reynolds and his group were exceptions and, although the courts survived the creation of the Newsome Sports Complex in 1990 – and indeed were re-roofed – their demise was not far off. In 2004 the site became a café.

At Marlborough two courts remain but two have been converted into a weights room – the conversion even took the master-in-charge by surprise when he returned from his summer holidays. One of The Leys courts has become a climbing wall; the other is a canoe store.

The Oxford University team of 2003: left to right, back row: Simon Randall (Eton & Trinity), Sanjaya Ranasinghe (St.Olave's & St.John's), Hedi Young (Highgate & Worcester). Front row: James Toop (St.Olave's & Jesus), Tom Dunbar (Harrow & Balliol), Ewan Thompson (Berkhamsted & Wadham)

So the ups and downs of the spiky graph continued. In 2005 Mill Hill replaced their old courts with three beautifully appointed courts in a new development, and in 2010 the two run-down courts at the Royal Grammar School High Wycombe, built in 1918 as a memorial to the fallen in the Great War, were refurbished. Similar court improvements were carried out at Emanuel and St Bartholomew's in 2005, the latter seeing their first use for twenty years, and at Rydal (now known as Rydal Penrhos). In the most extensive programme of all, the entire block of fourteen courts at Shrewsbury has been restored to the highest standards; there was a re-opening ceremony in 2010.

The two outstanding players of the first decade of the twenty-first century were James Toop and Tom Dunbar. James Toop was a Kinnaird Cup winner three times and a runner-up five times between 2003 and 2010 with various Old Olavian partners: Chris Cooley, Matthew Wiseman and Howard Wiseman. He also record-

ed a singular success by winning the Rugby Fives Singles Championship in 2009, the first time this 'double' had been achieved since Kenneth Gandar Dower in 1929. Robin Mason, deprived of his former partner Jonathan Mole, who had begun working as a doctor in Southampton, struck up a successful new partnership with Tom Dunbar, to win again in 2002, 2003 and 2004. Tom Dunbar and his brother Peter, who had won the Schools' Championships together in 2000, then re-formed to win in 2006, 2007 and 2009.

The expansion of the Schools competitions has been matched by an explosion of adult tournaments. By 1987 there were 23 teams playing in four divisions of the League and in 1989 the EFA Trophy, a competition for less good players, was added. With the Shortland-Jones Cup for Veterans (over-40s) and the Walters Cup for over-60s, it is now possible to keep the sideboard populated with silverware right up to the threshold of senility.

Not least of Michael Constantinidi's contributions to the game was the procurement of his successor, Richard Barber, OBE, nephew of Alan. Richard Barber, an Old Salopian, had been Commercial Director of Corus, formerly British Steel, and he brought with him the skills honed in a career in industry. Richard Barber's first move was to conduct a wide consultation. He began by visiting the Headmasters of every Eton fives-playing school in the country and asking them, players, officials, coaches, club secretaries and any one with an interest in Eton fives, their opinion of the game as it existed and what they thought the way forward should be. Agreement of the objective was soon reached: "to achieve a significant and sustainable increase in the number of people, both men and women, playing Eton fives regularly wherever there are fives courts in the UK."

Having arrived at a broad consensus, Richard Barber then delegated further lines of investigation to particular individuals, each of whom reported back to the Board. Some seriously weak points in the structure were exposed. It was found that at a number of schools Eton fives was an endangered species; many clubs were operating in small cliques with no more than a handful of active players; and although there were plenty of competitions, many of them, including the Kinnaird, were poorly supported. When these reports had been analysed, a 'Strategy for Eton Fives' was published in 2005. The following needs were highlighted: strengthening the links with schools; a code of practice for masters in charge and club secretaries; arrangement of a 'coaching weekend'; introduction of a 'fives ladder'; involvement with 'one-wall fives'; and the

Cambridge University team of 2005: Simon Purkis (KES, Birmingham & Churchill), Nick Gill (City of London & Magdalene), James O'Callaghan (Highgate & Christ's). Front row L to R: Aly Patel (Highgate & Trinity), Dexter Davis (Highgate & St. Catharine's), Peter Nichols (Shrewsbury & Emmanuel)

forging of closer ties with the Rugby Fives Association through the Fives Federation.

By 2008 there were some reasons for optimism: the number of pupils taking part in the schools competitions had reached a commendable 750; work had begun on establishing nationally recognised certification for fives coaches; a new plan had been put in place at Westway; and financial support had come from the Jesters in addition to the HSBC (of which Holmwoods had by then become a part) sponsorship of the Schools' Championships and the work of the Charitable Trust. However, the Chairman also underlined three concerns that he had: first, that Eton fives was still a very fragile game in some schools – including one or two where the game had been established for generations; second, that well over 90% of school fives players were lost to the game when they left school; and third, that many of the adult clubs were being run on a very flimsy basis without proper structure.

The popularity of the Marsh Insurance Schools' Championships (the most recent re-naming of Holmwoods) has increased year by year under the direction of Mark Williams. In 2011 over a thousand boys and girls competed in the Championships at Eton. The Championships by then consisted of the following competitions: Boys' Open, Under-16, Under-15, Under-14, Under-14 Beginners, Under-13, Under-12; Girls Open, Girls Under-17 Beginners, Girls Under-15, and Mixed. Shrewsbury and Highgate established themselves as the two top schools, between them winning every competition except the Boys' Under-15s, claimed by Eton. These three schools with Harrow have been in every Open Final since 2000.

James Toop joined K Gandar Dower as the only players to have won both the Kinnaird Cup and the Rugby Fives Singles Championships in the same season

The changes in the Preparatory Schools' Competition in the forty years since its inception were not unexpected and reflected the transformation of the preparatory school world over that period. The under-100-pupil all-boy all-boarding school had virtually disappeared; the survivors had usually become co-educational, day or part-boarding schools of over 200 pupils. So St Peter's and St Wilfrid's of Seaford had closed; Stoneygate had moved to a new site (without fives courts); St Andrew's and Aysgarth had pulled down their courts and Eagle House, the Wellington junior school, had also stopped playing.

On the positive side, Summer Fields, Oxford, traditionally a strong feeder to Eton fives-playing schools, built two new courts in 1995. The other additions to the original entrants were Orley Farm (playing in the Harrow Courts), Belmont

(Mill Hill Junior School) and Cranleigh Junior School. For the first twenty years, the most successful school in the competition was Sunningdale, who won on ten occasions. Since then the competition has been dominated by Highgate Junior School, a great credit to Tony Brunner the master-in-charge, but also a reflection of the status and importance given to Eton fives in the school. In the last ten years Highgate have produced both pairs in every final.

These days, pupils join a number of secondary schools at the age of 11 and this has also affected the demographics of fives competitions: an Under-12 competition was added in 1992. Of constant concern to the organisers of Eton fives over the years has been the feed-through of players from school to adult fives. The chief problem has been, of course, that more and more school leavers have been going on to university but a smaller proportion to Oxford and Cambridge, the only British universities to have Eton fives courts. An attempt was made to overcome this by introducing a universities' championship under the auspices of the British Universities Sports Federation (BUSF) in 1984. This ran for four years and succeeded in attracting pairs from Loughborough, Birmingham, St Andrews and Warwick as well as the predictable Oxford and Cambridge entries. It foundered more because of difficulties encountered by BUSF than for any other reason. It was reinvented in 2001, this time under the British Universities Sports Association (BUSA) but again only lasted three years. A third attempt to hook this elusive fish was made in 2008, this time for the newly presented Tony Hughes Cup.

A more successful tournament has been the Under-25 Championship which has been played since 1992, and recent additions have been a

Ladies' Under-25 and both Men's and Ladies' Under-21 Championships. Whether any of these competitions has actually fulfilled the original intention of keeping more young people in the game is doubtful; it may just be giving more fives to those playing regularly already.

So the view from the bridge in 2012 is of a spiky profile. The standard of play in the top echelons of the game is higher than ever: the Kinnaird Cup Final, the later rounds of the Barber Cup and the other main competitions provide a spectacle of athleticism and skill equal to that in any amateur sport. The involvement of women and girls in the game has been a triumph and their level of skill is improving all the time. Eton fives is played in some schools more keenly and to a higher standard than ever before – but there are leakages at the margins: in other schools, principally where there is little or no support from the Headmaster, few pupils play and the future looks bleak. It is salutary to compare the current status of Eton fives at three similar Midland schools, each with a long tradition and each a one-time centre of excellence: Shrewsbury, Uppingham and Repton. At Shrewsbury, Eton fives is flourishing throughout the school: a recent expensive refurbishment of the courts was funded by enthusiastic Old Salopians; the school plays a full programme of matches at every age level and the recent introduction of girls has simply enabled them to extend the range of excellence. Where expert coaching is lacking, the school employs outside coaches; over fifty pairs travel to Eton or Highgate for the Schools Championships.

At Uppingham on the other hand, the game is fragile, limited to pupils in just a few Houses. The courts are reduced to four in number and two slightly smaller courts attached to one House; there is a constantly changing rota of young masters-in-charge and although there are matches and

pairs do occasionally enter for the Schools Championships, they rarely achieve success.

Repton no longer plays school matches at all and although the block of twelve courts, the fifth largest number in the country, is maintained in good order, they are used for internal play only – not a regime designed to inspire young players. It seems that in the Spring term hockey is king – and soccer is crown prince. The experienced master-in-charge feels that he and fives are "victims of the siren call of specialisation".

Eton faced the challenge of a declining game with fewer masters to support it in an altogether more positive way. The Old Etonian Fives Club stepped in with financial support for a professional coach, sharing his salary with the school.

Oxford University Ladies 2009: Front row (L to R): Rosie Scott (Lancing & Magdalen) and Juliet Browning (Lancing & St.Peter's); Behind L to R: Hannah Cutmore-Scott (Westminster & Christ Church) and Emma Černis (Berkhamsted & St.Edmund Hall)

A Ladies Championships match from 2010 between Natalie Lilienthal (top step) and Charlie Farquharson-Roberts in white and Rosie Scott (top step) and Ashley Lumbard

where there are so many opportunities to spread the game – and so much need for meaningful, skill-enhancing, physical activity.

No account of Eton fives should fail to mention the huge part played by the Jesters. Founded in 1928 and expanded to include Eton fives in 1931, it has long been the only national 'open' club, and although squash has far outstripped the other court games, the Jesters have remained faithful to the intentions of its founder and embraced all its constituent games equally. The Jesters has maintained its missionary role, playing all Eton fives schools and in recent years has made generous grants to the EFA in support of the Universities and Under-25 Championships, and the Westway initiative. Its contribution to the continuing advance of Eton fives is immeasurable.

Media coverage of Eton fives is rare these days and usually only occurs when there is a particularly interesting story to tell. The days when the names and scores of every match submitted were published in the sports summary section of *The Times* and *Daily Telegraph* ended in the 1960s. Occasional references to Eton fives do pop up in unexpected places: Giles Coren, who among his many guises is a restaurant critic for *The Times*, has mentioned the game on more than one occasion.

Social fives outside the structured clubs and competitions is more difficult to assess because it is not recorded. There is not much 'country house fives' of the sort enjoyed in the 1920s and 1930s any more and nearly all fives is played on school courts. Even there the prescriptive tenta-

This has worked well and the generosity of the benefactors is to be applauded; the standard of fives at Eton and the number of boys playing have both risen significantly. Unfortunately such a rescue package is unlikely to be replicated elsewhere, simply because the resources of most Old Boys' clubs would not extend that far.

Stimulating and maintaining play in a minority school sport like fives is difficult without support; it is particularly difficult in schools that are on the fringes. Especial credit, therefore, must go to those at St Bees in Cumbria, Bryanston in Dorset and Rydal Penrhos in North Wales, and encouragement to Dover College.

Westway is an open question: at the time of writing, its success is not assured and there has been no breakthrough into the inner city schools

cles of modern life have found their way: not only are schools (quite rightly) expecting payment for the use of their facilities – something fives players have not been used to – but child protection legislation is threatening visitors to school premises, a point made by Giles Coren. That would be prohibitive and one can only hope that common sense will prevail. It would indeed be tragic if Eton fives turned out to be ambushed by a trip-wire of political correctness.

Meanwhile, there was an interesting sideline on court construction being explored by Nigel Cox and John Reynolds. One of the drawbacks to the building of new courts has been their cost, which is way beyond what one would expect for a simple structure and has been comparable to the cost of a small apartment. Cox had built two Eton fives courts – or to be more accurate one Eton fives court and a mirror image with the buttress on the right hand wall – at his home in Provence. Reynolds, Cox and his wife Jennifer Green, who ran a sports management consultancy, formed the Fives Court Company to develop some revolutionary ideas. Any means of reducing the cost would have to involve using methods

and materials different to those adopted by standard builders. The Fives Court Company produced a prototype prefabricated Eton fives court, which opened up opportunities that had hitherto appeared closed. The prototype court found its way to a private buyer and is now at the home of the Shawcross family at Friston Place in East Sussex. Meanwhile work on the commercial production of more such courts is in progress.

After seven years as Chairman, Richard Barber stood down in 2010. Again Eton fives was fortunate in his successor. Peter Worth, a Public Schools' Champion with Nick Pocock in the Shrewsbury pair of 1970, had spent his working life first with the sports management company IMG and latterly leading his own company, Quintus. He had a wealth of experience to bring to the game. Peter Worth's arrival followed Mike Fenn's handover of the administration to another Old Ipswichian, Gareth Hoskins.

There was much unfinished business to address: the matter of Westway; how to achieve an acceptable usage rate for the courts, but more especially how to attract the target group, inner city school children, had yet to be resolved,

Ladies Championships 2011. The winners were Kerry White (extreme left) and Dominique Redmond (on the right in the back row) who beat Charlotte Cooley and Marianne Rees in the final

Oxford University Ladies 2011. Back row (L to R): Emily Cornish (Benenden & Christ Church), Antonella Gorenflos (Oxford High School & Exeter), Constance Mantle (Highgate & Exeter), Hannah Cutmore-Scott (Westminster & Christ Church) . Middle row (L to R): Joanna Mason (Tiffin Girls' & Exeter), Izzy Watts (Woodbridge & Keble), Alice Walker (Shrewsbury & Lady Margaret Hall), Kate Millar (Marlborough & Lady Margaret Hall), Gina Ford (Westminster & Keble). Front row (L to R): Harriet Allan (Westminster & Queen's), Sophie Cowen (St.Mary's Shaftesbury & Exeter), Harriet Asquith (Wycombe Abbey & Corpus Christi)

attention of the board. The Charitable Trust, under the Chairmanship of Rodney Knight from 2002, has continued to provide a trickle of funding, boosted by occasional capital injections from legacies. These were almost entirely spent on sweeteners to schools for coaching and court maintenance. Holmwoods, later HSBC, had grown yet another skin and become Marsh Insurance and had continued their support. The new Chairman immediately noticed that a third source of income, perhaps the most fundamental of all, was woefully inadequate: members' subscriptions.

It has already been pointed out that generations of players had enjoyed Eton fives for the cost of travel and a pint after the game; most of them did not even belong to the Association.

although some local academies were showing interest. The work on establishing a national coaching certificate involved a huge amount of bureaucracy and was grinding ahead; the first actual courses took place in autumn 2011. Quite apart from the obvious need for a proper qualification for the games coaches – and the necessary safeguards that that implies – this is a step towards an appeal for lottery funding, which could lift Eton fives to a whole new level.

Financial matters continued to command the This just had not happened in any other game and needed to be put right. The Board therefore took three steps: first, they set themselves a target to double the membership, standing at less than 500 at the time, in four years; second, they insisted that any player entering an EFA-sponsored competition should be a member; thirdly they began to follow the Rugby Fives Association's lead in moving towards charitable status. Acceptance as a charity would effectively increase the subscription income by about a third.

Chapter 18

The Sardauna's Game

Eton Fives in Nigeria

One of the more curious legacies of the British Empire is the spread of Eton fives to Northern Nigeria. It is generally accepted that the first Eton fives courts in Nigeria were built in 1922, but the game there has developed along such a different path that there must be some doubt as to whether the versions played in the UK and Nigeria can be classified as the same game. However Eton fives is a broad church and there are many courts in the UK that vary significantly from those at Eton College yet are accepted to be Eton fives courts. One thinks of those at Rossall and St John's Leatherhead as particular examples of variations, but one must also realise that insisting on some concept of 'purity' would leave very few centres passing the test.

In 1922 JS Hogben, who was teaching at the Provincial Secondary School in Katsina, proposed and supervised the building of two mud courts, complete with ledges and buttresses, at Birnin Kebbi. This was the school where the Sardauna of Sokoto and a number of his Ministers were educated. The prime mover was the Premier of the Northern Region at that time, Alhaji Ahmadu, Sardauna of Sokoto, and for some years fives was known as 'The Sardauna's Game'. Although the original courts are in a state of decay, they have been augmented by three concrete courts.

Hogben had been in the Fives VI at Highgate in 1916, and was in Northern Nigeria from 1922-33; later he returned to London as Senior Lecturer at Goldsmith's College. In his book, *An Introduction to the History of the Islamic States of Northern Nigeria*, there is a photograph of the original mud courts. In his foreword to the book, Sir Ahmadu Bello, Sardauna of Sokoto, who was assassinated during the first Nigerian coup in January 1966, wrote about fives: "Not only is this my favourite recreation, but it is a game which has continued to grow in popularity in many parts of the country and has given pleasure and relaxation to thousands of people both young and old."

The essential difference in Eton fives as played in Nigeria is that there it is played with a tennis ball and bare hands. The reasons for this are both historical and cultural: Hogben's first courts and many later were built of mud and the standard Eton fives ball (at the time) marked and left indentations on the walls. His decision to use a tennis ball was pragmatic but also removed the need for protective gloves. Since that time courts have been built in brick and plaster but the suggestion that players should then conform to UK practice has been resisted on several grounds. First, as many mud courts still exist, it would be unsatisfactory to have two forms of Eton fives being played; second, the cost of Eton fives balls and gloves would put the game out of the reach of many young players; and third, in the climate of Northern Nigeria gloves are an unfamiliar item of clothing, which would have to be specially made.

Up until ten years ago there were Eton fives courts in eight of the thirty-six States of Nigeria, and also in the Federal Capital Territory. With the exception of the courts in Lagos, these were all to be found in the north-west quarter of the country. Most of the courts are in townships rather than in schools and are in use all the year round from dawn to dusk, seven days a week.

As spectators seem to be more important than the players, who are perceived as mere gladiators, courts in Nigeria all have a long run-out space terminating in a spectator stand. Tournaments draw important dignitaries such as Governors and Ministers and on such occasions the number of spectators will often exceed 500; the ceremonies involve speeches, refreshments and in some cases splendid cultural dances.

The first Eton fives courts were built at Birnin Kebbi Provincial School in 1922, at the instigation of JS Hogben, who had played at Highgate

There are about thirty Eton fives clubs. The premier competition is the annual Sardauna Challenge Cup Tournament, which is organised by the Fives Association of Nigeria (FAN) and is rotated among the States. The main Trophy was donated by Sir Ahmadu Bello, Sardauna of Sokoto, in 1959.

The first winners of the Sardauna Cup in 1960 were the Sardauna Fives Team, Kaduna, followed a year later by the Sokoto Fives Team. Between 1962 and 1985 the competition only took place on one occasion but it then returned to the fives calendar on a regular basis. The most successful team has been the Katsina Fives Club with six wins up to the year 2003, followed by the Gwandu Fives Club from Birnin Kebbi with four wins. A new event is a competition at the National Sports Festival, held every two years.

Over the years there have been several tours from England to Nigeria, and there have been a number of return visits too. In 1960 the Head Master of Eton, Dr Robert Birley, and the Sardauna of Sokoto, arranged a fives exchange between Eton and Nigeria. In January 1961, four

Etonians: GWP Barber, TP Shaw, JGM Walsh and WD Robson and the master-in-charge of fives, Mr SJ McWatters, flew to Kano for a ten-day tour. New courts were specially built in Zaria and Katsina for their visit, which was also timed to coincide with the final rounds of the inaugural Sardauna Cup Tournament, played at Kaduna. Not surprisingly, playing with a tennis ball and bare hands in temperatures of over 35°C, the two Etonian pairs lost their games on the first day but they steadily improved, drawing on the second day before winning at Katsina and Kano. Additional unexpected features were two referees for each court, a loudspeaker commentary and a phalanx of reporters and photographers. The Etonians were an integral part of the evening's ceremonies involving several hundred people.

The visit was then reciprocated with two boys from Sokoto Provincial Secondary School and two from the Government Technical Training School visiting Eton. Matches were played against Eton, Highgate, Charterhouse and Shrewsbury.

Four years later, the EFA was invited to send a

The courts at Sokoto Provincial School were built in 1923. These courts were made of mud that became pitted by the hard fives ball; this was then replaced by a tennis ball

who all those years ago had introduced the game to Nigeria with the first mud courts. Highgate won the match with the hard ball 2-1 but comfortably lost the follow-up match with tennis balls. Roger Beament wrote in a match report, "The [Highgate] boys were surprised by the speed of the Nigerian cuts and the Nigerians recovered well with some spectacular and occasionally unusual shots. The Nigerians hit the ball with a loose wrist which gives the shots considerable power, though less control. The Nigerians were much improved compared with their tour of 1961, and it was very entertaining, interesting fives which was played with a most pleasant spirit." They also played some matches in the Midlands against the Old Edwardians, King Edward's and Shrewsbury, and at Eton. In London they played the Old Citizens and they finished with matches against the Jesters (at Harrow), Lancing, the EFA (at Eton) and Westminster. With the hard ball the Nigerians managed to win three matches (Shrewsbury, Eton, Westminster) and draw one (Lancing), while with the tennis ball they proved unbeatable, only the Old Edwardians producing a close result.

party to tour Nigeria: the team selected was David Guilford, David Barton, Gordon Stringer, Martin Shortland-Jones, Monty Moss, Tony Baden Fuller and Anthony Negretti. The team travelled some 1,200 miles by road and played nine matches at Zaria, Sokoto, Birnin Kebbi, Gusau, Kano and Katsina. As David Guilford later wrote, "At each place the players were received at the palace with feudal splendour by the Emir and his Council in their robes of many colours; costumes and backcloths might well have been by courtesy of Kismet or the Arabian Nights. Even if the Emir could speak English, as most of them could, Hausa was spoken through an interpreter, and once accustomed to this novel style of communication the conversation flowed easily." Such was the interest in the tour that the players appeared twice on national television.

For the return visit in October 1966, the Nigerian tour party was MM Lagos, A Sambo, Y Abba, A Udu, H Ibrahim, S Musa and M Gayya. The team had a week's training camp in Nigeria and were entertained by the Deputy British High Commissioner in the North before setting off from Kano. Their first match was against Highgate, where one of the spectators was JS Hogben,

The Nigerian Civil War of 1967-70 led to some years without contact between the EFA and the FAN but news was received in 1975 from the Kaduna Club. The game had lost some of its former popularity since the overthrow of the last civilian regime but the players were doing their best to persuade the federal government to accord the game national recognition. Inter-state competitions were being held and although the Sardauna Cup was not being competed for, others were. Alhaji Abbas Dabo Sambo had donated a cup, which was intended for an annual inter-state championship, and Alhaji Tanimu Saulawa donated another cup for the North Central State (now Kaduna State) Championship. Kaduna were the strongest team in 1975 with Kano and Sokoto Clubs their greatest rivals. Tennis balls were still being used although there was a wish to revert to the hard ball.

In December 1988 Tony Hughes and Richard Tyler embarked on a three-week tour in which they played in the seven main centres. They found that many of the courts were by then built of brick and that the Nigerians had been busily practising with the fives gloves and balls that had been sent out in advance. Hughes and Tyler experienced all the predictable cultural shocks: the pre-match and post-match ceremonies; the presence of various dignitaries, whose importance far outweighed that of the players; the spectator stand brimming with up to a thousand faces; the dominance of the umpire; the television cameras, the interviews and the closing prayers. It must have been quite disconcerting, even if they were prepared for it. Matches were played with both hard and soft ball. Unsurprisingly the British pair found that they were usually outclassed with the tennis ball but generally gave a good account of themselves with the hard ball. Afterwards they wrote, "We certainly felt that we had, after many years, re-established links with a country that is keen to develop the game, both nationally and internationally. Indeed, during our visit to Sokoto, the local District Commissioner sanctioned the building of thirty new courts in the town over the next twelve months."

One of the British pair's matches had been played against the local champions at the Governor's palace in Katsina: "The Governor of the State, on the evidence of one hard ball game, was convinced that his pair would return to England in March and win the British championship. We therefore accepted the challenge, on behalf of the Eton Fives Association. There was, however, a greater lasting benefit to the game, in that the State Governor decided, simply on the spot, to build two further courts in the town to host the

State championships later on in the year. Such is the rapid development of fives in Nigeria."

Later in that same year, 1989, the Katsina team made the trip to England to mount their challenge for the Kinnaird Cup. The party consisted of two players, Muazu Turaki and Abdu Mamman, and two officials, Dr Yushau Armiyau, Chairman of the Katsina Fives Association and Adamu Yakabu, Secretary of the Fives Association of Nigeria. Their experience of the recent Hughes and Tyler visit and the belief in their own ability had convinced them that they would win the trophy. An opening match was played at King Edward's, Birmingham, and it was immediately obvious that the Nigerians were less at home in England than in their own country but, despite this, they achieved a two-all draw against Hughes and Tyler. The following week they played at Highgate and performed very creditably, beating four strong club pairs and only losing to Brian Matthews and John Reynolds, the reigning Kinnaird champions. Their prospects for the championships looked bright. Unfortunately, however, a dispute had arisen between the Nigerian officials and the players and when it came to the Kinnaird, the Katsina pair deliberately lost every game and were ignominiously eliminated in the first round. This was a huge disappointment to the many who had invested time and money into their visit and to Hughes and Tyler in particular. On return to Nigeria, Muazu Turaki and Abdu Mamman were disciplined by the Association and received a life ban. It was a very sad end to what had been such a potentially exciting episode.

Through the 1990s, reports of the Sardauna Cup were sent by Adamu Yakabu, Secretary of FAN, for publication in the EFA *Annual Review*. In spite of the difficulties in organising a national championship with limited resources in a country the size of Nigeria, enthusiasm usually wins the day. In the last decade the National Sports Festival, in which Eton fives plays a significant part, has been a vehicle for a rapid expansion of the game, which is no longer limited to the north-west states. In 2006 the venue was Ogun State, just north of Lagos, and a new court was built there for the event. Seventeen states were represented in the 2007 National Schools Sports Festival, including Abia, Edo and Imo in the south; Ekiti, Lagos, Ogun, Osun and Oyo in the southwest; and Plateau in the east of Nigeria. No doubt new courts have sprung up in all these other states as well: a situation at which observers in the UK can only marvel.

Although there have been no more reported visits between the two Associations in the last twenty years, it has not been for want of trying: numerous initiatives have foundered on the rocks of bureaucracy. But it would appear that Eton fives in Nigeria continues to flourish. The following description of Nigerian fives appeared in a Reuters article in June 2011 and gives a flavour of the modern game in the country:

> In a dusty Nigerian park, dozens of youths dodge goats and rusting cars to be first on to crumbling courts built to replicate the side of the chapel at one of England's most elite Public Schools so that they can play the ancient game of Eton fives. Introduced nearly a century ago, this peculiar form of handball pulls in the crowds in impoverished Nigeria, "An English schoolteacher may have brought the game here but Nigerians are the best now," said Usman Yusuf, a

civil servant and local Eton fives favourite in the northern state of Katsina, where many people live on less than $2 a day. "We love it. Every day after school we come here and fight to get on the court," said Yusuf, standing in front of crowds of barefooted schoolchildren shouting instructions to players dashing around graffiti-covered courts.... "It looks simple but it has subtle skills that take

Eton fives in modern Nigeria

intelligence. This is why Nigerians are so good at it," Umar Kabir, the secretary to the Emir of Katsina state, told Reuters. "The Emir has a court in the palace and every evening he goes out to play. He still plays to win. ...Some people here don't have much but you can see how the children are when they play the game, so we'll always keep the courts ready for them," Kabir said. "Nigeria loves fives."

Tony Hughes and Richard Tyler in ceremonial dress, Nigeria 1988

Chapter 19

The Spencer Legacy

Eton Fives in Switzerland & Germany

It requires a strange eye for architecture to consider a row of Eton fives courts to be an object of beauty. Be that as it may, the setting of the courts at the Lyceum Alpinum, just outside the tiny village of Zuoz and not far from the winter resort of St Moritz, is spectacular. The view from the courts across the Upper Engadin Valley is nothing short of stunning. In 1923 Mr Edward Gordon Spencer, who had been appointed Games Master, was responsible for the construction of three Eton fives courts at the Lyceum. These courts, known as the Rondell courts, are within the complex of the school buildings and are approached through an attractive stone archway. Plaques at the side of the courts show that the first House Fives Championships were held in 1923, and provide an immediate link with England since one of the first school pair that year was Nigel Blakstad, a schoolboy from King Edward's School, Birmingham.

One does not immediately associate the English games of cricket and fives with the Swiss Alps. Indeed the climate forces fives and football to become summer sports; in the winter the football field is flooded for ice hockey and skiing is the major sport. Flat ground is at a premium at 1700 metres in the Upper Engadin Valley and grass a rarity, but this did nothing to deter Mr Gordon Spencer.

Cricket is played on an artificial wicket set in an outfield, whose main crop is plantains, down by the river, which is more of a fast-rushing stream at this altitude. The first fives courts were built without roofs in the belief that in winter a glass roof would not withstand the frequently experienced weight of snow.

Such was the enthusiasm of 'Bones' Gordon Spencer that the pupils of the Lyceum embraced both Eton fives and cricket with alacrity. In the early days all competition had to be internal but Gordon Spencer soon began to organise tours to Britain: the 1929 tour, just six years after the courts had been built, included matches at Eton, Harrow, Lancing and Stowe, and also against the Old Citizens. The Old Citizens' match was played at Queen's Club and it was reported that "the Swiss team were very keen and promise to

The Rondell courts at the Lyceum Alpinum, Zuoz are right in the centre of the school. The view across the Upper Engadin Valley is spectacular

Edward Gordon Spencer

Edward Gordon Spencer (1889-1963). To think that cricket and Eton fives are the ideal activities for a school perched on the side of a mountain in the Alps, one either has to be a hopelessly optimistic fanatic or completely mad. It was Edward Gordon Spencer who was responsible for introducing both these games to the Lyceum Alpinum at Zuoz in 1923. So who was he? Where had he gained his love of these games? Where did he come from and what was his background?

Tracing Edward Gordon-Spencer's background proved to be more difficult than it might have been, because he not only changed his name by deed poll; he also changed his 'known name'. The Old Members' Records Office at Exeter College, Oxford found that there had indeed been a Gordon Spencer at the College: Ernest Gordon Spencer was the "first son of The Rev John Spencer Jones" and had been educated at Taunton School and in Zurich; he matriculated in October 1925.

Taunton School's records confirm that Ernest Spencer Jones and his brother Vernon Orlando Jones left in December 1908. Vernon Jones went on to "an International School". Incidentally, it was in 1909 that Taunton School opened a three-walled fives court (without a step or buttress, as far as one can see from the only available photograph).

What happened to Ernest Spencer Jones in the next fifteen years is unknown: he may have taken a degree at Zurich University but he certainly spent some time in Zurich as a private tutor of the Schwarzenbach family, who were

alumni of the Lyceum Alpinum. Presumably he joined the teaching staff at the Lyceum. And he changed his name....

Then it seems that he went up to Oxford at the age of 37. The Oxford University Archive confirmed that Ernest Gordon Spencer matriculated from Exeter College on 5 November 1925. On the form he filled in at the time, he signed himself as Ernest Gordon Spencer-Jones and stated that he had been previously educated at Zurich University. The graduate register recorded that he changed his name from 'Spencer-Jones' to 'Spencer' by deed poll. He was admitted for a B.Litt by the Faculty Board of Medieval and Modern Languages and his branch of study is recorded as being the relation between English and Swiss Literature in the eighteenth century. The records at Lancing College and Westminster School show that an EJ Gordon Spencer played fives against these schools for Oxford in 1926. At Westminster he and his partner GE Buckley were beaten 15-1, 15-3, 15-7, suggesting at best a mediocre standard.

Gordon Spencer allowed his academic course to lapse and he was readmitted in 1929. The Archivist was unable to find, however, any record of Ernest Gordon Spencer having applied for examination or having the B.Litt conferred upon him by the University.

So it seems that Edward Gordon Spencer was actually Ernest Spencer Jones from Pontypool in Wales, educated at Taunton School, but this sheds no light on why he thought the Lyceum Alpinum should have Eton fives courts in 1923. But what a legacy!

reach a high standard of fives".

A return visit to the Lyceum was undertaken in 1933 by a pair described as representatives of the 'British Fives Association' – probably one of the first EFA teams. By then Swiss visits to the UK had become annual events. Maybe they had aroused the disapproval of Herr Rektor, as Gordon Spencer chose to describe them as "tours of study"; they included cricket coaching at Somerset CCC and fives matches against various schools and clubs.

Inevitably, the war brought an interruption to these visits but in October 1954 the Old Citizens EFC made their first visit to Zuoz. Two years later they noticed "an extraordinary advance in the standard of play and keenness" and players from the Lyceum did, in fact, participate in the English Public Schools Championships in both 1956 and 1957. A Highgate pair visited Zuoz in 1958 and the Old Citizens, through the efforts of their enthusiastic Hon Secretary, Gordon Stringer, continued to make annual visits into the 1960s. Berkhamsted School, under master-in-charge Paul Dicker, also became regular visitors at this time. These contacts spread to Eton, Harrow, Birmingham's Old Edwardians, Highgate, Westminster, City of London School and Cranleigh.

The winter of 1961 was severe in Switzerland

– even by their standards – and by March there was still snow to a depth of five feet in the fives courts. This exonerated the original planners, who had been loath to fit glass roofs to the courts, but by then technology had advanced and the proposal was made to rebuild the courts on a different site, with an additional two courts, all to be covered and lit. In fact that plan changed and on the death of Mr Gordon Spencer in 1963, the Old Zuozers Club decided to erect a further three courts in his memory. In 1965 these were constructed on a site away from the school buildings and are known as the 'Spencer courts'. The Lyceum now has six standard Eton fives courts – more than in most British schools.

In 1978 Tony Hughes began a series of annual two-week visits to Zuoz to give the boys intensive coaching. Initially he was assisted by Richard Lambert and later by Richard Tyler. The Zuoz Fives Club reported that "this helped immeasurably to maintain a fair standard at the School and to ensure a flow of younger players. As many other sports are played at Zuoz such as athletics, tennis, field hockey, football and, as the fives courts are covered with snow during winter, Eton fives can only be kept flourishing by constant efforts such as those made by Tony Hughes."

The Old Zuozers continued to make periodic

The Old Zuozers' courts at Geeren near Zurich. The second court was added on the site of the former pigsty in 2001

The two Eton fives courts at Veigny, near Geneva, were built as part of a sports complex in the 1990s

Whitsun weekend trips to England where regular hosts were Tony Hughes of the Old Edwardians and Dale Vargas of the Hill Club at Harrow. From time to time Zuoz players also participated in both the Midland Tournament and the Kinnaird Cup. By 1981 the general standard of play had reached a very good level and girls had started to play. In April of that year, the Keeper of Fives, Christof Marpmann, went to England for individual coaching prior to the International Team Championships, which were held at Eton College in May. Together with G Paffrath, the pair represented Germany in these championships and M Hoegl and T Luxemberger were selected for the Rest of the World side. Although these players met with little success in the Tournament, they gathered a wealth of experience which was greatly to their benefit and to the development of fives at Zuoz.

A report from the college in 1981 noted that, "The game is played with enthusiasm, the Rondell courts being constantly in use, and the lighting facilities enable the game to be played throughout the darker evenings. The coaching has produced several up-and-coming young players... the standard of today's fives is higher than ever before."

The first Engadin Challenge Tournament was played at Zuoz on the 12 and 13 September 1992. This was the largest and most international fives tournament ever held in continental Europe with twenty-six pairs. Men and women from Switzerland, Germany, the United Kingdom, France, Italy, the Netherlands, Austria, Brazil, Peru, Singapore and Finland participated; many of these players were of course former pupils at Zuoz. The winning pair was G Stucki and G Turner. The tournament continues to be held at regular intervals.

The Lyceum Alpinum now visit England regularly to participate in the Schools Championships and in recent years the girls have been particularly successful, reaching the Final twice before F Kuenburg and S Becker won the Ladies' Trophy in 2009.

The enthusiasm for fives at Zuoz did not stop at school and in 1963 the inaugural meeting of the Zuoz Fives Club Zurich was held in the

Restaurant Geeren on the outskirts of Zurich. Edward Freytag was elected President and Johnny Grob as Honorary Secretary. Thanks to a gift from Andres Bechtler's father, the Old Zuozers (as they styled themselves) were able to build a court at Geeren in the following year. This was on the edge of a farm field and visitors to the court will chiefly remember it for its position next to a pigsty. Not only were the squeals of delight from the fives court replicated in the sty next door but the various flying and stinging insects that besieged the pigs found sweating fives players equally attractive. The court was roofed and lighting added in 1971. Great relief was provided when a second court was opened on the site of the former pigsty in 2001; the court was built of 'poured concrete' and is thought to play particularly well. Over the years Zurich has become the main fives centre for the Old Zuozers.

Several Old Zuozers built Eton fives courts at their private homes: the Veicht family built a court in the grounds of their residence in Salzburg in the 1920s. The house was later sold and became the Hotel Monchstein but some time later part of the hotel grounds including the court was sold off and a private house built on the site. The court was still useable in 1958 but by 1984 it had become a wood store. The current owner, the proprietor of a jeweller's in the centre of Salzburg, was more than a little surprised when some English tourists started asking probing questions about her wood store.

Fürst Fugger-Babenhausen, another Old Zuozer, built an Eton fives court in the grounds of his schloss at Wellenburg, near Augsburg in 1954. Two years later the Old Citizens played there in a "Grand Festival of Fives", a triangular contest between teams of Old Zuozers, Wellenburgers

Mark Mettler and Seb Galperti, winners of the Engadin Challenge in 2000

(foresters on the estate) and England, represented by the Old Citizens. The local players had only experience of playing among themselves and found the English style of play confusing. The Old Citizens continued to visit annually and in 1959 found that the court had been much used by foresters – fortunately for its proper purpose, unlike the foresters of Salzburg. This visit led to the employment of Old Citizen, Geoff Bates, as tutor in mathematics and Eton fives to the Fugger-Babenhausen children. There were grandiose plans to build further courts in Zurich, Munich and Milan but ultimately only the former became a reality.

The Zuoz-Rhineland Eton Fives Club in Hansa-Allee, Dusseldorf, had a short life. Richard and Edward Dorrenberg erected two courts at their May-Dorrenberg factory manufacturing motor parts in 1982. Unfortunately the company went into liquidation in 1985 and the courts went the way of the factory.

The Underberg Schnapps family presented a sports ground to the city of Rheinberg and included an Eton fives court. The court is part of the Rheinberg Turn und Sportverein Club and is available to the public. Several clubs have stopped off there on their drive through Germany and the Hill EFC made two visits in 1983 and 1984. They found fifteen or so regular players at Rheinberg and all, uniquely on the continent, with no Zuoz connection. As at Geeren, the fives club had forged a link with a nearby hostelry, Gasthof Prophet, and a cabinet in the bar displayed some Eton fives memorabilia. Both venues were used for the German Championships, which were first played in 1980. These lasted for five years but ended with the demise of the Dusseldorf courts. C Marpmann and G Paffrath won on three occasions and W Ahrens and H Muller once.

In the late 1920s, two other schools in Switzerland followed the Lyceum's lead and built Eton fives courts: Alpine College, a preparatory school at Arvey just outside Villars near Bex, had one court but the school no longer exists. Institut Montana at Zugerberg near Zug built four courts at about the same time; the Old Citizens played there "unofficially" in 1961 and were asked to give an exhibition game the following year. By 2005 two of the courts were declared derelict, the other two remain intact. Of the playable courts, one is used as the groundsman's shed, a story that is all too familiar; the other is currently the official school smoking area. This is a new departure: in the UK, school courts are regularly used as **unofficial** smoking areas, but 'official': that's a new concept. There appears to be some enthusiasm for re-establishing fives at the Institut.

The Geneva branch of the Old Zuozers built two Eton fives courts in Veigy, near Geneva, as part of a sports complex during the 1990s. There is now a festival of fives held there each year, too.

If these courts had been the only legacy of Edward Gordon Spencer, it would be already a remarkable achievement, but former pupils of Zuoz are spread far and wide – even as far as South America. The date of the court built by Curt Lindemann in Buenos Aires is not known, although it was certainly before 1985. The extent of its use is also unknown but apparently the court is situated in a factory and access is by climbing over a wall. In a sharply contrasting location is the "Maybud Fives Court" at Terravista Golf Club, Bahia, Brazil. This court, located near to the clubhouse, was built by Orlando Kohn Martinez, Director of Terravista, and was opened in 2008. It was named in honour of Cyrus Maybud, who arrived from Europe with fifteen other Old Zuoz players for the opening event. Dr Michael Rumpf Gail, President of the Terravista Complex, participated in the opening game.

Fives in the Rondell courts at the Lyceum Alpinum, Zuoz

Chapter 20

Whither the Rolling Circle?

Although a history must by definition look back, it would be wrong to end this story of Eton fives giving an impression of termination or closure. In the small corner of the world in which it operates, fives is a thriving game – but it is a small corner – and so it is instructive to try to trace back through its history to see what factors have led to its popularity or demise, and to try to gain some directives as to its future. Let us return to Thomas Gray's question at the beginning of Chapter 3: "Whither the rolling circle and the flying ball?"

It is interesting to note that, apart from association football, very few games are played worldwide. Of the other great Victorian team games, cricket is still confined to the former British colonies, and rugby, although it has a similar former colonial base, has only spread across parts of Europe with outposts in Argentina and Japan. Hockey is the third most widely played game (after soccer and cricket) and has gained this position by modern technology more than perhaps any other game: the artificial pitch has become a *sine qua non*. The North American games of baseball and American football clearly have the same genesis as cricket and rugby but they have taken different turnings and are not widely played outside their homeland.

This gives us the first clue as to why the seed of a game germinates: natural conditions. The

Lord Kingsdown has his own Eton fives court at Torry Hill. He has been Patron of the EFA since 1997

reason why the Calcutta Cup was sent to the UK for competition between England and Scotland was because the grounds of Bengal were found to be most unsuitable for the game of rugby football; it was overtaken by lawn tennis and polo. The code of football played at Harrow School in the nineteenth century had evolved for conditions of deep mud as found on London clay at the bottom of a hill. It was never going to be transferable to a dry, porous, sandy or chalky surface, in the way that the versions played at Charterhouse and Westminster were. Games adapt to the natural environments in which they are played.

For court games the situation is only slightly different. Except for lawn tennis and badminton, something more than a field and a ball is required: the need for a court restricts where a game can be played. We noted in the introduction to this story that almost every culture has a handball game of some sort, but of the 'wall games', only squash has broken through the 'glass ceiling' of international recognition. We have seen how Eton fives has been adapted in Nigeria, but even squash is played with a different ball in a different-sized court in the USA. The recent introduction of 'one-wall fives' as a formal game – really just getting back to basics – has created access and opened up opportunities to almost everyone. In the UK the administrators of both Eton and

Rugby fives hope that players beginning in this way will graduate to a three- or four-wall game later. This is an exciting prospect.

The second factor that nurtures sport is social environment: people need to have the affluence and the leisure time to devote to it. Many of the Victorian games evolved from boredom. These days, for better or for worse, there is a wide range of distractions for the young and unoccupied: some of these are destructive or damaging to self, people or property, some are passive such as television-watching, others are sedentary such as computer games. This has led to government concerns about the lack of direction in the lives of some young people and about social disorder and obesity, but there are also athletic opportunities as never before. Some schools may have sold off their playing fields but there are clubs and sports centres across the country offering a whole range of physical activities. Moreover, independent schools are keener than ever to open up their facilities for public or state school use. This is partly for philanthropic reasons, and partly due to some sabre rattling by the Charity Commissioners who suggested that independent schools were not justifying their charitable status by providing significant public benefit. It is in the independent schools, of course, that the majority of Eton fives courts lie.

If these two factors were the only ones, then Eton fives would be being tossed about on an ocean of chance and uncertainty. But there is a third factor that, in the modern world, far outweighs the other two: it is human intervention or leadership. In this respect Eton fives has been very fortunate and the quality of leadership, all voluntary and unpaid, would be the envy of other much bigger sports – if they but knew about it. The three most recent Chairmen have been Eton fives players, who had just

Gareth Hoskins. Secretary of the EFA since 2010

emerged from successful careers, with the time, the energy, the ideas and the skills to take on a new challenge. It may also have helped that they came unencumbered with the background of service on the Board. Strong leadership has a very uplifting effect on morale and has nurtured a clutch of enthusiasts, too numerous to name here, who have carried out the many unseen tasks, such as organising competitions, raising funds or picking a way through the minefield of government legislation. The building of the Westway courts, the introduction of one-wall fives, the creation of a nationally recognised coaching certificate, the provision of coaching through the REFCA, all backed by funding from the EFCT, have brought Eton fives to within reach of the glass ceiling. Moreover, recent cooperation with the Rugby Fives Association and the merging of forces to promote fives in all its forms is likely to produce a much louder voice in the clamour for recognition, and hence Government funding and commercial sponsorship.

Let us now attempt to answer the tripartite question posed in Chapter 1:

Why did the game break out from Eton College to be adopted by other schools?
In the second half of the nineteenth century there was perceived to be a need to codify and formalise what had been previously 'messing about in a playground'. Eton fives was seen to be a good game and the prestige of Eton College and the influence of Old Etonians as Headmasters, teachers or Governors in other schools led to courts being built or adapted to the Eton model.

Having broken out, why did it not become a universal game?
(i) The complicated court and rules give a first impression of a weird and unfathomable game.

(ii) There is the requirement of four players for a proper game.

(iii) The attraction to spectators, sponsors, television presenters and the media in general of a one-against-one individual battle with a single champion at the end, is lacking.

(iv) An unsatisfactory feature of the game is that, for most of the time, the players present a rear view to the spectators (a disadvantage that has been overcome in squash by the introduction of glass-walled courts).

Peter Worth. Chairman of the EFA since 2010

(v) For many years the players and organisers of Eton fives were totally unconcerned with the image and accessibility of the game. It was a game for **players**; if it was an elite game, so much the better. This was a situation that faced rugby union football in the 1970s and, to a lesser extent, cricket before the arrival of Kerry Packer. The solution in each case was professionalisation and commercialisation.

How has it managed to survive as a minority pursuit?

On its merits as a game. Those who play Eton fives love it. They like the fun of playing with a ball that bounces off ledges, corners and edges in seemingly unpredictable ways; they like the sheer pleasure of hitting a ball hard or the subtlety of spinning it out of reach; the dominance of brain over brawn; they like the teamwork required on court and camaraderie off it; they enjoy the exercise. As in most games,

Winners of the Schools Open Competition 2012, Shrewsbury: Jack Hudson-Williams and Henry Lewis, who is the grandson of PBH May (see page 91)

there is pleasure to be derived by playing it at any level of skill.

Finally there must be no shirking the question: *what is the future for Eton fives?* Is it a Victorian anachronism or will it adapt to the needs of the twenty-first century?

Everything will depend on the attitude of the schools that own the courts where the game is played. If they take a positive approach to fives and each appoints one of the coaches, who will be qualified with a coaching certificate under the scheme newly implemented (in the same way that rackets has for decades), then the recruiting of pupils as players – now expanded to include female pupils – should be able to engage their enthusiasm and withstand the host of other sports bidding for their attention. All school sports facilities are grossly underused and a resident coach should be able to attract at least two other groups of players: first, children from nearby state primary and secondary schools, and preparatory schools. Second, there should be lunchtime, evening and weekend clubs (as appropriate to the circumstances) open to local residents and staff in local businesses. If these external players pay a court or coaching fee, the cost of the coach will be defrayed. Finally, there must be a proactive programme in the existing club structure to ensure that school players of all standards are drawn into adult fives.

The next generation of fives players? Coaching at Westway

professionals take charge (and are incentivised by bonuses for court occupation) activity should be greatly increased. And so will the game go professional? Well, of course the coaches on school staffs are professional so, as in other sports, there will be two tiers of players, with professional, amateur and open championships.

And the Eton Fives Association? Will it do more than encourage, promote and organise? If the game achieves official recognition, Government funds should become available and the role of the EFA will become infinitely more challenging. The quality of current leadership gives reason for optimism that it will meet these challenges. Unquestionably, with external funding may come indigestible commitments and difficult decisions, many of which may be distasteful to those who have grown up in the game's amateur comfort zone. But then a lot of dead bodies had to be climbed over before rugby players realised that beer swilling was not the main occupation of the day,

If all this seems fanciful, it should be pointed out that it has happened before and is happening now, but piecemeal and in patches, because the organisation is being done by amateurs. Once the tennis players began to play hard ball, metaphorically if not literally, and amateur and professional cricketers were able to emerge from the same dressing room.

Hic noster ludus in perpetuam floreat
(May this our game flourish for ever)

Appendices, Bibliography and Index

Appendices

Appendix 1 – Eminent Victorians & Edwardians

The most important players on the Eton fives stage up to the Great War

AC Ainger, See biography on page 16.

CA Alington, See biography on page 46.

AE Allcock, at King Edward's, Birmingham; Emmanuel College, Cambridge; Assistant Master at KES 1874-1880; at Wellington 1880-1893; Headmaster of Highgate 1893-1908; won "Scratch Fives" 1895; responsible for six new courts.

CH Allcock, at King Edward's, Birmingham; younger brother of Arthur; Assistant Master at Eton 1884-1910; House Master 1890-1905. In a famous match he and Lionel Ford beat Townsend Warner and EM Butler in their prime, 3-2.

Duke of Argyll, See Campbell.

Sir Ralph Assheton, Bt, at Eton; of Downham and Cuerdale, co. Lancaster; DL. He built an Eton fives court at Downham Court, Clitheroe.

GT Atkinson, Assistant Master at Highgate 1879-1903; winner of "Scratch Fives"1887; composed fives song *Hard Lines on a Fives Ball.*

EC Austen-Leigh, at Eton; Assistant Master 1862-1905; one of AC Ainger's drafting committee for the laws of fives in 1866.

Baron Avebury, See John Lubbock.

HD Bache, See biography on page 49.

TE Bagge, at Eton; winner of the first School Fives in 1857; CU cricket XI 1859-61; captain in 1861.

MT Baines, at Harrow 1877-81; in Fives Ties at Cambridge in 1886 with L Sanderson, beat Meyrick and Hall, winners of the 1885 School Fives at Eton.

C Barclay, at Eton; winner of the School Fives 1885; played in first recorded inter-school match v Harrow.

JRL Emilius Bayley, at Eton; cricket XI 1838-41, captain in 1841; scored 152 against Harrow at Lord's in 1841.

Hon Ivo Bligh, See biography on page 18.

WD Bodkin, at King's College, Cambridge; Assistant Master at Highgate 1867-1884; several times winner of "Scratch Fives".

Canon HT Bowlby, at Charterhouse; Balliol College Oxford; Assistant Master at Eton 1897-1909; Headmaster of Lancing 1909-25.

Albert Brassey, at Eton; rowed bow in the Eton VIII of 1862; the fourth son of the railway contractor Thomas Brassey; University College, Oxford; Colonel in the Queen's Own Oxfordshire Hussars; High Sheriff of Oxfordshire 1878; MP for Banbury 1895-1906. He built his own Eton fives court at Heythrop Park, Enstone.

Henry Broadbent, Assistant Master at Eton 1876-1914, Master-in-College 1879-86, and a House Master 1886-1914. Regular fives partner of Lionel Ford, "a safe but rather slow-moving player and his main contribution was, from his own wish, one of exhortation to, or of praise and sometimes abuse of his partner."

EM Butler, at Harrow 1880-85; son of Head Master, Dr Montagu Butler; captain of fives 1885; winner of Public Schools Rackets 1884, 1885; Trinity College, Cambridge; CUCC 1888-9; CU Tennis 1888; CU Rackets 1888-9; Amateur Rackets Champion 1889; Assistant Master at Harrow 1891-1919. Outstanding fives pair with G Townsend Warner.

HF Buxton, at Harrow 1889-94; Trinity College, Cambridge; Director of Truman, Hanbury, Buxton & Co., Brewers. Joint donor of a fives court to the London Hospital.

JGEHDS Campbell, Duke of Argyll KG, KT, GCMG, GCVO, PC, at Eton, where he was known as Marquess of Lorne; donated challenge cup for junior fives in 1865. He was the fourth Governor General of Canada from 1878 to 1883.

WNF Cobbold, at Charterhouse; winner of House Fives for Verites 1882; "Nuts" Cobbold played for CUAFC for 4 years; CUCC, CU Tennis; International football for England; won 9 caps; played cricket for Kent.

Viscount Cobham, See Hon G Charles Lyttelton.

WC Compton, Headmaster of Dover College, responsible for introducing Eton fives in 1895; previously Assistant Master at Uppingham.

JC Craigie, at Eton; winner of the School Fives 1909; awarded MC in the Great War.

EH Crake, with RE Eiloart in Harrow fives pair 1904-06 that beat Eton and Charterhouse home and away in all three years.

RH Crake, at Harrow 1896-1900; in fives pair with FB Wilson that beat Eton home and away 1900. Awarded DSO in 1918.

GR Dupuis, at Eton; CUCC 1854-57; Assistant Master at Eton 1861.

JB Dyne, Headmaster of Highgate 1838-74; responsible for the first Eton fives courts in the new buildings of 1865.

WJ Earle, 'Usher' at Uppingham 1850; House Master of Broadlands 1861-80, where two fives courts still exist.

RE Eiloart, with EH Crake in Harrow fives pair 1904-06 that beat Eton and Charterhouse home and away in all three years.

EW Foljambe, at Eton; winner of the School Fives 1909; OU AFC 1918.

Lionel Ford, See biography on page 42.

WH Gladstone, at Eton; winner of the School Fives with WM Hoare in 1858; eldest son of WEG, Prime Minister; played for Scotland v England in the first soccer international in 1870.

G Hamilton-Fletcher, at Eton; winner of the School Fives 1913; in the Great War; killed at Cuinchy 1915.

EC Hawtrey, at Eton; King's College, Cambridge; Head Master of Eton 1834-53; Provost 1853; responsible for building the first courts at Eton.

JW Hely-Hutchinson, at Eton; winner of the School Fives 1901; Newcastle Select; Exhibitioner to Trinity College, Oxford.

Quintin Hogg, at Eton; winner of the School Fives with A Lubbock in 1863. donated challenge cup for junior fives in 1865.

HM Jackson, at Harrow 1869-72; Trinity College, Cambridge; barrister; succeeded his father (also Henry Mather Jackson) as 3rd baronet 1881; assumed the name Mather-Jackson, 1886.

Hon FS Jackson, See biography on page 40.

JL Joynes, Assistant Master at Eton 1849-77; donated challenge cup for School Fives in 1865. Henry Salt, his son-in-law, wrote a chapter on him in *Memories of Bygone Eton*, published in 1928. The Lubbocks and Quintin Hogg were in his House.

Arthur, 11th Lord Kinnaird KT, at Eton; Trinity College, Cambridge; CU tennis 1868-69; played football in nine FA Cup finals for the Wanderers and the Old Etonians; international cap for Scotland v England, 1873; President of the Football Association, 1890-1923; a director of Ransom, Bouverie & Co, 1870; of Barclays Bank, 1896-1923.

Hon KF Kinnaird, later 12th Lord Kinnaird, at Eton; winner of the School Fives 1898, 1899; donated the Kinnaird Cup for the Amateur Championship.

GHC Lewis, at City of London; a one-armed player, who was said to have been "able to do more with one hand than many could with two".

Marquess of Lorne, See Campbell.

Alfred Lubbock, at Eton; winner of the School Fives 1861, 1862, 1863, described by his contemporaries as the best player of his era; cricket XI 1861-2-3, captain in 1863, when he scored 80 against Harrow at Lord's. The Lubbock family had their own Eton fives court at High Elms, Orpington.

Edgar Lubbock, at Eton; younger brother of Alfred; winner of the School Fives 1882, 1885, 1886; cricket XI 1864-5-6, captain in 1866. He was involved in an incident when batting at Lord's against Harrow in 1866: a small boy from the crowd fielded the ball, leading to the run out of Lubbock's partner. Lubbock lost his temper, refused to go on and the game was abandoned for the day.

John Lubbock, 1st Baron Avebury PC, FRS, at Eton. Sir John Lubbock, 4th Bt., was a polymath and Liberal politician and MP. He was a banker with his family's firm, but was also involved in entomology, botany, biology, and evolutionary theory. In 1865 he published his seminal work *Prehistoric Times*, which became a standard textbook on archaeology. He built his own Eton fives court at High Elms, Orpington.

Hon Alfred Lyttelton, at Eton; winner of the School Fives 1873; played for England at both cricket & football; later a barrister, QC.

Hon G Charles Lyttelton, at Eton; winner of School Fives 1860; later 5th Baron Lyttelton, Viscount Cobham.

Hon GWS Lyttelton, at Eton; winner of the School Fives 1865.

Hon Edward H Lyttelton, at Eton; winner of the School Fives 1873, 1874; Head Master of Haileybury 1890-1905; of Eton 1905-16. Played cricket for Middlesex and for Gentlemen v Players; Association football for England.

HV Macnaghten, Assistant Master at Eton 1886-1920; Vice-Provost 1920-29; prolific author; described by his ex-pupil Sir Charles Tennyson as 'a saint and a poet.' He drowned in the Thames; the coroner's verdict was 'suicide while temporarily insane'.

SM Macnaghten, at Eton; winner of the School Fives with the Hon KF Kinnaird in 1899; said to be 'the strongest pair for some years'.

CHK Marten, later Sir Henry Marten KCVO, at Eton; Balliol College, Oxford, 1st class Mod History; Eton Master 1895-1929; Vice-Provost; Provost 1945-48. Tutor to Princess Elizabeth, later Queen Elizabeth II. Co-author with G T Warner of *Groundwork of British History*,1912, 'one of the most used text books of the 20th century'. He was knighted on the Chapel steps at Eton.

RAH Mitchell, at Eton; cricket XI 1858-61, captain 1861; Balliol College, Oxford; OUCC 1862-65, captain 1863-65; Assistant Master at Eton 1866-1901; Master i/c cricket 1866-97. His third son Frank H Mitchell (b1879), OUCC 1898, was winner of the School Fives with GA Akers-Douglas in1897.

A Moon, at Eton; winner of the School Fives, 1901.

George Mount, at Eton; Assistant Master at Eton 1894-1900; "he and his partner, Lionel Ford, never suffered defeat against the School pair, or had any fear of it."

JG Mountain, Assistant Master at Eton; associated with the building of the first fives courts.

DR Napier, at Harrow; played with FS Jackson in the pair of 1889 and with AM Porter in 1890; won the Sword of Honour at Sandhurst but died from wounds received on the Indian Frontier in 1898. Porter was killed in the Boer War in 1900.

FE Norman, at Eton; winner of the first School Fives in 1857; CU cricket XI 1858-60.

Cuthbert Ottaway, at Eton (KS); winner of the School Fives 1868, 1869; Public Schools' Rackets Doubles Championship1868,1869; Brasenose College, Oxford; OUAFC 1874, OUCC 1870-73, rackets (1870-3), athletics (1873) and real tennis (1870-2). After his death an Oxford newspaper wrote, "Ottaway was a great cricketer… the best amateur racquet player of his time, a capital football player and a fair sprint runner. It has fallen to the lot of few amateur cricketers to attain greater popularity, and his reception on the day when he took his degree at Oxford was something to be remembered."

TE Page, at Lincoln GS & Shrewsbury; Fellow of St John's College, Cambridge; Assistant Master at Charterhouse; House Master of Pageites 1875-80, Hodgsonites 1881-1910; Governor of Shrewsbury 1914 -36; of Charterhouse 1916-36; credited with the building of the first courts at Charterhouse.

Walter Phillimore, 1st Baron Phillimore of Shiplake, at Westminster; High Court judge, Lord Justice of Appeal; governor of Westminster, largely responsible for the building of the first Westminster fives courts in 1886.

EH Pickering, at Eton; captain of CUCC 1829; Assistant Master at Eton 1830-52; associated with the building of the first fives courts.

FT Prior, Shrewsbury Master 1891-1933; the most important influence on Eton fives at Shrewsbury until the arrival of Dr Alington as Headmaster; first President of the Old Salopian Eton Fives Club in 1929.

GB Raikes, at Shrewsbury; OUAFC 1893-96; OUCC 1894-95; international footballer England v Wales 1895-96; v Scotland, Ireland 1896; played cricket for Norfolk, Hampshire, for English XI v Australia.

HS Salt, at Eton; Cambridge; Assistant Master at Eton 1875-84; an influential writer and campaigner for social reform in prisons, schools, economic institutions and the treatment of animals; anti-vivisectionist and pacifist; literary critic, biographer, classical scholar and naturalist. Henry Salt was son-in-law of the Rev JL Joynes (above).

Lancelot Sanderson, at Harrow (1878-82); cricket XI 1882; CU rackets 1885; in Fives Ties at Cambridge in 1886 with MT Baines, beat Meyrick and Hall, winners of the 1885 School Fives at Eton.

GO Smith, at Charterhouse; winner of the House Fives for Hodgsonites 1892; Keble College, Oxford; OU AFC 1893-96, captain 1896; International footballer; gained 20 caps for England, captain on 11 occasions. Joint Headmaster of Ludgrove Prep School 1901-18, first with Arthur Dunn, then William Oakley.

RSA Straus, at Harrow 1896-1901; fives pair 1901; natural science scholar at Pembroke College, Cambridge; later a biographer and novelist.

CT Studd, at Eton; winner of the School Fives 1879; Trinity College, Cambridge; CUCC 1880-83, captain in 1883; played five test matches for England; became a missionary first in China and later as founder of the Heart of Africa Mission, which became the Worldwide Evangelisation Crusade.

GB Studd, at Eton; winner of the School Fives 1878; Trinity College, Cambridge; CUCC 1879-82, captain 1882; also OU tennis 1881, 1882. He toured Australia with England in 1882/3 and played in four tests; he was called to the bar 1886; later a missionary in a squalid area of southern Los Angeles, California, USA.

JK Tancock, one of two Cheam masters, Tancock and Wilson, who year after year challenged and defeated the Eton Keepers with only one defeat. The Cheam men evolved a technique of their own; a perfect system of collaboration, mostly "on-wall" play, whereas the Eton tradition was a free and open game, almost as much "off-wall" as "on.

Freeman Thomas, See biography on page 19.

CI Thornton, at Eton; winner of the School Fives 1867, 1868; cricket eleven 1866-68, captain 1868; Trinity College, Cambridge; CUCC 1869-72, captain 1872; played in 216 first-class cricket matches, including 18 for Kent and 29 for Middlesex. "Buns" Thornton was a tremendous hitter of the ball'. Originator of the Scarborough Cricket Festival.

Edward Thring, at Eton; Headmaster of Uppingham 1853-87; author of educational books; founder of the Headmasters' Conference; introduced Eton fives to Uppingham.

JRR Tolkien, at King Edward's, Birmingham; fives player; Secretary of Football (Rugby) in 1910; later a well known author.

G Townsend Warner, at Harrow 1880-83; Assistant Master at Harrow 1891-1916. Author of *Landmarks of English Industrial History*, joint editor of *Harrow School*; co-author with CHK Marten of *Groundwork of British History*,1912, 'one of the most used text books of the 20th century'. Author of *Hints on Eton Fives*; Townsend Warner and EM Butler became an outstanding fives pair when they were teaching together at Harrow.

BR Warren, at Harrow 1883-86; fives pair 1885, 1886; played in first recorded inter-school fives match v Eton.

AK Watson, at Harrow; Headmaster of Ipswich School; responsible for introducing Eton fives in 1908.

Charles White Talbot, at Highgate; Fives VI 1889-90; co-founder Old Cholmeleian Society; responsible for starting OC Fives and Football Clubs.

FB Wilson, at Harrow 1895 -1900; fives pair 1899, 1900; with RH Crake beat Eton home and away 1900; CUCC 1902-4, captain 1904; CU tennis and rackets 1902-03. Sports correspondent for *The Times*; author of *Sporting Pie*. He wrote numerous articles on Eton fives.

WF Witts, at Eton; cricket XI 1836-37; 'Daddy' Witts was an Assistant Master at Uppingham and frequent fives partner of Edward Thring.

JE Yonge, at Eton; Assistant Master 1840-75; a "Johnnie Yonge" was the name given to a shot that clipped the edge of the top step and was unreturnable.

EM Young, at Eton; Scholar and Fellow of Trinity College, Cambridge; Assistant Master Harrow 1863-77; credited with introducing Eton fives to Harrow; later Headmaster of Sherborne.

Appendix 2 – Heroes of the Golden Age

The most important players on the Eton fives stage between the Two World Wars

Lord Aberconway, at Eton; Keeper of Fives; Captain of the Oppidans; Chairman, President of the OEFC. Presenter of the Aberconway Cup for father-and-son pairs.

JJ Adie, at Shrewsbury; finalist with EA Barlow in the Public Schools' Handicaps 1931.

MJ Adler, at Eton; won the Public Schools' Handicaps with FST Barnado in 1937.

J Aguirre, at Highgate; later described by the Eton Head Master, Oliver Van Oss, as 'a freak Basque pelota player whose left hand produced magic'. He won the Kinnaird Cup with Howard Fabian at the age of nineteen but was killed in 1938 in the Spanish Civil War.

Sir Lionel Alexander, The first Chairman of the EFA, from 1924-33. He was High Sheriff of Huntingdonshire in 1929.

CA Alington, See biography on page 46.

SR Allsopp, at Eton; reached the 1937 Kinnaird Cup final with RHV Cavendish.

DM Backhouse, at Shrewsbury; winner with Alan Barber of the Kinnaird Cup in 1934 and 1936. He also played international squash for England.

FG Baddeley, at Highgate; fives VI 1919-20-21, football XI 1919-20, captain of both games for two years. He played in the first Kinnaird Cup competition in 1925.

AT Barber, See biography on page 103.

AC Baring, at Eton; finalist with RA Paget-Cooke in the Public Schools' Handicaps Competition in 1938.

EA Barlow, at Shrewsbury; finalist with JJ Adie in the Public Schools' Handicaps 1931; OUEFC; OUCC 1932-34; OUAFC 1933-34; played cricket, lawn tennis, squash for Lancashire; lawn tennis for Wales.

FST Barnado, at Eton; won the Public Schools' Handicaps with MJ Adler in 1937.

FH Barnard, at Charterhouse; 1st pair with GB Garnett, beat Eton, Harrow and Highgate in 1920.

FW Barnes, at Highgate; fives VI for four years, the last two as captain. Finalist in the Kinnaird Cup with AH Fabian in 1929.

JM Barrell, at Aldenham; finalist in the Public Schools' Handicaps with JAU Warwick in 1934.

BD Barton, at Eton; finalist with JA Ponsonby in the Public Schools' Handicaps in 1939.

JH Beale, at City of London; Secretary of the Old Citizens Fives Club and organiser of the Queen's Club Competition 1932-37.

JH Bevan, at Eton; winner of the School Fives with G Hamilton-Fletcher in 1913; Christ Church, Oxford; awarded MC in the Great War; finalist with BS Hill-Wood in the second Kinnaird Cup Championship in 1928.

RA Blair, at Highgate; fives VI for two years; afterwards was the strongest player in the London Hospital team; reached the Kinnaird Cup final with AH Fabian in 1935 and with AGA Turnbull in 1938. He was a consultant psychiatrist.

EA Bland, at Uppingham; finalist with ACS Gibson in the Public Schools' Handicaps in 1937.

D Boumphrey, at Shrewsbury; cricket XI 1909-12. Donald Boumphrey, awarded MC in the Great War, coached cricket and rugby at Rydal from 1918. Responsible for first two courts built there in 1935. Played cricket for Wales v West Indies in 1928.

CW Bower, at Highgate; fives VI 1913-4, captain; played with FW Barnes in the first Kinnaird Cup competition in 1925; instrumental in establishing the Old Cholmeleian Fives Club.

JF Burnet, at St Paul's; founder of The Jesters Club.

GM Butler, at Harrow; Guy Butler was Head of School, captain of football, cricket and fives; son of EM Butler (see Eminent Victorians and Edwardians); President of the CUAC 1920-21; amateur champion Quarter-Mile 1919; 220 yards 1926; Olympic medalist: 400 metres silver, 4x400 relay gold (1920 Antwerp) and two bronze in same events (1924 Paris). Jointly with Sebastian Coe, Butler holds the British record for the most (4) Olympic athletics medals. Assistant Master at Lancing 1922-28; Secretary of the EFA from 1934-8.

RHV Cavendish, at Eton; reached the 1937 Kinnaird Cup final with SR Allsopp.

APF Chapman, at Uppingham, 1st pair 1919. In the Shrewsbury match of 1919, *The Salopian* wrote, 'A feature was Chapman's brilliant play' and the Uppingham magazine wrote: 'We have not seen many better players.' He also had a 1st XI batting average of 111 in 1917. Percy Chapman later captained Cambridge, Kent and England.

JAS Collins, at Harrow; won the Public Schools' Handicaps with AH Henderson in 1933; losing finalist with GFD Haslewood in 1932; OUEFC 1934; OULTC 1935-37 (captain 1936).

AJ Conyers, at Aldenham; reached the Kinnaird Cup final with AWS Sim in 1934 and with TG Lund in 1936; reached at least the semi-final of the inaugural competition in 1925.

AP Cox, at Harrow; won the Public Schools' Handicaps with DJQ Henriques in 1936; CUEFC 1937.

HG Crabtree, at Charterhouse; first Hon Sec of Old Carthusians Fives Club 1931; organiser of the Kinnaird Cup Championships 1934-38.

Roald Dahl, See biography on page 78.

HG de Grey Warter, at Harrow; won the first Public Schools' Handicaps with WM Welch in 1929; this pair also won the Kinnaird Cup in 1931 and 1933.

RG de Quetteville, at Eton; Kinnaird Cup Winner with RA Redhead in 1925 and 1928, losing finalists in 1930; Chairman of the EFA 1934-47; President until 1965.

Lord Dunglass, Alec Douglas-Home, later Lord Home of The Hirsel. See biography on page 110.

DG Egerton, at Lancing; Hon Sec of EFA 1931-33; founder of the Wyverns; author of articles and chapters on Eton fives.

AH Fabian, See biography on page 89.

BM Fisher, at Eton; won the School Fives with RVC Westmacott and the Public Schools' Handicaps in 1935.

StJO Forbes, at Eton; winner of the School Fives with CNJ Hill-Wood in 1926; played with D'A Lambton in an Old Etonians v Old Harrovians match when the score in the final game was 21-18.

NM Ford, at Harrow; son of Head Master Lionel Ford; 1st pair fives 1924-26; Head of School, captain of cricket 1925-26; winner of Public Schools' Rackets 1925; OUEFC 1928; OUCC 1928-30.

KAF Frost, at Highgate; losing finalist in Public Schools' Handicaps with HKS Lindsay in 1933.

KC Gandar Dower, See biography on page 72.

GB Garnett, at Charterhouse; 1st pair with FH Barnard, beat Eton, Harrow and Highgate in 1920.

JA Gaywood, at Highgate; Hon Sec, President OCEFC; Hon Auditor EFA.

WE Gerrish, at Westminster; "Ebbie" Gerrish co-founder, Hon. Sec. OWEFC.

ACS Gibson, at Uppingham; finalist with EA Bland in the Public Schools' Handicaps in 1937.

JV Gillespie, at Uppingham; won the Public Schools' Handicaps with NS Knight in 1932.

CH Gosling, at Eton; winner of the School Fives with JM Carnegie in 1927.

RN Grant, at Charterhouse; winner of the Public Schools' Handicaps with PL Richards in 1934.

TS Hankey, at Eton; the first long term Secretary of the EFA, serving from 1924-9.

GFD Haslewood, at Harrow; won the Public Schools' Handicaps with JFM Lightly in 1931; losing finalist with with JAS Collins in 1932.

JSO Haslewood, at Shrewsbury; finalist with DN Moore in the first Public Schools' Handicaps Competition in 1929.

Lord Hazlerigg, at Eton; AG Hazlerigg was winner of the School Fives with CEW Sheepshanks in 1929; was responsible for Eton fives becoming a Jesters game in 1931.

GW Headlam, at Eton; 'Tuppy' Headlam was an Assistant Master from 1905-1935, mainly teaching history. He was a keen supporter of fives and served on the original committee of the OE Fives Club. *The Times* said of him, 'He had the reputation, not wholly undeserved, of being the laziest master on the staff. He alone taught his division in a room in his own house, which meant that there was no need for him to go out of doors in inclement weather. He would appear from the private side of the house, probably rather late, a small, bright-eyed, dapper figure.'

DJQ Henriques, at Harrow; won the Public Schools' Handicaps with AP Cox in 1936; killed in action in Belgium in 1940.

HL Higgins, at King Edward's, Birmingham; captain of fives in 1911; played cricket for Gentlemen v Players in 1920.

CNJ Hill-Wood, at Eton; winner of the School Fives with StJO Forbes in 1926; played with NM Ford in the 1st Oxford pair in the first Varsity match in 1928.

BS Hill-Wood, at Eton; Winner of the School Fives in 1917, 1918 with T Bevan; finalist with JH Bevan in the second Kinnaird Cup Championship in 1928.

RB Hodgkinson, at Harrow; 1st pair 1928; Lt Col Welsh Guards MC.

JS Hogben, at Highgate; Fives VI 1916; introduced Eton fives to Nigeria 1922, building 2 mud courts; wrote *An Introduction to the History of the Islamic States of Northern Nigeria.*

RL Holdsworth, at Repton; OUCC 1920-22; OU AFC 1919-21; Assistant Master at Harrow, coaching fives 1922-33.

ASC Hulton, at Charterhouse; finalist with C Middleton in Public Schools' Handicaps 1930.

KRG Hunt, at Wolverhampton GS; Assistant Master at Highgate 1908-45, Housemaster 1920-43, coaching cricket, football and fives. The Rev Kenneth Hunt played for Wolverhampton Wanderers, scoring the first goal in the 1908 Cup Final, and won two full international caps for England in 1911. He played with a fellow master, HJ Gibbon, in the first Kinnaird Cup competition in 1925.

RG Kerrison, at Eton; finalist with RVC Westmacott in the Public Schools' Handicaps 1936.

Lord Kinnaird, at Eton; Kenneth Kinnaird presented the trophy for the Eton Fives Amateur Championships; Committee member of the original Fives Association; Patron of EFA. See also Eminent Victorians and Edwardians.

NS Knight, at Uppingham; won the Public Schools' Handicaps with JV Gillespie in 1932.

D'A Lambton, at Eton; co-founder of the 'White Rabbits'; played with StJ Forbes in an Old Etonians v Old Harrovians match when the score in the final game was 21-18.

HW Leatham, at Charterhouse; 1st XI cricket, rackets pair, fives pair; Public Schools rackets 1909-10; Exhibitioner, Trinity College, Cambridge; CU rackets (singles and doubles); CU tennis (singles and doubles) 1912-14; Amateur rackets champion (singles) 1914, 1924; (doubles) 1912, 1921, 1924-27, 1930; St Thomas's Hospital; Medical Officer, Charterhouse 1923-51.

JFM Lightly, at Harrow; won the Public Schools' Handicaps with WM Welch in 1930; with GFD Haslewood in 1931; CUEFC; CUSRC; CUAAA.

HKS Lindsay, at Highgate; fives VI 1932-3-4 and captain, football XI and captain; losing finalist in Public Schools' Handicaps with KAF Frost in 1933. Knighted as Sir James Lindsay.

TC Longfield, at Aldenham; Tom Longfield was five years in the cricket XI; CUAFC; CUCC 1927-28 (captain); played cricket for Kent off and on up to 1939; one of the best fives players Aldenham had produced.

DGA Lowe, at Highgate; Head of School from 1919-21, captain of football and cricket and a member of the fives VI. Douglas Lowe won Olympic Gold medals in the 800 metres in both Paris (1924) and Amsterdam (1928) games. He wrote several books on athletics and was on the council of the IAAF. Later he was President of the Bar Council and a QC.

TG Lund, at Westminster; reached the final of the Kinnaird Cup with AJ Conyers in 1936; Hon Treasurer of the EFA from 1934-47. Later Deputy Registrar of Solicitors.

George Mallory, at Winchester; later a Charterhouse Master; mountaineer; when his body was recovered on Mount Everest, a receipt for a pair of fives gloves was found in the pocket.

Gerald Mander, Donor of the Eton fives courts to Wolverhampton Grammar School.

EH Mariette, at Aldenham; also Assistant Master; bequeathed £1000 in 1923 for the building of Eton fives courts.

JSF Marriott, at Charterhouse; 1st XI cricket (Capt) and football; fives pair; CUCC 1912, 1914 (Capt 1919); CU AFC 1913-14 (Capt 1919); CU golf 1919. Somerset cricket 1920; amateur international football, England v Wales 1920; international golf, England 1930.

Sir Henry Marten, Vice-Provost, then Provost of Eton. He chaired the original committee of the Old Etonian Fives Club. (See also Eminent Victorians and Edwardians.)

GR McConnell, at Harrow; OUEFC 1928; winner of the Kinnaird Cup with KC Gandar Dower in 1929 and 1932, and losing finalists in 1931 and 1939. McConnell was Hon Treasurer of the EFA briefly in 1934 and later became a Harrow Master.

William McLean, at Repton; fives team; played in the first Kinnaird Cup competition in 1925. Alpine climber and medical officer on the 1933 Everest Expedition.

C Middleton, at Charterhouse; finalist with ASC Hulton in Public Schools' Handicaps 1930.

LN Minford, at Shrewsbury; winner of the Public Schools' Handicaps with JCF Quinn in 1938, with RDR Walker in 1939.

JW Moir, at Eton (Newcastle Scholar); Balliol College, Oxford; 1st class hons in 'Greats'; Assistant Master at Harrow 1922-48; died while playing fives.

DN Moore, at Shrewsbury; finalist with JSO Haslewood in first Public Schools' Handicaps Competition in 1929; OUCC 1930-31 (captain).

JAA Morton, at Highgate; fives VI 1937-8, cricket XI 1936-7-8; partnered JKG Webb in the "best Highgate pair since 1929". Killed in action 1941.

GW Nickson, at Shrewsbury; Assistant Master at Eton; Nickson and Peterson, another Salopian housemaster at Eton, were undefeated for a quarter of a century.

EB Noel, at Winchester; briefly Hon Secretary of the EFA in 1924. He was a celebrated tennis and rackets player; also erudite scholar of tennis and related games, he was co-author of *History of Tennis*, first published in 1924 and recently reprinted.

MR Norman, at Eton; co-founder of the 'White Rabbits'.

HC Owen, at Shrewsbury; cricket XI, football XI, fives team, Head of School; classical scholar at Clare College, Cambridge. Bertie Owen was a Berkhamsted master 1937-39, 1945-57, coaching fives, and Headmaster of the Junior School 1957-77.

RA Paget-Cooke, at Eton; finalist with AC Baring in the Public Schools' Handicaps 1938.

FA Peet, at Charterhouse; Head Boy; captain of the football XI, cricket XI; fives VI; OUEFC; OUAFC; founder member of the Pegasus Football Club; played cricket for Cornwall in 1947; later senior district commissioner in the Colonial Service in Mombasa. Although called to the Bar in 1952, after Kenya's independence he qualified as a solicitor and practised in Oxford until his retirement in 1988.

JM Peterson, See biography on page 80.

ED Portu, at Highgate; Fives VI 1927-8-9, captain; with his brother EN Portu was unbeaten against school and club first pairs; playing with J Aguirre he beat the Kinnaird Cup holders (Gandar Dower & McConnell) twice in the 1929 season.

JA Ponsonby, at Eton; finalist with BD Barton in the Public Schools' Handicaps in 1939.

R Pulbrook, at Harrow; Head of School; winner of Public Schools' Rackets Championships with JM Lightly in 1932, with JH Pawle in 1933; OU rackets, lawn tennis & squash; Assistant Master at Bryanston 1937-40, 1945, coaching fives.

JCF Quinn, at Shrewsbury; winner of the Public Schools' Handicaps with LM Minford in 1938.

RA Redhead, at Eton; winner of the School Fives with PD Lindsay in 1919; Kinnaird Cup winner with RG de Quetteville in 1925 and 1928, losing finalists in 1930.

Hon PF Remnant, at Eton; won the School Fives with NA Pearson in 1916; finalist with Hon RJF Remnant in the Kinnaird Cup Competition of 1932; probably also reached the final of the inaugural Kinnaird Cup in 1925.

Hon RJF Remnant, at Eton; won the School Fives with FJL Johnstone in 1914; finalist with Hon PF Remnant in the Kinnaird Cup Competition of 1932; probably also reached the final of the inaugural Kinnaird Cup in 1925.

PL Richards, at Charterhouse; winner of the Public Schools' Handicaps with RN Grant in 1934.

RWV Robins, at Highgate; four years in cricket and football XI, fives VI 1923-4-5, captain of all 3 sports. Walter Robins was captain of the England cricket XI in 1937 and captain of Middlesex between 1935 and 1950. He was also Wisden Cricketer of the Year in 1930. Played football for Nottingham Forest.

HF Robinson, at Shrewsbury; in the 1st pair with AT Barber that beat Eton in 1923. 'Robinson was the best player on court.'

CEW Sheepshanks, at Eton; won the School Fives with AG Hazlerigg in 1929 and with HS Gosling in 1930. Assistant Master at Eton; a gifted all-round sportsman, he was one of the great artists of Eton fives and "revelled in the intricacies of the game, and using to great effect the rubber facing of the gloves prevalent at the time, he baffled all but the most wary with his science and cunning - few effected such cut and such spin". With JM Peterson he won the Kinnaird Cup in 1935, 1938 and 1950.

AWS Sim, at Aldenham; reached the 1934 Kinnaird Cup final partnered by AJ Conyers.

EJ Gordon Spencer, See biography on page 142.

JS Stephenson, See biography on page 69.

AJA Turnbull, at Highgate; finalist in the Kinnaird Cup Competition with RA Blair in 1938.

MT Turnbull, at Harrow; finalist with GRR Wilson in the Public Schools' Handicaps in 1935; played squash for England in 1949.

TL Twidell, at Shrewsbury; Assistant Master at Highgate 1922-62, partnered Jack Peterson for Old Salopians against Highgate; played with a fellow master in the first Kinnaird Cup competition in 1925. He was in charge of the 100 or so boys who remained at Highgate during the Second World War.

BH Valentine, at Repton; fives VI 1925. Bryan Valentine won blues for soccer and cricket at Cambridge in 1928-29, then played cricket for Kent (captain) and England (7 Tests, batting average 64.85).

RDR Walker, at Shrewsbury; winner of the Public Schools' Handicaps with LM Minford in 1939.

JAU Warwick, at Aldenham; finalist in the Public Schools' Handicaps with JM Barrell in 1934.

JKG Webb, at Highgate; Head of School 1936-7, captain of football, cricket and fives; OUAFC; OUEFC; won the Kinnaird Cup three times with Howard Fabian, first in 1937 while still at school. Later Professor of Child Health at Newcastle University.

WH Webster, at Highgate; Head of School 1928-9, five years in cricket XI and four in football XI, captain of both; fives VI 1929; CUAFC, CUCC; played cricket for Middlesex; amateur football for England and played for Casuals in the Amateur Cup win of 1936. He later became President of the MCC.

WM Welch, at Harrow; won the Public Schools' Handicaps with HG de Grey Warter in 1929; with JFM Lightly in 1930; won the Kinnaird Cup with HG de Grey Warter in 1931 and 1933; England squash international 1938. Died of wounds at Calais in 1940.

RVC Westmacott, at Eton; won the School Fives with BM Fisher; winners of the Public Schools' Handicaps in 1935, finalist with RG Kerrison in 1936.

FB Wilson, at Harrow; Sports correspondent for *The Times* who wrote many articles in support of Eton fives. (See also Eminent Victorians and Edwardians).

GRR Wilson, at Harrow; finalist with MT Turnbull in the Public Schools' Handicaps in 1935.

Appendix 3 – Dramatis Personae of Eton Fives

1945-2012

This list comprises the winners and finalists of the Amateur Championship for the Kinnaird Cup; of the Ladies' Championships; winners and finalists of the Schools' Open Championship; of the Schools' Girls' Championship; Masters in charge of school fives for a significant period; Officers of the Eton Fives Association; Trustees of Eton Fives Charitable Trust; Editors of the EFA Annual Booklet; holders of other administrative posts and other former players of general interest

Lord Aberconway, See Heroes of the Golden Age

NO Addy, Schools Winner 1990, Finalist 1991 (Highgate)

MLY Ainsworth, Shrewsbury 1st pair 1939-41 (captain); Kinnaird Cup Finalist 1959; Master at Ludgrove

B J Alderson, Schools Finalist 2005 (Shrewsbury)

A Aldous, Master i/c Fives at Oakham 2001-

H Allen, Schools Girls Finalist 2012 (Highgate)

HD Amos, Master i/c Fives at Wellington 1977-82

TJC Anderson, Schools Finalist 1981 (Shrewsbury)

CE Arkell, Master i/c Fives at Aldenham 1979-91

J N Attree, Schools Finalist 2002 (Shrewsbury)

G Audley, Schools Girls Finalist 2003 (Mill Hill)

C J Austin, Schools Winner 1993 (Wolverhampton)

AT Baden Fuller, Uppingham 1st pair; CUEFC 1958-59; Inventor of the modern Eton fives ball; EFA tour to Nigeria 1965

D M G Bailey, Public Schools Winner 1952 (Eton)

N A Bailey, Schools Winner 1996 (Eton)

G Baker, Schools Winner 1982 (Wolverhampton); CUEFC 1984-86; Kinnaird Cup Winner 1992

H Bancroft, Ladies' Championships Finalist 1992-94

AT Barber, EFA Chairman 1950-71; President 1972-84. See also Heroes of the Golden Age

GWP Barber, Winner of School Fives at Eton 1961; Eton tour to Nigeria 1960; Kinnaird Cup Finalist 1965; OUEFC; Headmaster of Ludgrove

RPF Barber, at Shrewsbury; OUEFC; EFA Chairman 2004-10; President 2010-

SWT Barber, Triple Winner of the School Fives at Eton. Headmaster of Ludgrove

DR Barker, Public Schools Winner 1957, 1959 (Aldenham); CUEFC 1960-62; Master i/c Fives at Aldenham 1966 -1979

AS Barnard, Master i/c Fives at Shrewsbury

FM Barnes, Ladies' Championships Finalist 1996-97, 1999, 2008

D Barnes, Public Schools Winner 1975 (King Edward's Birmingham)

BD Barton, at Eton; EFA tour to Nigeria 1965; EFA Hon Treasurer 1952-71; Vice President 1972-2009

AS Bates, Schools Winner 1980, Public Schools Finalist 1979 (Wolverhampton)

JP Batting, at Harrow; CUEFC 1978-80; EFCT Trustee

A Bhattacharya, at Highgate; professional fives coach at Rydal Penrhos 2010-11

R Beament, at Lancing; EFA Hon Secretary 1996-98; Master i/c Fives at Highgate 1959-75

JDIS Beardmore-Grey, at Eton; OUEFC 1949-50 (captain); Master coaching at Ludgrove

S Becker, Schools Girls Winner 2009 (Lyceum Alpinum, Zuoz)

AFH Bell, Public Schools Finalist 1977 (Harrow)

JF Bell, Master i/c Fives at Lancing

LA Bell, Schools Girls Finalist 2007-08 (Lancing)

S Benson, (formerly Sandy) Ladies' Championships Finalist 1984-85

TGW Best, Public Schools Winner 1962 (Eton); Kinnaird Cup finalist 1966

AJ Betts, Master i/c Fives at Lancing 1991-

JW Biggs, at St Olave's; Kinnaird Cup Winner 1957, 1961, 1962, 1964; Finalist 1955, 1956, 1958, 1963, 1967, 1968, 1976

R Binz, Schools Girls Finalist 2001 (Lyceum Alpinum, Zuoz)

APW Bishop, Master i/c Fives at Summer Fields

RNL Black, at Lancing; EFA Chairman 1991-95; Vice-President 1997-; EFCT Chairman

WS Blackshaw, Master i/c Fives at Repton 1958-65

MC Blundell, Public Schools Winner 1972 (Berkhamsted)

GR Bolt, Master i/c Fives at Aldenham 1947-70; at Cranleigh 1970-80; Organiser of the Public Schools Championships

GPT Bond, Public Schools Winner 1971(Highgate)

B Boobyer, Uppingham 1st pair 1945-46; OURFC, OUCC, nine England International rugby caps 1950-52

ROI Borradaile, at Westminster; captain of fives and cricket; played cricket for British Empire XI; Assistant Master at Wellington 1948 -87, Master i/c Fives

PV Boughton, at Ipswich; Master i/c Fives at Ipswich 2007-

PR Bowden, Master i/c Fives at Stowe 1977-80, at Mill Hill 1980-89

C Bowen, Schools Finalist 2003 (Harrow)

JRC Bowen, Schools Winner 1981, Finalist 1980 (Berkhamsted)

LFF Boyall, Public Schools Winner 1969 (City of London)

PN Bradburn, Master i/c Fives at Repton 1986-

JM Brearley, City of London 1st pair 1959; Public Schools Championships Semi-Finals; Captain of Middlesex & England cricket teams

OGC Broome, Triple Winner of the School Fives at Eton: Schools Finalist 1999 (Eton)

NC Brown, Public Schools Winner 1953, (King Edward's, Birmingham)

J Browning, Schools Girls Winner 2005; Finalist 2006 (Lancing); OUEFC 2007-8

AJ Brunner, Master i/c Fives at Highgate Junior School 1981- ; at Highgate 2004-

RJ Bryan, Schools Finalist 1997 (Harrow); CUEFC 1999

JDG Buchanan, Public Schools Finalist 1954 (Highgate)

K Buhler, Schools Girls Finalist 2000 (Lyceum Alpinum, Zuoz)

O Bull, Schools Winner 1983 (Highgate)

AE Bundy, Public Schools Finalist 1962 (Highgate); Kinnaird Cup winner1971, 1972; Kinnaird Cup finalist 1973

FT Burgess, Schools Winner 2006 (Eton); OUEFC 2011

JF Burnet, at St Paul's; Founder, Hon Sec, President of Jesters

ARB Burrows, Triple Winner of the School Fives at Eton; Public Schools Winner 1956, Finalist 1955

RJP Burton, Schools Finalist 1982 (Shrewsbury)

M Burton-Brown, Public Schools Winner 1950 (Charterhouse); OUEFC; Master coaching at Ludgrove

AP Buxton, Schools Winner 1984 (King Edward's, Birmingham)

PA Byrne, Public Schools Finalist 1979 (Wolverhampton)

AJG Campbell, Public Schools Winner 1953 (King Edward's Birmingham) ; Kinnaird Cup Winner 1958, 1965-68, 1971, 1973, 1975; Kinnaird Cup Finalist 1960, 1961, 1964, 1969, 1974

G Campbell, at Lancing; professional fives coach at KES Birmingham, at Zuoz

J Carr, Master i/c Fives at Cranleigh 2003-08

K Carvell, Ladies' Championships Winner 1988, Finalist 1986

D Cattenach, Public Schools Winner 1968 (Highgate)

D Cecil, Master i/c Fives at St Paul's, Darjeeling

A Chadwick, Master i/c Fives at St Olave's 1988-92

DAJ Chamberlain, Public Schools Winner 1966 (Highgate)

JMS Chapman, Schools Winner 1985 (Highgate)

TJ Chappell, at Marlborough; Master i/c Fives at St Peter's, Seaford

ML Charlesworth, at Shrewsbury; Assistant Master at Shrewsbury 1947-61, 1967-81; Master i/c Fives at various periods; Headmaster of Lawrence College in Pakistan, 1961-67; responsible for introducing Eton fives to Geelong GS, Melbourne

NR Chelleram, Schools Winner 1988 (Harrow); CUEFC 1991-92

BJ Chesters, Schools Finalist 1995, 1996 (Shrewsbury)

WJ Chiang, Schools Finalist 2000 (Shrewsbury)

J Clegg, Shrewsbury 1st pair 1948-9, Captain; OUAFC 1950-52; OUEFC

WGA Clegg, Public Schools Finalist 1958 (Eton)

HPD Clive, Schools Finalist 2002 (Shrewsbury)

JA Cogan, at Liverpool College; Deputy Head at Westminster; principal instigator of the fives courts at Westway

PM Cohen, at St Olave's; Eton Fives Development Officer at Westway Sports Centre; professional fives coach

MI Collins, at Highgate; Master coaching at Highgate

NR Colquhoun, Public Schools Finalist 1966 (Eton); OUEFC; Master i/c Fives at Eton

MD Constantinidi, Winner of School Fives at Eton 1946; OUEFC 1949-51; EFA Chairman 1996-2003; Vice President 2004-06; President 2006-11

CEM Cooley, Schools Girls Finalist 2001, Winner 2002-04 (Newstead Wood, St Olave's); Ladies' Championships Winner 2004, Finalist 2002-03, 2005, 2007, 2009-12

SKP Cooley, Schools Winner 1999 (St Olave's); Kinnaird Cup Finalist 2004, Winner 2011-12; Professional EF coach at Zuoz, at Eton, at Shrewsbury

RM Corner, Public Schools Finalist 1951 (Uppingham); Jesters Eton Fives Representative

J Courier, Schools Finalist 1987 (King Edward's, Birmingham)

SH Courtney, Public Schools Finalist 1967, 1968 (City of London) ; Kinnaird Cup Winner 1969, 1970, Finalist 1972. Great Britain & England squash international; England squash team manager

NL Cox, at Lancing; Director of The Fives Court Company; builder and owner of two courts in Northern Provence, France

TWP Cox, Schools Winner 2004, Finalist 2005 (Shrewsbury)

EJ Craig, Charterhouse 1st pair 1959-60; CUEFC 1963-64; CUCC 1962-64

P Cramer, Schools Girls Finalist 2000 (Lyceum Alpinum Zuoz)

DH Crook, Master i/c Fives at Rydal -1978

AW Culverhouse, Public Schools Finalist 1972 (City of London)

PC Curtis, at Repton; CUEFC 1947; Kinnaird Cup Winner 1957, Finalist 1955, 1958; EFA Hon Treasurer 1947-51; Hon Secretary 1952-60; Vice President 1964-84; President 1985-91; EFCT Founder Chairman

PE Cushing, Public Schools Finalist 1969 (Highgate)

HR Cutmore-Scott, Schools Girls Winner 2008 (Westminster); OUEFC 2010-12

Sir James Darling, at Repton; Head Master of Geelong GS, Melbourne 1953, when Eton fives court was built

MJ Darlington, Master i/c Fives at Rydal 1979-85

NG Darrah, at Wrekin; Master i/c Fives at Shrewsbury

TN Darrell, Master i/c Fives at Oakham 1987-2000

GA Das Gupta, Schools Winner 1989 (Wolverhampton)

CJ Davies, at Highgate; Master coaching at Highgate 1985-99

AJN Dawson, at Eton; Headmaster of Sunningdale; Organiser of Preparatory Schools Eton Fives Championships

TACN Dawson, Winner of the School Fives at Eton 1992; Headmaster of Sunningdale; Master i/c Fives at Harrow 1999-2003

TME Dawson, at Eton; Headmaster of Sunningdale

AS Day, at Harrow; Captain of Fives; Master i/c Fives at Charterhouse 1959-69

HL de Quetteville, Public Schools Finalist 1948 (Eton)

RG de Quetteville, EFA President 1934-65; Chairman 1934-47. See also Heroes of the Golden Age

MBTdeC de Souza Girao, Schools Winner 1988 (Harrow); CUEFC 1989-91; Kinnaird Cup Winner 1991

S Demierre, Ladies' Championships Finalist 1996-97

SM de Zoete Winner of the School Fives at Eton 1958, 1959; Chairman of the OEFC 2012-

PK Dicker, at City of London; EFA Hon Secretary 1995; Master i/c Fives at Berkhamsted, 1961-92

HH Dixon, Schools Winner 1996 (Eton)

JE Doley, Ladies' Championships Winner 2000, Finalist 1999

EH Donger, Schools Girls Winner 2008 (Westminster)

Sir Alec Douglas-Home, EFA President 1966-71; Patron 1972-96. See also Heroes of the Golden Age

AF Downie, Public Schools Winner 1974 (Highgate)

CD Dryborough, Highgate 1st pair 1956-7, Captain; OUEFC 1960-2; OUAFC 1961; OUCC 1960-2; Middlesex CCC captain

LJ Duckham, Master i/c Fives at Oakham 1975-80

PG Dunbar, Schools Finalist 1975 (Highgate); OUEFC; Master-in-charge of Fives at Harrow 1982-98, 2004-

PR Dunbar, Schools Winner (Harrow) 2000; Kinnaird Cup winner 2006-07, 2009, Finalist 2005, 2008, 2010; OUEFC 2004-7

TG Dunbar, Schools Finalist 1998; Schools Winner (Harrow) 2000; Kinnaird Cup Winner 2002-04, 2006-07, 2009, 2011-12, Kinnaird Cup Finalist 2005, 2008, 2010. OUEFC

TR Dunbar, Ladies' Championships Finalist 1988, 1990, 1998, 2006

HD Duncan, Schools Winner 1991 (Harrow)

MJ Duncan, Master i/c Fives at Harrow 1969-74; EFA Membership Secretary

EJ Dyson, Public Schools Winner 1954, 1955 (Aldenham); CUEFC 1958-60

JM Eaton, Schools Finalist 1982, 1984 (Shrewsbury)

MJ Edmonds, Public Schools Finalist 1964 (City of London)

JD Eggar, Master i/c Fives at Repton 1948-58; played cricket for Derbyshire

GA Eleftheriou, Schools Finalist 2001 (Highgate); CUEFC

AH Fabian, at Highgate; Kinnaird Cup Winner 1948; Finalist 1949. See also Heroes of the Golden Age

J K Fawcett, Public Schools Finalist 1954 (Highgate)

R Felce, Games Master at Lyceum Alpinum, Zuoz

MR Fenn, at Ipswich; EFA Hon Secretary 1999-2009; Vice President 2010- ; Editor of Annual Review; founder of Old Ipswichian EFC

JW Finnett, at Chigwell; Master i/c who revived fives at Queen Elizabeth's, Barnet from 1954

DC Firth, at Berkhamsted; Kinnaird Cup Winner 1974, 1976-77, 1979, 1980; Kinnaird Cup Finalist 1975. 1978, 1981

SG Flavell, Schools Finalist 1986 (Wolverhampton); CUEFC 1988

JG Fleming, Schools Winner 1991 (Harrow)

IR Fletcher, Public Schools Finalist 1974 (Berkhamsted)

L Foch, Ladies' Championships Finalist 2011

RPC Forman, Master coaching Fives at Eton

AMT Fortt, Public Schools Finalist 1956 (Cranleigh)

D Foster, at Lancing; professional fives coach at Berkhamsted, at Emanuel

AJ Fowler-Watt, at Eton; Master i/c Fives at Cranleigh 1991-96

TF Gales, Public Schools Finalist 1972 (City of London)

A Ganguly, Schools Girls Finalist 2001, Winner 2002-04 (Newstead Wood, St Olave's) ;Winner Ladies' Championships 2004, Finalist 2002-03, 2005

TR Garnett, at Charterhouse; Kinnaird Cup Winner 1949; Master i/c Fives at Charterhouse 1946-52; played cricket for Somerset; Master of Marlborough 1952-61, of Geelong GS 1962 See also Heroes of the Golden Age

GE Gergaud, Master i/c Fives at Charterhouse 1990-98

TD Gerrard, Schools Winner 2004 (Shrewsbury)

PNH Gibbs, Public Schools Winner 1967, Finalist 1965, 1966 (Eton); OUEFC

AE Gibson, at Highgate; Kinnaird Cup Winner 1978; Finalist 1977, 1979, 1984, 1985

CD Gilbert, Public Schools Winner 1971, Finalist 1970 (Highgate)

RMC Gilliatt, Charterhouse 1st pair 1962-63; Master i/c Fives at Charterhouse 1986-90; OUEFC 1964-66; OUCC 1964-67; OUAFC 1963-65; Captain of Hampshire CCC 1971-78

D Gooderick, Master i/c Fives at Aldenham, 1992-2004

DHG Goodliffe, Public Schools Finalist 1949 (Charterhouse)

PC Gordos, Schools Finalist 1988 (Wolverhampton)

PBJ Gould, Public Schools Finalist 1971 (Repton)

JA Green, Public Schools Winner 1978 (Highgate)

JC Green, Public Schools Finalist 1957 (King Edward's, Birmingham); CUEFC 1960-61

B Greenslade, Ladies' Championships Finalist 1985

RF Griffiths, Schools Finalist 2008 (Shrewsbury); CUEFC 2011-12

DJS Guilford, Public Schools Finalist 1950 (Harrow); CUEFC 1952-54; Kinnaird Cup Winner 1959, 1960, 1963; Finalist 1953, 1957, 1962; EFA to Nigeria 1965; EFA Hon Secretary 1961-68; Vice President 1975-2011; Jesters Eton Fives Representative

PA Hall, Public Schools Winner 1963 (City of London)

BM Halstead, Ladies' Championships Winner 1987

JC Halstead, at Highgate; Kinnaird Cup Winner 1996, 1997, 2001; Finalist 1994, 1995, 2002

CSH Hampton, Public Schools Winner 1963, Finalist 1964 (City of London); Kinnaird Cup Winner 1969, 1970; Finalist 1972

RA Harris, Schools Winner 1987 (Wolverhampton)

L Harvey, Schools Girls Finalist 2005 (St Olave's)

HA Hatchwell, Schools Winner 2009 (Highgate)

J Hatteea, Ladies' Championships Winner 1985-86

AP Hawkes, Public Schools Winner 1969 (City of London)

MF Hayes, Public Schools Finalist 1962, 1963 (Highgate); Kinnaird Cup Winner 1971, 1972; Finalist 1973

MR Herring, at Berkhamsted; professional fives coach

NMJ Hewens, Public Schools Finalist 1977 (Harrow)

JR Ho, Schools Finalist 2007, Winner 2008 (Highgate)

RJ Hobbs, Schools Winner 1989 (Wolverhampton)

JC Hodgkinson, at Uppingham; CUEFC 1964; Master i/c Fives at Uppingham 1975-87; Headmaster of Aysgarth

DA Hollinrake, Public Schools Winner 1958 (Highgate)

Earl Home of the Hirsel, See Sir Alec Douglas-Home

FB Hooper, at Westminster; EFA Chairman 1972-79; Vice President 1983-93

BJ Hoskins, Master i/c Fives at Ipswich, 1975-2007

GJ Hoskins, at Ipswich; EFA Secretary 2010 - ; CUEFC 1992-95

KM Hoskins (formerly Runnacles), Ladies' Championships Winner 1988-98, Finalist 2006

Rev DA Howard, Rector of St Paul's Darjeeling; responsible for court refurbishment 2007

JG Hudson-Williams, Schools Winner 2011-12 (Shrewsbury)

A Hughes, Public Schools Finalist 1957 (King Edward's, Birmingham); Kinnaird Cup Winner 1958, 1963, 1965, 1966-68, 1971, 1973, 1975; Finalist 1960-62, 1964, 1969, 1974, 1983, 1986, 1987, 1990; founder of the Old Edwardian Fives Club 1957. Coach and ambassador for Eton fives overseas

KR Hughes, at Berkhamsted; Master i/c Fives at City of London 1965-69, at Eton 1973-75; Administrator of EFA fives ball supply

MP Hughes, at Shrewsbury; professional EF coach at Shrewsbury -2011, at Eton 2011-

IJF Hutchinson, at Shrewsbury; Kinnaird Cup Finalist 2000; professional EF Coach

AH Illingworth, Winner of the School Fives at Eton 1992, 1993; Jesters Eton Fives Representative 2003-

JHH Illingworth, Public Schools Finalist 1952, 1953 (Eton)

ACD Ingleby-Mackenzie, Winner of School Fives at Eton and Public Schools Championships 1951, Chairman of Holmwoods Insurance, sponsors of Schools Fives; captained Hampshire CCC to Championship 1961

JGK Ingram, Master i/c Fives at Harrow 1960-65

AG Irwin, Public Schools Winner 1961 (Aldenham)

S Ishmael, Schools Girls Finalist 1998 (City of Norwich)

VJ Jeffrey, Ladies' Championships Winner 1998; Finalist 1987, 1989, 1995

K Johnson, Schools Girls Finalist 2002 (St Olave's)

T P Johnson, Public Schools Winner 1958 (Highgate)

DE Jones, Schools Winner 1992 (Wolverhampton)

S Katz-Roberts, Schools Girls Finalist 2011 (Highgate)

DJL Keeble, at St Olave's; presenter of the Douglas Keeble Cup for the League

MR Keeling, at Berkhamsted; Kinnaird Cup Winner 1977, 1979, 1980; Finalist 1978, 1981

PA Kelland, at Repton; Master i/c Fives at Highgate Junior School 1955-81

PSS Kerr, Public Schools Finalist 1978 (Aldenham)

SM Khan, Schools Finalist 1994, Winner 1995 (Highgate)

TA Kiggell, Master i/c Fives at Marlborough 2006-

SEA Kimmins, Charterhouse 1st pair 1947-8; played cricket for Kent CCC 1950-51

DJ King, Schools Finalist 1993, 1994; Winner 1995 (Highgate)

J King, Ladies' Championships Finalist 1991-92

Lord Kingsdown, at Eton; EFA Patron 1997-; NatWest Bank Chairman, sponsors of Eton Fives County Championship

Lord Kinnaird, EFA Patron 1947-71. See also Heroes of the Golden Age

AR Kittermaster, at Shrewsbury; CUEFC 1949-51; Kinnaird Cup Winner 1954, 1955, 1956; Finalist 1950, 1951, 1952

RM Knight, at Repton; EFA Hon Secretary 1979-89, Vice President 2000- ; Jesters Eton Fives Representative; EFCT Chairman; CUEFC President

RD Knight, Master i/c Fives at Cranleigh 1987-91, 97-99

PJ Knowles, at King Edward's, Birmingham; coaching fives at Shrewsbury 1973-4; Master i/c Fives at Highgate 1975-81, coaching 1981-2005; coaching at Bryanston 2005-; Organiser of Schools Eton Fives Championships; EFA Archivist; EFCT Hon Secretary

MJ Kovar, Schools Finalist 2011 (Highgate)

F Kuenburg, Schools Girls Winner 2009 (Lyceum Alpinum, Zuoz)

RJ Lambert, at King Edward's, Birmingham; Kinnaird Cup Finalist 1983, 1986, 1987

MJ Lamping, at King Edward's, Birmingham; Master i/c Fives at St Bees

HS Langton, Public Schools Winner 1956, Finalist 1955 (Eton)

MJ Lascelles, Master i/c Fives at Shrewsbury 1994-2003

H Le Bas, Charterhouse 1st pair 1944-45; CUEFC 1947-48; EFA Hon Secretary 1947-51

JF Leaf, at Harrow; CUEFC 1949; Master i/c Fives at Harrow 1950-59

DS Lee, Public Schools Finalist 1951 (Uppingham)

J Leigh, Master i/c Fives at Cranleigh 1980-86

R Leigh-Pemberton, See Lord Kingsdown

AP Lewis, Marlborough 1st pair 1959-60; Master i/c Fives at Repton 1975-85

H Lewis, Schools Winner 2012 (Shrewsbury)

JB Lewis, Schools Finalist 1995, 1996 (Shrewsbury)

RAC Linzee, Public Schools Winner 1948 (Eton)

MR Little, Schools Winner 2005 (Highgate); CUEFC

SC Little, Schools Finalist 2007, Winner 2008, 2009 (Highgate)

JD Luddy, Public Schools Winner 1976 (Repton)

AC Lumbard, Schools Girls Winner 2006-07 (Lancing)

JR Lumbard, Schools Girls Finalist 2007 (Lancing)

DTG Luxford, Public Schools Finalist 1969 (Highgate)

J MacDonagh, Schools Finalist 2009 (Eton); OUEFC

DR Maclean, Public Schools Finalist 1952, 1953 (Eton)

SIJ Maguire, Schools Girls Finalist 2008 (Lancing)

TE Manning, Master i/c Fives at City of London

C Mantle, Schools Girls Finalist 2009 (Highgate); OUEFC 2010-12

PN Markkanen, Schools Finalist 1992 (St Olave's)

DAC Marr, Public Schools Winner 1952 (Eton)

DJ Marshall, at Brighton, Master i/c Fives at St Bees

J Marston, at Eton, Master i/c Fives at Aysgarth -1988, Jeremy Marston Plate annually awarded in Preparatory Schools Championship

Sir Henry Marten, Provost of Eton; knighted on the Chapel steps, below the original fives court. See also Heroes of the Golden Age

RJ Mason, Schools Winner 1986 (King Edward's, Birmingham); CUEFC 1987-9, 92-5; Kinnaird Cup Winner 1993-95, 1998, 1999, 2002-04; Finalist 1992

R Matland, Director of the Westway Trust, responsible for the construction of courts at the Westway Sports Centre

BC Matthews, at City of London; Kinnaird Cup Winner 1981-90; Kinnaird Cup Finalist 1980; Master i/c Fives at Highgate 1982-2004

R Matthews, Public Schools Winner 1979 (City of London)

DRH Maughan, Master i/c Fives at Queen Elizabeth's, Barnet 1979-2000

GS May, at Berkhamsted; CUEFC 1968-70; Kinnaird Cup Winner 1974, 1976; Finalist 1975

JWH May, Public Schools Winner 1949, 1950 (Charterhouse); Kinnaird Cup Winner 1951, 1952, 1953

PBH May, Charterhouse 1st pair 1945-47; CUEFC 1950-52; Kinnaird Cup Winner 1951, 1952, 1953. England cricket captain

DH Macindoe, Winner of School Fives at Eton 1936; OUCC; a Master and Vice Provost at Eton; co-author with CH Taylor of *Cricket Dialogue*

J Maclean, at Lancing; professional coach at Rydal Penrhos

MM McKeever, Schools Finalist 2008 (Shrewsbury)

SJ McWatters, Master i/c Fives at Eton; Manager of Eton College tour to Nigeria 1961; later Headmaster of Clifton

DG Mew, at St Olave's; professional coach at Westway

MOMcL Mills, Public Schools Finalist 1973 (Eton)

BAS Mitchell, Public Schools Finalist 1961 (Berkhamsted)

F Mitchell, Ladies' Championships Finalist 1991-92

U Mohammadu, Public Schools Winner 1959 (Aldenham); first played Eton fives in Northern Nigeria

JR Mole, Schools Winner 1986 (King Edward's, Birmingham); CUEFC 1988-91; Kinnaird Cup Winner 1993-95, 1998, 1999, 2002-04; Finalist 1992

MJ Moore, at Wolverhampton; CUEFC 1981-84; Kinnaird Cup Winner 1992; Finalist 1993; Master i/c Fives at Eton 1990-92. Headmaster of Clifton

AS Morrison, at Eton; Master i/c Fives at Charterhouse 1970-80

E Morrison, Schools Finalist 2009 (Eton)

MG Moss, at Harrow; EFA tour to Nigeria 1965; President OHEFC

C Most, Schools Finalist 2011 (Highgate)

ARB Moulsdale, at Shrewsbury; CUEFC 1949-51; Kinnaird Cup Winner 1954, 1955, 1956; Finalist 1950, 1951, 1952; Master coaching fives at Shrewsbury

R Myrsep, Games Master at Lyceum Alpinum, Zuoz

R Nagy, Master i/c Fives at City of London 1998-2003

AST Negretti, Public Schools Winner 1964 (Eton); EFA tour to Nigeria 1965

CPA Nissen, Triple Winner of School Fives at Eton: Schools Winner 2003 (Eton)

EFJ Nissen, Schools Winner 2003 (Eton)

RE Norman, Public Schools Winner 1965, 1966 (Highgate)

RMW Norris, Schools Winner 1994 (Harrow)

K Nunn, Schools Girls Finalist 2003 (Mill Hill)

AA O'Callaghan, Schools Winner 2005 (Highgate)

J O'Callaghan, Schools Finalist 2004 (Highgate); CUEFC 2005-8

HC 'Bertie' Owen, at Shrewsbury; Master i/c Fives at Berkhamsted 1945-56

BJ Pack, Public Schools Finalist 1970 (Highgate)

RM Packham, Public Schools Finalist 1949 (Charterhouse)

S Palmer, Schools Girls Winner 2005, Finalist 2006 (Lancing)

L Parker, Ladies' Championships Winner 1994-97

AT Parker, Schools Finalist 2006, Winner 2007 (Shrewsbury)

MJ Parsons, Schools Winner 1981, Finalist 1980 (Berkhamsted)

RW Parsons, Public Schools Finalist 1976 (Berkhamsted)

A Patel, Schools Finalist 2004 (Highgate); CUEFC 2005-7

RSR Pattison, at Charterhouse; EFA Vice Chairman

A Paul, School Girls Winner 2011-12 (Highgate)

SJ Peaker, Schools Finalist 1983 (Wolverhampton)

JM Pearson, Schools Winner 1987, Finalist 1988 (Wolverhampton)

DRV Pedley, at Wolverhampton; Master i/c Fives at Wolverhampton 1978-97

FA Peet, at Charterhouse; Kinnaird Cup Finalist 1948; OUEFC 1946; OUAFC 1947

Hon MC Penney, Public Schools Finalist 1956 (Cranleigh); CUEFC 1960

MT Peplow, Master i/c Fives at Queen Elizabeth's, Barnet 2001-

J Pepper, Master coaching Fives at Rydal -1985

MJ Perkins, Public Schools Winner 1949 (Charterhouse)

R Perrie, Professional coach at Westway

JM Peterson, Kinnaird Cup Winner 1950; EFA Chairman 1948-50; Vice President 1948-77; Headmaster of Shrewsbury. See also Heroes of the Golden Age

NF Peterson, Schools Winner 1959 (Eton)

MS Pett, Master i/c Fives at Berkhamsted 2000-

AH Phillips, at Shrewsbury; Assistant Master at Shrewsbury 1925-64

AG Phillips, at Shrewsbury; Kinnaird Cup Finalist 1954; Master coaching Fives at Shrewsbury 1961-76

TC Pilkington, Public Schools Finalist 1958, 1959 (Eton)

CR Pilkington, Public Schools Finalist 1960 (Repton)

JMA Pinner, Schools Winner 1985 (Highgate)

ST Plummer, Master i/c Fives at Mill Hill 1990-

NEJ Pocock, Public Schools Winner 1970 (Shrewsbury); Captain Hampshire CCC

DJ Pollock, Schools Finalist 1984 (Shrewsbury)

CS Poole, Master i/c Fives at Bryanston 1975-2012

WG Poole, Public Schools Winner 1965 (Highgate)

BLH Powell, Public Schools Winner 1967 (Eton)

MP Powell, at Eton; EFA Hon Secretary 1990-95; Hon Treasurer 1995-

MWG Pryke, at Highgate; Kinnaird Cup Finalist 1949

MS Rasheed, Schools Winner 1990 (Highgate)

NC Rathbone, Schools Winner 1983 (Highgate); Kinnaird Cup Finalist 1991, 1993

RNE Raven, at Shrewsbury; Master coaching fives at Shrewsbury

CTA Ray, at Charterhouse; Master i/c Fives at Lancing 1951-58, at Charterhouse 1980-81

DEA Redmond, Schools Girls Finalist 2003 (Kingston College); Ladies' Championships Winner 2005-12; professional fives coach

L Redmond, Ladies' Championships 2008 Finalist, Winner 2012

M Rees, Schools Girls Finalist 1999, Winner 2000 (St. Olave's); Ladies' Championships 2000-01, 2007, 2009-12

JR Rees, Schools Winner 1998 (St Olave's)

A Reimer, Schools Girls Finalist 2011 (Highgate)

Hon PF Remnant, Public Schools Finalist 1973 (Eton)

JP Reynolds, Public Schools Winner 1979 (City of London); Kinnaird Cup Winner 1981-91; Finalist 1980; author of Eton Fives Coaching Manual; Director of The Fives Court Company

PE Reynolds, Public Schools Winner 1954, 1955 (Aldenham); CUEFC 1958-60

JD Rimer, at Aldenham; EFCT Hon Treasurer

DS Ritchie, Public Schools Winner 1968 (Highgate)

MJ Robinson, Schools Winner 1993 (Highgate)

NF Robinson, at Eton; Public Schools Winner 1951; CUEFC 1954-56

WD Robson, Eton tour to Nigeria 1960; Winner of the School Fives at Eton 1962; Kinnaird Cup Finalist 1966

OD Rodwell, Schools Finalist 2001, Winner 2002 (Highgate)

MO Ross, Schools Winner 1992 (Wolverhampton)

NJ Rossi, Ladies' Championships Finalist 1993-95

JR Rowland-Clark, Schools Winner 2006 (Eton)

K Rudman, Schools Finalist 1992 (St Olave's)

N Rumph, Schools Girls Finalist 2001 (Lyceum Alpinum, Zuoz)

RB Rumsam, Public Schools Finalist 1963 (Highgate)

K Rymarz, Schools Girls Finalist 1998 (City of Norwich)

R Sale, Master i/c Fives at Repton 1945-60; OUEFC 1939

AJ Sanghrajka, Master i/c Fives at Bryanston 2012-

DRS Saunders, at Shrewsbury; Kinnaird Cup Finalist 1959

DJ Saunders, Schools Finalist 1981 (Shrewsbury)

H Schofield, Ladies' Championships Finalist 1987, 1989

RE Scott, Schools Girls Winner 2006-07 (Lancing); OUEFC 2008-9

GDP Scott, Public Schools Finalist 1978 (Aldenham)

RS Scott, Public Schools Finalist 1971 (Repton)

A Shams, Schools Finalist 1990 (Highgate)

BH Shaw, at King Edward's, Birmingham; Kinnaird Cup Finalist 1962

NR Shaw, Schools Winner 1994 (Harrow); CUEFC 1996-9

TP Shaw, Eton tour to Nigeria 1960; Kinnaird Cup Finalist 1965

CEW Sheepshanks, at Eton; Kinnaird Cup Winner 1950. See also Heroes of the Golden Age

A Shelley, Schools Girls Finalist 2005 (St Olave's)

SP Sherrard, Public Schools Winner 1964, Finalist 1965 (Eton)

JM Shorrocks, Public Schools Finalist 1974, 1976, Winner 1977 (Berkhamsted)

MJ Shortland-Jones, at Harrow; CUEFC 1950-53; Kinnaird Cup Winner 1959, 60; Finalist 1953, 1957, 1967, 1968; EFA tour to Nigeria 1965; EFA President 1992-2000; Vice President 1983-91; Hon Secretary 1975-78; Master i/c Fives at Ipswich, Berkhamsted, Eton

WP Shovelton, Charterhouse 1st pair, 1938; OUEFC; Jesters Hon Secretary 1952-56; Under-Sec Dept Trade & Industry 1972-78

AS Simmons, Schools Winner 1993 (Wolverhampton)

RA Skeels, Schools Finalist 1985, 1986 (Wolverhampton)

CA Sloan, Public Schools Winner 1961 (Aldenham)

RW Smart, Public Schools Finalist 1950 (Harrow)

AC Smith, King Edward's, Birmingham 1st pair 1955; Warwickshire CCC; England cricketer; Chief Executive of the TCCB

MR Smith, Public Schools Winner 1978 (Highgate)

PM Smith, Public Schools Winner 1975 (King Edward's Birmingham)

E Smith-Bingham, Schools Girls Winner 2011-12 (Highgate)

JR Smithers, Public Schools Finalist 1959 (Eton)

CW Sorrell, Schools Finalist 1999 (Eton)

AM Stanton, Schools Finalist 1989 (Highgate)

SR Stephens, Triple Winner of School Fives at Eton 1986-88

AP Stephenson, Schools Winner 1980, 1982, Finalist 1983 (Wolverhampton)

JM Steward, Master i/c Fives at Oakham 1981-86

RA Streatfield, Public Schools Finalist 1948 (Eton)

RE Strickland, at Shrewsbury; CUEFC 1952-55; Kinnaird Cup Finalist 1954

GD Stringer, at City of London; EFA tour to Nigeria 1965; EFA Hon Secretary 1969-74; Vice President 1993-

AV Sutton, Charterhouse 1st pair 1954-56; EFA Hon Treasurer 1980-84

E Tadman, Schools Girls Winner (Bullers Wood) 1998-99; Ladies' Championships Winner 1999, 2001-03, Finalist 2004

JDP Tanner, Charterhouse 1st pair, 1940; OUEFC 1949; OUAFC 1948; Amateur Cup Winners medal (Pegasus AFC) 1951; 3 England Amateur caps 1947-48

EO Taylor, at Shrewsbury; Kinnaird Cup Finalist 1998, 2000

C Temple, Ladies' Championships Finalist 1984

AJ Tennant, Public Schools Winner 1948 (Eton); CUEFC 1952-53

A Theodossi, at Emanuel; professional EF coach at Berkhamsted 2009-

G Thomason, Schools Winner 2011 (Shrewsbury); professional coach at Rydal Penrhos

N Tindale, Schools Girls Finalist 2012 (Highgate)

RM Tinn, Public Schools Finalist 1960 (Repton)

ATR Titchener-Barrett, Schools Finalist 1997, 1998 (Harrow)

JG Tolchard, at Malvern; Master i/c Fives at Berkhamsted 1994-99

RL Toomey, at St Olave's; Kinnaird Cup Finalist 1976

H Toop, Schools Girls Finalist 2002 (St Olave's)

JP Toop, Schools Finalist 1997, Winner 1998-99 (St Olave's); Kinnaird Cup Winner 2000, 2005, 2008, 2010; Finalist 1999, 2001, 2003, 2004, 2006, 2007, 2009, 2011, 2012; Rugby Fives Singles Champion 2008-11

JC Troy, Master i/c Fives at Westminster 1994-98, at Charterhouse 1999-

RDN Topham, at Shrewsbury; OUEFC; Master coaching fives at Eton

MW Tudor, Schools Finalist 1990, 1991 (Highgate)

RMG Turnbull, at Eton; EFA Chairman 1980-85; Hon Treasurer 1972-79, 1985-95

J Turnbull, Schools Finalist 1987 (King Edward's, Birmingham)

JM Turner, Schools Girls Finalist 2004 (Kingston College)

JRM Turner, Public Schools Winner 1977 (Berkhamsted)

RC Tyler, Schools Winner 1984 (King Edward's, Birmingham); Kinnaird Cup Finalist 1990, 1998; CUEFC

JDC Vargas, at Harrow; CUEFC 1961; EFA Chairman 1986 -90, President 2001-06, Vice President 1993-2001, 2007- ; Master i/c Fives at Harrow 1975-82; EFCT Trustee; President OHEFC

K Vargas, Ladies' Championships Winner 1984-87, Finalist 1990,1998

J Varma, Schools Girls Finalist 2009 (Highgate)

AS Varma, Schools Winner 2001, 2002 (Highgate); CUEFC 2007

V Vernon, (formerly Hothersall) Ladies' Championships Winner 1984-87

GB Vine, Public Schools Winner 1957 (Aldenham); CUEFC 1959-61

JK Waddell, at Aldenham; Hon Sec OAEFC; Master coaching fives at Aldenham

AR Wagg, Public Schools Winner 1959 (Eton); EFA Vice Chairman; Jesters Eton Fives Representative

WG Wainwright, Public Schools Finalist 1967, 1968 (City of London)

DB Wainwright, Public Schools Winner 1973, 1974; Finalist 1975 (Highgate); Kinnaird Cup Winner 1978; Finalist 1977, 1979, 1982, 1985, 1988, 1989

LD Walker, Public Schools Finalist 1961 (Berkhamsted)

JC Wallis, at St Olave's; Kinnaird Cup Winner 1961, 1962, 1964; Finalist 1963

JGM Walsh, Eton tour to Nigeria 1960; Winner of School Fives at Eton 1961; Public Schools Winner 1962 (Eton)

JJ Walters, Schools Finalist 2000 (Shrewsbury)

EA Wass, Schools Finalist 1989 (Highgate); Kinnaird Cup Winner 1996, 1997, 2001; Finalist 1991, 1994, 1995, 2002

JKG Webb, at Highgate; Kinnaird Cup Winner 1948; Finalist 1949. See also Heroes of the Golden Age

A Wells, Schools Girls Finalist 1999, Winner 2000 (St. Olave's); Ladies' Championships Finalist 2000-01

D Wells Cole, Master i/c Fives at St John's, Leatherhead 1991-2006

S Welti, Schools Finalist 2012 (Shrewsbury)

KL White, Schools Girls Winner (Bullers Wood) 1998-99; Ladies' Championships Winner 1999-2003, 2005-11, Finalist 2004

D Whitehead, at Berhamsted; EFA Vice-President 2004-; EFCT Hon Secretary; Administrator of Eton Fives Ball Supply

CMB Williams, Public Schools Winner 1973 (Highgate); Kinnaird Cup Finalist 1982, 1984; Master i/c Fives at Shrewsbury, Harrow, Eton; Organiser of the Schools Championships 1989-

G Williams, Schools Finalist 2012 (Shrewsbury)

GDP Williams, at Highgate; Professional EF coach at Shrewsbury -2011

RJ Williams, Public Schools Winner 1972 (Berkhamsted)

CRC Wimble, Master i/c Fives at Lancing 1975-80

HME Wiseman, at St. Olave's; Kinnaird Cup Winner 2008; Finalist 2006, 2009, 2012. Founder & Proprietor of the Rugby & Eton Fives Coaching Agency

MCT Wiseman, Schools Winner 1997 (St Olave's); Kinnaird Cup Winner 2005, 2010; Finalist 1999, 2001, 2003, 2006, 2007, 2011; professional coach

RJ Wood, Public Schools Winner 1976 (Repton)

TJ Wood, at City of London; Clerk to Wax Chandlers, hosts to EFA Committee meetings in the 1980s

J Woodcock, at Uppingham; coached fives at Ludgrove, Summer Fields; CUEFC

L Wootten, Ladies' Championships Winner 1989-93

RJStJ Worth, Schools Finalist 2006, Winner 2007 (Shrewsbury); OUEFC 2009-12

PStJ Worth, Public Schools Winner 1970 (Shrewsbury); EFA Chairman 2010-

GA Worthington, Master i/c at King Edward's, Birmingham

AJ Wreford-Brown, at Charterhouse; Kinnaird Cup Winner 1949; Finalist 1948

MA Yates, Schools Finalist 1985 (Wolverhampton)

MW Yates, at Wolverhampton; developed Eton Fives Coaching Certificates; professional coach at Wolverhampton, at Wrekin, at KES Birmingham

H Young, Schools Winner 2001 (Highgate); OUEFC 2004-2005

Sir Brian Young, at Eton; CUEFC 1947; Headmaster of Charterhouse 1952-64

Appendix 4 – The Path of the Eton Fives Ball

The early history of fives is closely entwined with that of rackets: not only were the balls used for rackets, Eton and Rugby fives almost identical except for size, they were usually produced by the same manufacturers.

The earliest known maker of rackets racquets and balls was Pittman in 1834. After his death, production was taken over by a Mitchell, father of the rackets champion in 1846, John Mitchell.

The first school to take up rackets was Harrow where the game had been played in the School Yard since its enlargement in 1821. The game was played with 'leather-covered' balls known – oddly enough – as 'best fives', which were purchased from a shop in the High Street owned by a Mrs Arnold, known as 'Old Polly'. Later they were supplied by Sam Hoare, Custos from 1848-85, although presumably neither of these people actually made them.

Around 1850, so the story goes, a certain Mr Malings, was committed to prison for the incurring of debts. Because of the often quoted passage in Charles Dickens's *Pickwick Papers*, it is well known that the inmates of the Fleet Debtors' Prison occupied themselves with the playing of rackets. Less well known is the King's Bench Prison where Mr Malings found himself. The prisoners there also played rackets and fives and were of course obliged to manufacture their own balls for their games. Mr Malings proved more than usually adept at this craft and on release turned his skill into a business. The firm, Jefferies & Malings, suppliers of balls for rackets, rounders, stoolball, yardball and fives, was founded by Mr Henry Malings, a relation of the above, in 1852.

Another early supplier of rackets balls were the brothers Frank and George Erwood. Both were professional rackets players, Frank an instructor at the military college at Woolwich, George at Hampstead. In 1862 TH Prosser came on the scene, his firm later to trade as Clarence Prosser of Holloway. Prosser claimed at the head of his invoice sheets that he had been trained at Jefferies & Malings, and also that he was patronised by the Prince's Club (which had both rackets and fives courts). In 1882 he also claimed to be supplying Oxford and Cambridge Universities, Harrow, Eton, Rugby, Cheltenham, Marlborough, Winchester and Haileybury.

In 1873, Henry Malings of Woolwich, describing himself as 'late of the firm of Jefferies & Malings, and 'by special appointment to the Marylebone Club' (cricket and real tennis) appears. Then HJ Gray of Cambridge, calling himself 'Racquet Manufacturer' in 1878 had become 'Racquet & Lawn Tennis Manufacturer'

by 1882. He charged eighteen shillings and sixpence a gross for rackets balls and forty-eight shillings a gross for fives balls.

In 1890 The Rev JAA Tait, who was teaching at Charterhouse, wrote an essay on fives, which included an authoritative paragraph on fives balls. "The balls used at Eton are invariably by Gradidge of Woolwich, weight 1¼ oz. To my mind however, none are equal to Prosser's best Eton Fives balls, price 36 shillings the gross (the cheaper quality are not to be relied on), for weight durability and liveliness. For the Rugby games, the small-sized ball is the one always used: weight 1 1/8 oz; price about 28 shillings the gross. It is not so difficult to obtain satisfactory ones in this size and there is the choice of makers: Prosser, Jefferies, Malings, Gray and Ayres are all reliable, and doubtless many others;

Tony Baden-Fuller, who developed the formula for the modern Eton fives ball in his lunch hours while working for Shell

but for the Eton game it is exceedingly difficult to get good balls – at least that is my experience after trying many makers. The great point is to see that they are new balls not second-hand ones re-covered; keep them in a warm, dry place, for cold and damp are fatal; sprinkle a little flour, powdered chalk, or white lead over them that they may be clean and white when wanted for use."

Early in the 20th century the manufacture of both rackets and fives balls was taken over by Jeffery Malings of Woolwich. John Armitage, in a very erudite article written in 1933 entitled *The Craft of the Ball Maker*, writes, "With the craft of ball-making the name of Malings has long been connected.... To the best of our knowledge there is no other manufacturer of these balls in the whole world, who carries on this craft under the same old-world conditions as do Malings. Other

big sports manufacturers, such as Messrs. Gradidge and Messrs Prosser, make these balls in their factories, as a small side-line to their greater activities, but Malings confine themselves to the making of balls alone." He goes on to describe the process in some detail.

"The centre of a Fives or Rackets ball is a small piece of cork. Taking this piece of cork in his hand the craftsman folds around it strips of pure wool listing. Listings are less than an inch wide and are from the best possible cloth. Pure wool uniforms, such as pre-war Army Red and Blues and many officers' uniforms have ended their days beneath the cover of a ball but the present-day Khaki contains cotton and is useless. Billiard cloth is also used when it can be obtained. The wool listing is the most important material in the manufacture of a ball. The entire bounce of a ball is derived from the wool and the liveliness of each individual ball is dependent upon the amount of pressure to which it has been subjected. Far more wool than one could easily imagine from the size is embodied in the manufacture of a ball. Nine pounds of cloth are used in every gross of fives balls and one pound of worsted for winding. Both the listings and the worsted have to be worked wet, as the ball is made rather bigger than its ultimate size and shrunk later by drying.

"After the craftsman has wound the listing round the centre of cork, he stands in front of his bench and press. The press is a simple machine with an arrangement of cups shaped to size. Taking the ball between his fingers the craftsman begins to wind, twisting the ball round and round, working his fingers like a spider's legs. He is moulding the shape of the ball in his hand. He binds the worsted tight, stretching it to twice its natural length and every now and again he presses the embryo ball between the cups of his machine. Soon the first stage of the procedure is completed, the ball is a perfect round and although still big the listing has been covered with an equal layer of worsted. Although many weeks will go by before this ball is ready for play the most difficult task in its manufacture has been accomplished. It takes two years or more, rarely less, for the craftsman to learn to shape the ball between his fingers as he winds. Five out of seven boys who apprentice themselves to this craft prove quite unfit for the work, for it requires nimbleness of the fingers, which few possess.

"The ball is then taken to the drying room, where it is placed alongside many of its fellows on a rack. There is no artificial heating in this room and the balls lie like so many apples in the loft, gradually drying beneath the roof. Here they remain for four, five or six weeks before having a final baking in a warm oven. If the ball has been badly moulded, it will have shrunk out of shape and will now be discarded for reconstruction. If it is a good ball, it will have shrunk to the right size, quite round. The ball is now placed in the hands of the finisher. The finisher takes the ball between his fingers but instead of twisting the ball and winding the worsted round and round, he winds straight, first in one direction and then at right angles to the original line. He, too, uses the press from time to time. Once more the ball is replaced in the oven to make quite sure that every vestige of dampness has disappeared, for if the wool is wet, the ball will not bounce. The ball is now ready to be covered.

"Covering is done by women workers, who do their work in their own homes. Stitching rackets and fives balls is not the easiest of tasks, and since no woman can be expected to ply her needle for more than two hours at a time, it has been deemed wisest to let them work at home at piece rates. Accordingly a woman will call for so many uncovered balls and the same number of coverings. The coverings are made of the best sheepskin. First they are cut into squares of regulation size for the type of ball required; next they are thoroughly damped; then, when the ball has been placed in the centre of the square the four corners are joined together at the top, in much the same way as an orange is sometimes peeled by stripping the skin off in four quarters. The waste skin is cut off and the seams stitched as close as possible. It would be impossible to get a tight skin if the covering was worked dry. As it is, the damp skin stretches for the worker and grows tighter and tighter as it dries.

"The covering is very difficult and important work, but however good it is, the seam will stand up slightly from the skin, causing the bouncing ball to break at awkward angles. Hence the next step is to roll down the seams. This again is done by hand. Half-a-dozen balls are taken together and placed inside a specially grooved cover. A similar cover but with a handle is placed on top so that the balls are sandwiched between the two. The top cover is then wound round and round, fast and furiously, first in one direction then in the other, while inside the balls are having their seams rubbed down.

"The important business of testing then begins, and those which pass this eager scrutiny are stamped with the name of the maker and made ready for sale."

Armitage gives further information about the old fives ball: "There are eleven thousand stitches in the coverings of a gross of fives balls or an average of 84 stitches per ball. A good woman coverer may do as many as ten balls an hour, others as few as four or five. It takes a long time to gain the required knack for a coverer mainly because the stitches must be small and a small ball is a difficult object to handle. The speed of a ball is usually in relation to the number of times

it has been returned for recovering. …The harder type of fives ball has usually been re-made."

It is clear from reports and letters to school magazines that in the early days the type of ball used was far from standard. The *Eton College Chronicle* claimed that the ball used at Harrow was larger than the Eton ball. In 1890 a letter to *The Carthusian* asks, "Why don't we use Eton balls here, since we play in Eton courts?" And as late as 1925, fives at Shrewsbury was still being played with a smaller ball.

These balls were made by the old 'wound thread and stitched leather cover' method. They were replaced by the composition cork and rubber ball, designed by Tony Baden-Fuller in the 1960s

In 1918 Eton announced that, for the first time ever, fives balls were unprocurable due to war. However by 1921 they were back on sale at 10 pence each.

In spite of the lengthy process and skill of the craftsmen, the performance of the Malings ball was variable. Often the stitching would come adrift. Especially when the courts were at all damp, the skin would split at the stitches. If the stitching survived, eventually the skin would stretch and become very loose. In matches it was customary to start each game with a new ball. Of course balls could be, and were, re-covered – at about half the cost of new.

When, at last, Malings was obliged to retire through ill-health he handed on the business to Mr. EJ Bailey, his manager. The business carried on in the same house. Edmund Bailey had his office and testing room combined in the front room. Armitage describes the scene: "Huge baskets, full of rackets, fives and rounders balls,

stand about the room, and Mr Bailey tests each ball himself at an amazing speed. He stands facing the fireplace with an empty basket on either side of him. Then, from another basket he takes a large handful of new balls. Like lightning he bounces these balls one after another on the hearthstone, testing each one partly by the bounce but more especially by the sound. With another flick of the wrist the ball drops neatly into the correct basket, according to its merit, sound or rejected."

Bailey had a couple of anecdotes about the players of Eton and Rugby Fives. In the old debtors prison, fives balls were known among the inmates as 'Bench Balls', that is King's Bench Balls. In the trade the name persisted – but it seems only for Rugby balls. Asked for a fives ball, the craftsman knew that an Eton ball was meant, but a Bench Ball, light or heavy, was always used to signify the two kinds of Rugby ball.

Apparently Rugby fives players were content to have their balls delivered in a large sack. "This sack," he said, "would stand in the corner of the tuck-shop whence the boys would choose their ball by bouncing one or two upon the floor. Not so the Eton fives player. He not only desired his balls to be packed in boxes of a dozen so that he might carry them about under his arm, but demanded also that they should be individually wrapped and sealed in blue paper."

Unsurprisingly, problems of supply occurred again during the Second World War but this time it was more serious. Although the Malings premises was hit by a bomb and Mrs Bailey was killed, the firm went on producing fives balls for another fifteen years. It seems that there were several companies selling fives balls at this time: Lillywhites, Gradidge, Slazenger, and the less well-known Webber Bros of London SE25 and Jabez Cliff of Walsall. In 1947 it became an EFA committee matter when it was reported that the balls supplied by Lillywhites were "unsuitable" and were returned. By 1954 it was reported in the minutes that "Jefferies Malings is now a one-man band". Edmund Bailey went on until 1962 but died a year later. In 1961 balls from Webber Bros were selling at 10s each, re-covers 3s 6d; Slazenger's were much cheaper at 60s a dozen, re-covers 31s 8d a dozen.

Some years before then the EFA committee had realised that a crisis point had been reached. In 1957 they formed a sub-committee to look into the whole business as a matter of urgency. There were two main problems: first the thread winding and pressing was a very labour-intensive business and second, the cover and stitching required skills that were no longer being passed on. After the demise of Malings, hopes were pinned on Cliff's who had some up-to-date machines. The Cliff ball was quite hard and had a wooden core, and efforts were made to get them to modify it.

Two ideas were tried to solve the problem of

covering: one was to stick the skin cover to the ball, thus avoiding the need to stitch. Another was to replace the skin with thin sticking plaster. Maybe one of these two methods would have been developed further as in rackets and Rugby fives, but the problem of making the inner part of the ball still remained. The sub-committee then approached W Gordon, the rackets professional at Marlborough, who had "perfected" a plastic rackets ball. John Armitage of the Rugby Fives Association was also interested in a plastic ball so, in 1958, Gordon began working on a plastic fives ball. Various manufacturers were contacted including ICI Plastics and Craxford's of Broadstairs, who were making the plastic rackets balls. A few experiments were carried out without success; one of the difficulties was that the projected sales were not large enough to justify experimentation without financial support from the Eton Fives Association – who did not have any money. The plastic fives ball was never perfected and after much delay the idea was abandoned.

In 1960, Anthony Baden-Fuller, who had played Eton fives at Uppingham and Cambridge, began to investigate a new idea, that of finding a composition substance to mould a completely different ball. He had just graduated from the university and had begun employment with Shell. The development work was done in his lunch hour – actually over a hundred lunch hours. By 1963 Baden-Fuller had devised a satisfactory combination of cork and rubber, covered with a specially formulated white paint to resist scuffing. This was marketed as the EFA ball.

The approximate proportions of the ingredients of the new ball were cork (30%) and rubber (50%). Needless to say, there were some teething problems, largely caused by the variability of the texture of the cork. Several firms were approached to manufacture the new composition ball. Negotiations were conducted with

Volcrepe Ltd of Glossop, Woodville Rubber of Ross on Wye, and Sparkbrook. Sparkbrook set up a production stream for a while but the quantities involved did not make a contract worth their while. Then, in 1977, a family firm near Bath agreed to work on the new ball. Derek Price, the Managing Director, had always been interested in sporting equipment and the company was a manufacturer of many other types of ball. Price

The modern Eton fives ball is manufactured by J. Price (Bath) Ltd.

himself took a personal interest in the project and the company became the sole supplier of the EFA ball.

Although the composition ball was different to its predecessor, being faster and smoother so taking less 'cut', after initial dissatisfaction, players soon adjusted to it. The Malings ball bounced approximately 18 inches when dropped from 50 inches; originally the new ball had a similar

bounce, but over the years the demand for a faster ball has resulted in a bounce of between 22 and 24 inches.

In 1988 C King Chemicals agreed to re-coat balls in small quantities, but after a short while this proved uneconomic. From 1989 onwards Derek Whitehead has taken on this task himself. Initially it was quite an involved process, which involved heating the coated balls to dry the paint properly. However around 1993/4 Price acquired a paint from America that no longer required the heating process.

Despite several crises brought about by uncertain supply and quality of cork, the EFA ball has been in constant use to this day. From a manufacturer's point of view, the major problem remains: the small quantity required. Only about 3000 new balls are made each year, and mixing small batches of cork and rubber inevitably results in a few rogue balls that either bounce too high, too low or wobble. However the manufacturer has reduced rejects to less than 2 per 100, and currently there is general acceptance that the balls are very good.

Strangely and as an example of how fragmented the organisation of Eton fives still was, in 1970 Hymers College, Hull were still using Cliff's balls, which they considered suitable for the rough surfaces of their courts. Cliff's were not recommended by the EFA at that time because they were harder and more expensive than the EFA ball, but were described as "better than ten years ago".

Nowadays the EFA ball is in universal usage – except in Nigeria. It has proved to be an excellent successor to the old ball. Furthermore few players complain of bruised hands, a very common occurrence during the 1960s and 1970s. The Malings ball too frequently had players padding their gloves with anything from cotton wool and penny coins to plasticine and raw steak.

Appendix 5 – Glossary of Terms

Absence	a roll call at Eton where boys have to answer their names
Ace	a serve that is not returned, thus winning a point. This is not possible in Eton fives. In old terminology 'ace' was sometimes used instead of 'point'
After 12	a period between noon and lunch – a time for playing fives
Bag, to	to claim (for example a fives court)
Ball-fagging	junior boy duty, collecting balls hit out of the court
Battledore	a bat used in the original game of badminton (called battledore & shuttlecock')
Beak	a master at Eton (also used at Harrow)
Blackguard cut	a first cut that hits the front wall to the left of the vertical line, without first hitting the side wall (a 'blackguard')
Bully	old term for 'rally'
Bureian	a pupil of King Edward VI Grammar School, Bury St Edmunds – also the name of the school magazine
Carrying	prolonged contact with the ball, not a clean hit; also known as 'lifting'
Carthusian	a pupil of Charterhouse School – also the name of the school magazine
Choice	one of a select few of the best players (Eton term), often called a 'colour' or a 'scarf' at other schools
Cholmeleian	a pupil of Highgate School – also the name of the school magazine
Citizen	a pupil of the City of London School
Colleger	a King's Scholar at Eton
Coping	layer of stone across the top of a wall of an Eton fives court
Cut, to	(i) to return the ball from a serve, sometimes known as 'first cut'
	(ii) to hit the ball with under spin
Dead Man's hole	the space, originally a drain, between the step of a fives court and the buttress
Down, to be	(i) a ball hitting the front wall below the line is said to be 'down'
	(ii) a player who loses a point when 'up' is then 'down'
Edwardian	a pupil of King Edward's School, Birmingham
Fagging	junior boy duties
Finge	"not me" (old Eton slang)
First cut	the return of service by the cutter
Game ball	the situation when one team reaches a point short of game (usually 11)
Good 'un	term to describe a ball hit out of court (obsolete)
Half	a school term (Eton word); for example 'Michaelmas half' or 'fives half'
Harrovian	a pupil of Harrow School - also the name of the school magazine
Hole	short for Dead Man's Hole
Holes, in	to be cutting (old Eton term)
Holes innings	old term for "to be serving" (Eton term)
Jesters	A court games' club founded in 1928
Keeper	one of the first fives pair at Eton (and sometimes elsewhere); captain of fives
Kill the ball	to hit the ball into the join of wall and floor so that it does not bounce up
Kinnaird	'The Kinnaird' refers to the national Eton fives championships at which players compete for the Kinnaird Cup (presented in 1924 & first competed for in 1925)
Let	a let is given when a player is prevented from playing a shot due to obstruction by his opponent. The point is played again without penalty
Liberties	permission to go out of bounds (Eton term)
Lifting	see 'carrying'
Lob	a soft shot – usually over the 'pepper'
Lower boy	a boy in the lower part of the School (Eton term)
Marlburian	a pupil of Marlborough College
Olavian	a pupil of St Olave's Grammar School, Orpington
Old Etonian, etc	a former pupil of Eton College, etc
Oppidan	a pupil at Eton, who is not a King's Scholar
Pepper	short for 'pepper pot'
Pepper box	alternative to 'pepper pot'
Pepper pot	the buttress on the left hand side of an Eton fives court
Philathletic	liking games (esp. Philathletic Club at Harrow, a club for games players)
Portsmuthian	a pupil of Portsmouth Grammar School – also the name of the school magazine
Rally	sequence of shots between players in a game of fives
Salopian	a pupil of Shrewsbury School - also the name of the school magazine
Sardauna	traditional, now honorary, title of the chief of a state in Nigeria
Set, to	at 'game ball' the cutting team have a choice to play an extended game
Slam	word used for 'first cut' in some schools
Smash	word used for 'first cut' in some schools
Smite	word used for 'first cut' in some schools
Sudden death	at game ball, the cutting team may choose not to extend the game but to decide it on the next point
Swipe	word used for 'first cut' in some schools
Tambour	a feature of a real tennis court where the side wall angles at 135 degrees for a few inches
Tie	match; for example House ties were inter-House matches
Up	(i) a ball hitting the front wall above the line is said to be 'up'
	(ii) a player serving is said to be 'up'
Varsity	university esp Oxford and Cambridge; 'Varsity match' between these two
Volley	a shot when the ball is hit before it bounces on the floor
Wellingtonian	pupil of Wellington College, Berkshire
Wykehamist	a pupil of Winchester College
Wall	original word for a fives court (Eton term)
Wet-bob	Eton name for a boy who rows
Wulfrunian	a pupil of Wolverhampton Grammar School
White Rabbits	an Eton fives club founded by some members of Magdalen College Oxford in the 1930s
Wyverns	an Eton Fives club founded in 1930. It continued as a social club for the members of Magdalene College, Cambridge

Latin translations

Nugae Etonienses	Eton trifles
Mens sana in corpore sano	A healthy mind in a healthy body
Floreat Etona et hic noster ludus esto perpetuus	May Eton and this our game flourish for ever
Etona et hic noster ludus	Eton and this our game
Tectum	A roof (a covered play ground at Uppingham)
Facile princeps	Grammatically incorrect, but meaning "easily the best"
Hoc saxo per triennium uno tenore felicissimi consociati memoriae traduntur. MXCIV,V,VI	Memories of the most happy partnership over three years are borne by this stone, 1904, 5, 6
Hic noster ludus non iam floret	This our game flourishes no longer

Appendix 6 – The Laws of the Game of Eton Fives

(Revised in October 1981)

Definitions

The court is enclosed on three sides and open at the back. The 'front wall' is the wall facing the player, and the 'right-hand' and 'left-hand' walls are the walls on his right hand and left hand respectively.

The 'step' is a shallow step dividing the court into two portions, an 'upper' or 'top' and a 'lower' or 'bottom' 'court' or 'step'. The vertical face of the 'step' is not reckoned as part of the floor of the court.

The 'pepper-box' is a buttress projecting from the left-hand wall. With the 'step', it encloses a small square portion of the floor called 'Dead Man's Hole'.

The 'line' is the lower angle of the ledge running across the front wall, at a height of 4 feet 6 inches.

A vertical line is marked on the front wall at a distance of 3 feet 8 inches from the right-hand wall.

Where the context so permits a reference to the masculine shall be taken to include a reference to the feminine. A reference to the singular shall be taken as a reference to the plural.

Law I

The ball must in every case be hit up; i.e. it must be returned against the front wall on or above the line. Any ball which drops on the top of any of the walls or coping, or which hits any part of the roof or the sides of the court above the coping, or which touches the ground first outside the court, before the first bounce, except in the case of a Blackguard (see Law VI (b)) other than at Game Ball (see Law XI), or touches any person or object outside the court is out of court and counts against the striker. The sides and lower face of the coping shall be in.

Law II

The ball must be fairly hit with a single blow of the hand or wrist, and must not touch any other part of the striker's person under penalty of losing the stroke. It must not be caught, carried, or held in any way, except to serve or to stop a ball as provided for in Law VI. A ball taken with both hands or with a cupped hand may often be technically held, in which case the striker should declare a hold and allow the point to go against him.

Position of the Players

Law III

The game is played by four persons, two against two. Thus, if A and B (with first service) play C and D, A, the server, should stand in the upper court and his side is said to be up. C should stand in the lower court to return the service, and his side is said to be down. B and D also stand in the lower court, B having choice of position.

Choice of First Service

Law IV

The choice of first service shall be decided by one of the home side tossing a coin or placing the ball behind his back in one of his hands and one of the opposing side calling. The first server in each game also cuts first (see Law VI for definition of, and rules for, the first cut) for his side after he and his partner have been sent down; thereafter the player who has the second hand of a service cuts first. If in the first game A serves first and C cuts, then in the second game C serves first and A cuts; in the third game B serves first and D cuts; in the fourth game D serves first and B cuts; and in the fifth game A again serves first and C cuts.

The Service

Law V

The ball when served must hit first the front wall above the line and then the right-hand wall, and must fall in the lower court. The player who is cutting need not return the first or any service until he gets one to his mind, and if he fails to return the service above the line no stroke is counted. A service which goes out of court carries no penalty and may be taken by the player making the first cut.

The First Cut

Law VI

(a) Only the player who is cutting may return the service, and he may do so only between the first and second bounce. This return is called the 'First Cut'. He must return it so that it should hit either (1) first the right-hand wall and subsequently the front wall above the line; or (2) first the front wall above the line between the right-hand wall and the vertical line marked on the front wall. In both cases the ball may afterwards hit any wall or walls and may fall anywhere in the upper or lower court.

(b) If the first cut is hit in such a way that the ball will probably fall out of court, the side which is down may, without interference, touch the ball so that it falls within the court, or catch it, provided that the player touching or catching the ball has one or both feet on the floor of the court, or, if he jumps for the purpose, alights on the floor of the court with the foot which first touches the ground. The player may make only one attempt to touch or catch the ball. If the ball is caught, no stroke is counted; if only touched, one of the side which is up may, if he pleases, return the ball and neither of the opposing side may interfere with his shot; if he fails to return the ball up, no stroke is counted.

(c) If the first cut hits the front wall above the line but on or to the left of the vertical line marked on the front wall and without first touching the right hand wall, this shot is called a 'Blackguard'. It may be returned before the second bounce by either the server or his partner at their option, but if it is not returned above the line, no stroke is counted. The last sentence does not apply at Game Ball (see Law XI).

The Rally

Law VII

After the service and the first cut the ball is returned alternately by either side. It may be returned by either of the partners before the first or second bounce, and may or may not hit the side walls. A rally is lost to his side by the player who fails to return the ball above the line or hits it out of court.

Lets

Law VIII

(a) A let may be requested when a player is in any way prevented from returning or impeded in his attempt to return the ball by one of the opposite side, if he considers he could otherwise have returned it. A let may not be requested when a player is impeded by bystanders.

(b) A ball which would have hit the front wall above the line, but is prevented from doing so by one of the opposite side, counts as a let, unless it first strikes one of the opposite side, and thereafter the front wall above the line, in which case it counts as up; but if it first strikes one of the same side, it does not count as up, whether it goes up or not. A ball that was going to hit below the front line but first hits an opponent and then goes above the line shall be deemed to be up.

(c) If a ball after going up from a return by A or B strikes A or B before the second bounce, it shall count as a let if C or D consider that they could have returned it, if it had not hit A or B, except that if the ball clearly would have fallen out of court it shall count against A and B (subject to the provisions of Law VI relating to a first cut). C or D may, however, elect to return the ball and continue the rally. If not returned up, it counts as a let. If returned above the line, a let may not be requested, unless it falls out of court.

(d) Where a ball becomes lodged on any ledge within the court before the second bounce, it shall count as a let.

(e) A let may be requested when a player is in some way impeded in his attempt to return the ball by one of the opposite side, and after he has returned it up, the ball then falls out of court.

(f) If the first cut is hit in such a way that it will probably fall out of court and the side which is down tries to catch the ball or touch it so that it falls within the court, a let may be requested if the person touching or catching the ball is prevented from so doing or impeded in his attempt so to do by one of the opposite side and the ball falls out.

NB If there is no umpire, a request for a let is generally allowed, except where this Law expressly provides that no let can be claimed.

Scoring

Law IX

A game is won by the side which first obtains twelve points, except as provided in Law XII. Matches generally consist of the best of five games. Only the side which is up may score points. When A is put out B takes his place. When B is out, the side is out and their opponents go up, the player who has been cutting being the first hand to go up, except as provided in Law X. The result of each rally, except in the case of a let, is either to add one to the score of the side which is up, or to put one of them out, as the case may be.

Two Down

Law X

If C loses one point to the opposite side when he is cutting, he is said to be one down. If he loses a second point, he is said to be two down, and D takes his place: if D in turn loses two points, he is two down and C cuts again,

and so on until both A and B are put out; provided that he who was two down first is then the first to go up; but if through inadvertence or otherwise, he does not do so, the error cannot be corrected after the service has been returned. All balls which fall in the upper court belong to the player who is cutting. Failure to return a ball out of Dead Man's Hole does not count as one down against the player who is cutting. The player who is cutting cannot be two down at Game Ball.

Game Ball

Law XI

When the side which is serving requires one point for game, this is called Game Ball, and the following rules must be observed:

(a) The player serving must stand with at least one foot in the lower court, and he may not place both feet on the top step until the player who is cutting has hit the ball. If he forgets to stand thus, and serves the ball with both feet on the top step, the player who is cutting or his partner may try to catch the ball before it bounces. If they succeed in this, the side serving is out. If, however, they do not succeed in catching the ball, or if the player serving or his partner manage to touch the ball first, or if it hits the ground before being touched, it counts neither way. A player may remind his partner of this Law. Where the server places both feet on the top step after the first bounce but before the player who is cutting has hit the ball a let may be claimed by the side cutting.

(b) When the ball is properly served, the player who is cutting may return the first cut against any part of the front wall above the line, with or without hitting the side walls.

(c) The side which is down may not touch or catch a game ball cut which is going out of court (see Law VI (b)).

Setting

Law XII

If the score is at 10 all, the game may, at the option of the side which is cutting, be set to 5 or 3, or not at all; if it is 11 all, to 3 or not at all. If the game is set, Law XI shall apply at 4 or 2 respectively. At 14 all or 12 all in the first case, or at 13 all in the second case, or at 11 all if the game is not set, the game shall be decided by "sudden death", Law XI being observed on either side.

Bibliography

Bayley's Children: A History of Wrekin College 1880-2005 by Rodney Edrich; Ellingham Press 2005

Book of Racquets by JR Atkins, 1872

Boy: Tales of Childhood, by Roald Dahl; Jonathan Cape 1984

Carpenter's Children: History of the City of London School by Thomas Hinde; James & James, 1995

Distant Prospect of Eton College by Thomas Gray

Encyclopaedia of Sports & Games ed John Arlott – article by GD Stringer; Sampson, Low & Marston

Eton & Rugby Fives – Chapter 2, by David Egerton; Lonsdale Library; Seeley, Service and Co Ltd 1934

Eton College Chronicle

Eton College Magazine

Eton Fives, Lonsdale Library Volume XVI by David Egerton

Eton Guide, 1905

Eton Renewed by Tim Card; John Murray 1994

Eton Sixty Years Ago by AC Ainger; John Murray, 1917

Fifty Years of Sport at Eton Harrow & Winchester ed Hon FH Lyttelton, Arthur Page, etc.

Fives, Fairs and Football by Gereth Spriggs; Country Life

Floreat Etona: Anecdotes & Memoirs of Eton College, by Ralph Nevill; MacMillan 1911

The Forest of Dean, by Humphrey Phelps, 1982

Handball Games of the World by John Lolkama

Highgate School: A History by Thomas Hinde; James & James Ltd 1993

History of Emanuel School by CW Scott Giles, 1947; revised 1976

History of Eton College 1440 – 1910 by Maxwell Lyte; MacMillan 1889

History of Mill Hill School by Brett James, 1907

History of St Columba's College by Gregory K White, 1980

A History of Shrewsbury School by JB Oldham, 1952

An Introduction to the History of the Islamic States of Northern Nigeria by JS Hogben; OUP, Ibadan, 1967

The Jesters Club 1928-78 by JF Burnet

King Edward's School, Birmingham; published by Basil Blackwell, Oxford.

Life of Lord Metcalfe edited by JW Kaye, 1854

Lionel Ford by Cyril Alington; SPCK1934

Nugae Etonienses, 1766

Memories of Eton and Etonians by Alfred Lubbock, 1899

Manly & Muscular Diversions by Tony Money 1997; Gerald Duckworth & Co

Sport & the British by Richard Holt; Clarendon Press, Oxford, 1989

Physical Education at Thring's Uppingham by Malcolm Tozer, 1976, Uppingham School

Public School Life, Pitman, 1910

Ramblings in Retirement by David Guilford; Eton Fives Association

Records & Reminiscences of Repton by GS Messiter; 1907

Reminiscences by William Rogers, 1888

Reminiscences of an Etonian by HD Blake

Repton 1557 to 1957 by Bernard Thomas; Batsford, London 1957

Rugby since Arnold by JB Hope Simpson, 1967

A Short History of Repton by Alec Macdonald; Ernest Benn, 1929

Strikingly Alive; The History of the Mill Hill School Foundation 1807-2007 by Roderick Braithwaite; Phillimore & Co.

Tennis, Rackets and other Ball Games by Mike Garnett; Australia 1986

Things Ancient and Modern by CA Alington; Longman 1936

The Times Newspaper Archive

Oxford Dictionary of National Biography

Numerous school registers and magazines

Index

References to illustrations and their captions are in bold type